WHAT IS THE MATTER WITH US

Living with Self-Induced Existential Risks

Matt Henri

ISBN 979-8-89363-261-3

Dedicated to my Son

and

all the changemakers out there.

CONTENTS

PROLOGUE

A viral picture has been popping up in my news feed for over five years. It's a picture of a toddler hugging a huge Redwood Tree with a statement: I don't want to protect the environment. I want to create a World where the environment doesn't need protection.

In response, I asked the following question: If nobody wants and or denies climate change, biodiversity loss, pollution, mental health issues, and other human-caused illnesses, then why are all these manifestations happening?

This book attempts to figure out why and provide insights to transform how we think, talk, and act. The advice I often receive is that we need new stories. People are bound to stories. That makes us unique. Thanks to stories, we learn. Some even spread all over our planet. To understand humanity is to read all its stories, which would take several lifetimes of study. Add to that stories of our planet, and each of us will need to live for a hundred thousand years to understand it. We are not immortal. We are also a contradictory species. We choose the stories we like to read. When we are young, the stories we read are chosen for us. When we are older, we read what we like and are drawn to those that best fit within our culture and our lifestyles. I've tried to depart from the problem, context, conclusion, and recommendation approach and experimented with an alternative narrative that consciously may be confusing for a non-fiction book. It is an experiment, so the results of this form are unknown.

Many universal themes inspire people. These themes address injustice or, in some cases, a potential catastrophe and how an unlikely individual or a group of individuals are motivated to fight this injustice or potential doom. They are called David and Goliath stories, and our world is full of them. We love watching, listening, and reading these stories. They leave us feeling invincible and inspired to solve any and all predicaments, even wicked problems.

Another popular theme is adventure, where the protagonist goes on a journey and meets all sorts of impossible odds and disasters to return as a changed person. The protagonist's worldview completely changed.

This nonfiction book attempts to combine the theme of David and Goliath with a Journey into humanity's dark side to uncover what is the matter with us. We ignore and often forget humanity's dark side. For too long, we have ignored the warnings we have received every century since we came into existence. Why is that?

The Protagonist is Earth and its spheres. The Antagonist in this book is the one invited, not prescribed, to read and think. And please think for yourself. Do not rely on authority at face value. Conduct your own research and verify, verify, verify. The narrator offers no blue, red, or green pill. It's all up to you. We still live under Cassandra's curse for those familiar with Greek Mythology. People do not change when change is imposed upon them, at least not for long. They often fall to the dark side of power despite the knowledge and wisdom they acquired during the imposition. Civilizations have come and gone. People change when they are incentivized, inspired, and motivated to take action. People's strengths reside in themselves, families, and communities that unite and, with the right ingredients, embody true wisdom from which action emerges with good, true, and beautiful intentions.

This book does not cover War as part of the self-induced existential risks we face. Plenty of books have been published about the Cold War and how close we have come to mutually assured destruction. We understand an instant crisis, but what about those crises that are slow to manifest, like cancer or a virus that starts with a small molecule and spreads over a long time until it kills its host? What if this illness is global and affects All life and its supporting spheres? What if we don't feel that it is a potential catastrophe? How will humanity deal with that type of health crisis? How does the corruption of ideas, power, things, models, and our collective behavior manifest? What unseen forces are active here?

Portraying a doomed world for doom's sake has never worked except to draw protestors to the streets. Spreading doom and gloom is tempting. Doomist narratives tempt us, but they provide no value. A disaster makes it into the news, not the stages that preceded that disaster. Understanding our potential doom, which includes confronting impossible odds and how the protagonists will defeat it, holds more power. Watch the Matrix series, The Lord of the Rings, and Saving Private Ryan as examples of what I mean. But here, the Protagonist is Earth in all her beauty. The Antagonist is a contradictory being in a world that despises contradictions because we are taught to be rational administrative beings, which we are not. This book is not a rational rendition of mere facts, for we are humans and possess qualities that are much more than a mechanical, administrative being. We are not machines. We all share a common life. We all are living with self-induced global existential risks. Anyone born after August 6, 1945, has been living under self-induced existential risks. In the last 79 years, we have added more of those risks. Some would argue that we have become accustomed to it, and as a global civilization, we have accepted and resigned to living with these risks. Has this acceptance or avoidance of conscious thought about these risks psychologically affected us?

This book is a journey; compare it to when Bilbo left the Shire in the famous fantasy novel The Hobbit. I faced overwhelming odds, and even so, these did not discourage me from taking action and writing about it, fully aware of the potential criticism I would receive. Many gatekeepers out there would rather not see this work published, but thanks to the positive side of technology, I found a crack to wriggle this book through. You may be one of those gatekeepers, but I am an inhabitant of this planet just like you. We all live in spheres.

I was perfectly happy with my life inside my borders. I cared little for what was happening in the world. I had a busy life. When watching documentaries, I accept that nature is being destroyed because that is how Other humans behave. I felt sorry for the birds, fish, trees, and animals that were dying or being killed by humanity's actions and the pollution we caused. I even screamed at my flatscreen TV when I watched fishermen finning sharks alive. That rage and anger lasted for a few hours, perhaps even a day, until I went shopping or attended another business meeting or a party, which had nothing to do with the killing. Or did it? Was I also guilty of this killing indirectly? Out of sight, out of mind was my modus operandi, so why ask these questions?

It all changed in 2020, exactly twenty-three years after the last time I went diving. I found plastic bags and water bottles stuck on an otherwise beautiful, colorful reef with plenty of fish. That plastic had been there for a while because it was covered in green algae. No one had bothered to remove them. I wish I had never seen it because I could no longer unsee it. There were no reefs with plastic in the nineties. I was presented with a choice, and I took it. I joined the environmental movement. I entered a vortex. I went deep into the abyss of the underworld to find answers to the abovementioned questions. I provide a humble, imperfect layman's summary so that those who wish to become changemakers can take comfort in knowing that you don't need to know everything to start. You learn along the way.

My worldview has changed over the last five years. I've traveled thousands of kilometers, worked in many countries, and played on all continents, and I am not the same person I once was. Here, I aim to expose our potential doom and inspire you to build a worldview that provides a path to the post-tragic era. Until now, we have been lucky in the Age of Consequences. The way we think, talk, and act has consequences, and they manifest everywhere.

In Western culture, there is a saying: There are many paths to Rome. You can choose the one for you. Humanity's journey has never been easy, and as our combined history expands, so do our challenges, which we all must face eventually.

I have found no design in my search to solve our potential doom. We do not have a ring that we can cast in the fires of Mount Doom. Or do we? I invite you to take pen in hand and design what is good, true, and beautiful and how to acquire the wisdom to walk on its path. No one can do it for you or tell you how to become wise, but I hope those who do will find collective synergies. Each design will overlap within your family and community, which could hold the potential to unite us as a global civilization, living with self-induced, existential risks.

TRIUMPH

We shall require a substantially new manner of thinking if mankind is to survive.

Albert Einstein 1879-1955.

All birth emerges from the darkness.
It is also true that diving into darkness to find all that threatens us is
essential for us to emerge, see a new light, and grow from it.

The Author

The human species was not present for most of the planet's existence. Many species became extinct during that period, and even mass extinctions occurred in some periods. The extinctions occurred because some species failed to adapt to changing conditions, including competition from better-adapted species or running out of resources to sustain itself. Most species do not survive for substantial periods of geological time.

Why should the human species be the one that does?

The most commonly offered answers focus on human technology, economic prowess, sustained growth, creativity, and ingenuity. But these same attributes are creating problems faster than society can solve them. The least likely suggested answers are societal ethics, ethos, sense of individual responsibility, and compassion for other species. Yet, the human value system is an essential condition of sustainability. How can this conclusion of the need for value systems be valid when a reasoned approach is necessary to achieve sustainability with minimal trauma to humans and an actively caring relationship with natural systems?

The answer, of course, is a free and open discussion of all issues and substantively reducing or even eliminating taboos and denials. Even with a free and open debate, a clash between value systems and reasoned approaches may occur. Still, value systems are essential because every problem cannot be resolved by evidence produced by reductionist and holistic or integrative science.

The "least likely answer" mentioned previously is the least frequently used or offered because re-examining value systems or societal ethos is usually painful and contentious. Generally, a catastrophic event is essential to have an entire society involved in the discussion.

For example, The global restrictions on individual freedom that were considered unthinkable before the COVID-19 pandemic on freedom of movement, in particular, were implemented with what appears to be pretty strong citizen approval — at least for the short term.

Evidence and reason can often estimate risk reasonably, but only a value judgment can determine acceptable risk. It is also good to remember that, for a few people, prolonging the problem is profitable.

My question remains: Can our species change course before a catastrophe threatens our existence? The only hope I see lies in family, friends, and the local community, and from there, I hope to extend it to the rest of society and civilization.

Water that once was,

Air that was fair,

Soil brings forth no more,

Time, once abundant used up,

Erased all memory from whence we came.

During our short time on this planet, we have built many civilizations. They all started small and grew to huge empires; some were so large that they contained almost three-quarters of the total human population. All perished at some point. Many books have been written about these civilizations. They emerged through warfare with better weapons, strategy, and tactics, and they expanded and became so large that they eventually collapsed. The root causes of their collapse can be reduced to three.

Resource scarcity thanks to degradation, pollution, and disease.

Internal Conflict, social and cultural, and lack of coordination.

War. economical, and kinetic.

We are now a global Civilization and a young one since we've only emerged as a global civilization since WW2. Previous Civilizations lasted for centuries, some even for millennia, and ours? We've only been one Civilization for eight decades, and here we are. It does not matter if you are Asian, European, African, South American, North American, or Middle Eastern. We are all faced with the same phenomena:

Increase in resource scarcity, ecosystem degradation, pollution, and disease.

Wars and arms races, Social, Cultural, Economic, and proxy armed conflicts.

Increase in internal conflict and insufficient global coordination systems to resolve our global crisis.

Our global civilization, with an estimated 9.1 Billion people by 2050, has yet to fully understand that we are a global civilization with many cultures facing the same global risks.

Pieter Bruegel the Elder has always been one of my favorite painters, and I've always been fascinated by his painting Triumph of Death. I never knew why it fascinated me until recently.

I reference this painting because it represents the culmination of increased garbage in human society in the agricultural age that started 12000 years ago. The black death kills indiscriminately. It does not matter if you were a king, a bishop, a farmer, a cook, a husband, a wife, a daughter, or a son, or if you were rich or poor.

The first black death period started in 1346 and ended in 1351. It was spread by flees carrying a bacterial pathogen, Yersinia pestis, carried by rats who, along with trade goods, traveled on boats from Central Asia, the Middle East to Europe and back. It was the most advanced supply chain system at the time.

Humans carried these bacteria-infected flees in their hair, body, and clothes, and they got sick and died. Back then, health was a personal affair, not a public one. People generally were not hygienic; washing was considered unhealthy, and this belief lasted well into the early 20th century, especially in Europe. Humans carrying flees was common.

Sixty percent of the population in Central Asia, the Middle East, and Europe died between 1346 and 1351. Think about that for a minute. If that were to happen today in today's population numbers (1,276 Million), it would mean that 765 Million People would die in those three regions.

In 1350, the global population was estimated to be around 370 Million, of which approximately 70 million lived in Europe, 35 Million in the Middle East, and 10 Million in Central Asia.

So roughly 69 million people died between 1346 and 1351. From this experience of massive death in such a short period of time must have resulted in a change of worldview. This short, terrible period represented the end of the old world from the Dark Ages to the beginnings of a new world full of wonder and discovery that culminated in the Renaissance, scientific revolution, and the Enlightenment.

Could this happen again?

In the 14th century, we already had well-established cities where people lived close together. It was a melting pot of humanity who had no qualms about throwing their garbage onto the streets and into rivers. Even canals were built, mainly for access to drinking water. These canals also carried the trash to streams, rivulets, and rivers. The smell in the streets was so bad people even complained to the King and the Church, who were the authorities at the time. What attracts garbage? Rats of course, it's an easy source of food, water, and shelter from the cold. Waste produces heat, so it is an excellent solution for rats wanting to stay warm during the winter, especially for black rats carrying deadly flees. Back then, pollution was called corruption, and the causes were decaying carcasses, plague bodies, or garbage accumulating in the streets and waterways.

With so much education currently available in the 21st century, we should be better educated about garbage and what it can cause. We should have kept the meaning of the word corruption alive from those days. Corruption today has a different meaning, however the change of meaning did cause something else that we used to call garbage. We no longer like the word garbage in our current dominating Western discourse, so we changed it to waste. We use the term waste with everything: Time, food, space (air, land, water), energy, property, thoughts, beliefs, and many more. Language is our most powerful tool. Language can heal, entertain, neutralize, paralyze, and corrupt; we know how to use it well, so well, that we have become experts at it.

Humans have been producing waste for over 200,000 years and have mismanaged it ever since we started making it. Despite centuries of discovery and education that waste negatively affects us and our nature, we still have a challenge managing waste. We create waste with every process, and waste is the primary cause of pollution, yet we have a genius ability to "kick the can down the road."

Before you say that every animal produces waste, let me remind you that we have expert waste managers in nature and within ecosystems on land and in our ocean. On land, they are called scarabs, better known as dung beetles, who clean up after our fellow species. They even cleaned up after us a long time ago. Even in our ocean, some organisms process waste that comes from marine animals. It is a perfect system. Ever wondered why the ocean and African savannas are not covered in poop? Another killer waste management system we have on earth is fungi. That stuff is magical on so many levels. It's the largest organism on the planet. We don't even understand 1% of what it can do. Maybe eating magic mushrooms expands our understanding. After all, it's proving to be a magical substance that can replace plastic packaging. How cool is that? In the Ocean, we have sea urchins, sharks, and other species that clean up the mess their ecosystem creates. If you become a scuba diver, you can see the whole waste management system. The underwater world even has cleaning stations.

We, humans, are capable of incredible inventions that have benefitted us. While these inventions have done wonders for us, we now witness unintended consequences. The research is alarming.

Thanks to our technological prowess, we have evolved to become a species that can annihilate our host and all who live in it. In the context of our total time in existence, that technological power was only developed a few seconds ago. Before WW2, we did not have this capability. We were unable to destroy one another at scale. Realizing that mutually assured destruction is not an option, we were able to control nuclear proliferation by controlling as much as we could via treaties between those countries that had nukes. But we never got rid of them, even though no one wants a nuclear war. Why did we not get rid of them?

For the most part, war has almost always been about resources and power. As ingenious as we are, we developed a system that mitigated nuclear annihilation by providing mechanisms where everyone could participate in acquiring goods needed to develop each country and its people. Technology played a significant, if not dominant, role in this. Our financial system was another key characteristic. We could not have grown from 2 billion people after WW2 to 8 Billion people today without our capability to develop and finance technologies that enabled us to feed the population. We built bigger and better machines that could do more than any man could and developed chemicals to improve crop yields and kill non-food-related nature. For almost eight decades, we have had global peace. We have had many proxy wars but no WW3.

We have perfected our global supply chain for almost eight decades so that many critical products are no longer made in one country or continent. But what have been the unintended consequences of this phenomenon?

I often have conflicting thoughts because there is a flip side to an argument we cannot ignore. Our Global Civilization is still young. Our Civilization will change—no doubt about it. We are already trying to foresee what will emerge, which is odd when you think about it. Why do we think, feel, and talk as if things are changing at a fundamental level and that we need a new future? Almost every generation has said things need to change since the dawn of man. Change to what? We are more prosperous than ever, so why should we change? We have plenty of resources. We can fit the entire global population into Alaska. We might have to blow up and melt some glaciers for water. We can move polar bears further North. Why are we talking about sustainability and regeneration? We can geoengineer the troposphere, stratosphere, and mesosphere. The stock markets keep rising, corporations are making more money, and as long as we have energy, we will grow and produce even more. Whole population groups in Asia and Africa are motivated to emerge and wear shiny luxury goods, drive sleek cars, and live in beautiful homes. Climate change and pollution are not going to stop them. They want their share of the pie. Will you deny them the opportunity that you have enjoyed for decades?

Civilizations don't die overnight. It takes decades, sometimes centuries. You live your life, and I will live mine, and all will be fine. So why do I have this nagging feeling that not everything is fine? I see cracks appearing in the structures that we have built for ourselves. I see cracks in the earth with not a worm in sight, I see orange forests devouring all that lies around them like a demon from the underworld, I see farmland covered in silver shimmers reflecting the sky, and mirages appearing in cities and on the horizon that remain there for weeks. I see people shopping, partying, and shopping again without caring about what's happening worldwide. People flock to shows about zombies and superheroes as if Doctor Strange is going to save us from some zombie apocalypse. People worry about climate change, shrug, and go grocery shopping. People talk about Biodiversity loss but forget that we are part of biodiversity. If we are losing biodiversity and we are a part of it does that mean that we are losing ourselves? People talk about pollution, feel sorry about a bird or whale with plastics in their stomachs, and then return to work so they can meet their deadlines. People call for action but ignore causal effects when I ask what actions we should take. All I can say is that we live in weird and confusing times. Perhaps I'm not alone.

This time was not so different from a hundred years ago when idealism reigned supreme. The Spanish flu had ended, and people proclaimed that democracy, national socialism, imperialism, communism, capitalism, libertarianism, and freedom from colonialism were required to save the people from doom and that technology and enterprise would save us. We had serious problems back in the 1920s, and we have returned to a decade full of serious problems. Some call them wicked problems, meaning that they are frustratingly difficult to solve. The megaphones are howling nonstop about prosperity, wealth, growth, diversity, equality, integrity, climate change, pollution, biodiversity loss, and technology. It's hard to hear yourself think in all this noise. So I screamed a question, and all was quiet for a moment, which I had hoped would last longer than it actually did. Here is the question.

If no one wants war, climate change, pollution, biodiversity loss, species extinction, inequality, discrimination, polarization, or mental illness, then why is all this happening, and why are we not putting a halt to it and start to heal?

Before you answer, let me remind you that the answer is not as straightforward as it seems because we are now 8bn people, all with our own microphones. What I have found is what I will share here so you may find an answer for yourself. This journey of discovery all started with a piece of plastic stuck on a coral reef 22 meters deep in the ocean. I removed that piece, and it sucked me into a rabbit hole vortex from which I slowly emerged to find myself in between worlds; I cannot even begin to tell you how that feels. It borders on sheer horrors and wonders at the same time. None of them felt real, so I came up with the realization of spheres.

HYDROSPHERE

Our Precious.

Living with self-induced existential risks can be tailer to embody a crisis called the metacrisis. To understand our metacrisis, we should start from where we came from: the Hydrosphere. We all came into existence from a watery nature until we were big enough to be pushed onto our scary, dry world where we were forced to breathe and adapt to our new nature, which, given our capability to alter our nature, made us also the slowest species to stand on our feet at a young age. Each generation is born into a world different from our ancestors. The first thing we do is to imprint our surroundings before we can walk and talk. We are born vulnerable to nature so over 400,000 years we have embodied the notion of nature being hostile. This embodiment made us produce products to protect us from Nature from dead material that was once alive, like animal skins for clothing. That started the process of distancing ourselves further from nature for protection. Water binds the entire process; we can't do anything without it.

When I think of water, I always think of the ocean. It is vast as it stretches to the horizon when you sit on a beach. The ocean is my playground. Surfing and diving have been my passion since I was young. The ocean is beautiful, and I could not live without it. The ocean connects us even though we like to split it up and give it names like the North Sea, Java Sea, Pacific Ocean, Atlantic Ocean, Bering Sea, and many others. There is not one country which is not connected to the ocean. All landlocked countries have rivers that connect to the ocean, and the rest that don't have a river have a coastline. We live on a water planet. 71% of our planet is water, and that percentage will increase this century. So you better learn how to swim.

I was a competitive swimmer for many years and won several medals. I swan competitively in Africa and Europe. I always knew floating in salt water was easier than floating in fresh water. I swam faster in salt water than in freshwater. The difference was only 0.1 seconds over 25 meters, which is a lot for a competitive swimmer and can make the difference between winning and losing when competing in 100-meter events. Pools back in the day were treated with chlorine. Over the years, this has been improved by using more healthier salt-based chlorine. Adding salt makes you swim faster; swimming pools are now treated with salt versus chlorine. You can tell by tasting it, which I do not recommend. The water from swimming pools used for competitions now has strict salinity regulations to ensure fair competition globally.

What I did not realize when I was swimming ten times a week was that I would sweat and sweat a lot. I never realized this when swimming. Only when I was ordered to clean toilets in the army did I realize that I sweated more than most people. Even my platoon sergeant noticed. It was embarrassing, so maybe that's why I like spending my time close to and preferably in water. This book would have written itself if only I had a waterproof laptop.

Approximately 60% of the human body is water. Our body emits heat to stay warm, producing sweat to keep us cool. Today, we have housing and excellent air-conditioning to keep us cool. We don't like to sweat, so we use deodorants that stick to our bodies and mask our smell. Eat enough garlic, and you know what I mean.

However, heat, sweat, and body odor are essential to humans. We don't think about these things, yet they are critical. They are not by-products, even though now we seem to believe they are. Why do we have perfumes, for example?

But when it comes to Urine and Feces, that is pure waste, and we manage it well, or at least we trust that we do. We treat urine and feces as waste. We flush it down the toilet and forget about it. We never think about where it goes. Do you know where it goes?

You can now go to the bathroom in a plane and in space, but what is lacking on most roads? Access to a bathroom, so imagine what that was like centuries ago.

Ancient Mesopotamian settlements (40,000 BCE) often had clay structures made for squatting or sitting in the most private room of the house. Squatting is still popular today and can be found in many Asian countries. You could argue that Asians adopted the practice from the Mesopotamians.

The Romans, however, didn't care much for privacy as they used to gather in meeting houses where they would congregate and speak of current affairs and gossip while taking care of "urgent business." These houses could seat up to 20 Romans at a time. The urgent business: urine and feces fell to water conduits below the house and were carried off by water canals. Today, western cultures handle their "business" in more private settings. Some proudly have a calendar displayed where you can see the birthdays of the hosts' family members while you are taking a dump. Decades ago, you could find gossip magazines and newspapers in toilets. Today, you sit there browsing through social media or news apps or talk to your friends for hours until your butt is sore.

Thanks to our sewage systems, we can transport our waste far away. It's one of humanity's pivotal inventions. Our waste is disposed of differently in many countries. In some, our waste goes through a complicated filtration process; in others, it flows right into a river and even directly into the ocean. While many religious texts contain instructions to keep your waste away from drinking water and food sources, we have forgotten those texts.

In Mesopotamia, these squatting structures were connected to pipes that used running water to move "your business" into open street canals, which carried your waste to cesspits. Water systems like this flourished in the Bronze Age. In the Indus Valley, nearly every house had a toilet connected to a city-wide sewage system. As of yet, researchers are not sure what inspired these sewage systems. Maybe it was the smell. We do know that waste management is essential to public health. Untreated sewage is a dangerous breeding ground for micro-organisms, including those that cause cholera, dysentery, and typhoid. From research by Robert Koch and Louis Pasteur, we fully understand the relationship between sewage and sickness called the germ theory, which was argued, proved, and popularized in Europe and North America between 1850 and 1920.

We know from ancient texts that people back then knew that obnoxious odors from waste caused sickness as early as 100 BCE. By 100 AD, more complex sanitation systems began to emerge. The Roman Empire had continuously flowing aqueducts built to carry waste outside city walls. Chinese dynasties also had private and public toilets around the same time. Except their waste was immediately recycled. Most household toilets in China fed into pigsties, and at night specialized poop collectors carried the waste away from pigsties and public latrines to sell as fertilizer in the morning. In China, this type of waste management went on for centuries. In Europe, the fall of the Roman Empire brought sanitation into the dark ages. Pit latrines became commonplace, and chamber pots were frequently dumped into the street.

Castles ejected waste from tall windows into communal cesspits. At night, so-called Gong farmers would gather the waste, carry it beyond city limits, and dump it there.

However, toilets themselves underwent some significant changes during the Middle Ages. Wealthy families had commode stools, which were wooden boxes with seats and lids. In the royal court of England, the commodes were controlled by the king's Groom of the Stool, who also monitored the King's intestinal health. Thus, the groom's intimate relationship with the monarch made him an influential figure. Shit for knowledge turned to gold.

The next major toilet technology came in 1596 when Sir John Harrington invented the first modern flush toilet for Queen Elizabeth. It used levers to release water and drain the bowl, which is still found in contemporary designs. However, Harington's invention stank of sewage, but thankfully in 1775, Scottish inventor Alexander Cumming invented the bend in the drain pipe to contain water and limit odor. Thomas Crapper later improved this so-called S trap into the modern U bend.

Toilets in England during World War 1 were predominately made by the company Thomas Crapper & Co. Ltd. And those toilets displayed their company logo, so United States soldiers at the time started referring to the toilet as "the Crapper" and brought that slang back with them to the United States.

We can poop everywhere now unless you are on a road trip and desperately need to poop 200 km from your destination. Luckily, there are rest stops now in almost all countries, or if the need is too high, you can do "your business" by the side of the road, perhaps even use the river that runs alongside it should you find yourself stuck in a traffic jam on the way to Spain for your summer holiday.

By the 19th century, many modern cities had implemented modern sewage infrastructure and wastewater treatment plants. Today, we use the power of our most precious resource as the most efficient way to transport our bodies' waste to the ocean. However, according to the United Nations, 2.4 billion people today still do not have proper sanitation and wastewater management infrastructure. That is 30% of the global population. Most of their waste, as I've witnessed in Africa, ends up in the soil.

We have forgotten a little beetle called a scarab, better known today as the dung beetle. This incredible insect was revered in Egypt as they believed this beetle kept the earth revolving like a ball of dung. If an Egyptian from that era would jump out of their grave today, they would probably say something to the effect of " You see, the Earth does revolve from the shit we have produced these last 3000 years.

Scarabs were linked to Khepri, the god of the rising sun. These beetles were our Gong farmers when we were hunter-gatherers. They cleaned up after us and our fellow mammal species and still do today. They depend on dung entirely from birth to death. They are the most efficient waste disposal service on our planet. They can erase an elephant's "business" in less than 10 minutes. Knowing this now, I wished they were around when I had to scoop poop from the elephant enclosures at an East African national park's infirmary so I could spend more time feeding the sick animals. These beetles are still everywhere, although some species are in decline. They are the reason the vast planes of Africa, where migrant species like wildebeest, elephants, and zebras roam, are not full of poop. I never minded the smell of animal dung, but human waste is entirely different. If it weren't so obnoxious, I would promote these feces to be managed by dung beetles instead of our sewage system, but alas, dung beetles are hard to find in our cities these days. The good news is that the dung beetle is returning to regenerative farms, and farmers worldwide have known for centuries how beneficial these insects are.

Depending on where you are today, our sewage systems have significantly expanded to provide wastewater drainage from agriculture, industries, and households. So, we no longer talk about a sewage system that transports only "our business " down the pipe. Nowadays, our sewage wastewater contains all sorts of substances that are no longer organic. All this sewage from highly populated areas flows to water treatment plants. They should be the most sophisticated treatment facilities and treatment plants ever if you think of what flows through a sewage pipe today at each stage, from when it enters your sink, toilet or from a run-off in a slaughterhouse or fish processing plant or a livestock farm for example to the treatment plant. The amount of substances that need to be removed to turn that sewage into 100% clean water would be mind-blowing.

Another issue that occasionally occurs when wastewater treatment plants are oversupplied by wastewater is that the system allows overflow because of heavy rains. This means that when a wastewater treatment plant reaches total capacity, the excess capacity flows into nature. Usually, a river or a canal, and that wastewater flows into our Ocean. Sewage waste overflows are not uncommon these days as sewage systems have not been updated in most parts of the industrialized world, which means that waste overflows contaminate our rivers, our groundwater, and the ocean as the waste has to go somewhere. The United States Environmental Protection Agency has The National Pollutant Discharge Elimination System, a permit program created in 1972 by the Clean Water Act. is a permitting system delegated to the states to manage sewage treatment. It includes standards or limits on pollutants and overflow solutions, particularly from municipal sewers, which separate overflows between combined sewer and sanitary overflows.

Today, water samples from sewage systems anywhere in the world will contain the following substances: microplastics, including those from clothing, pesticides from households, industrial farming, and Industries. Medicines such as antibiotics and other drugs such as Xanax, ecstasy, and birth control pills. They also contain forever chemicals from household products found in varnish, furniture, carpets, dental floss, candy wrappers, pizza boxes, non-stick cookware, shampoo, and cosmetics. New Zealand banned forever chemicals in cosmetics starting Dec 31st 2026.

Since 1991, the European Union has enforced the Urban Wastewater Treatment Directive and is re-evaluating this directive as many pollutants are not covered. According to the European Union website, 90% of urban wastewater is dealt with in line with EU standards. 92% of toxic pollutants in wastewater come from the pharmaceutical and cosmetics sectors. What type of shampoo, facial cream, or lipstick do you use? And 10 million Europeans and 12 million Americans still lack access to essential sanitation services. The issue extends to the rest of the world as the definition of basic sanitation services differs in many countries. It mainly concerns the safe disposal of human waste (urine and feces). The United Nations defines it as improved sanitation not shared by other households. Poor Romans, so, nothing about safety. Dig deeper, and you will find significant differences in how wastewater is treated in many countries.

Furthermore, in many jurisdictions, the so-called sewage sludge, i.e., what remains after the wastewater has been cleaned, is used as agricultural fertilizer. Which, truth be known, is a common practice globally. Sewage sludge from wastewater treatment plants is left over, so all those substances I mentioned before are moved to land as fertilizer—the same thing when gong farmers moved the waste from cesspits to farmland. Sewage sludge is high in Nitrogen, an essential fertilizer in agriculture, thanks to intensive land use.

In high-income countries, using sewage sludge as fertilizer has been regulated. This sludge has been proven to cause diseases and penetrate our food, which ultimately lands on our plates. For the most part, wastewater treatment has been reactive, meaning that wastewater treatment was upgraded with better purification technology after new substances not captured during the previous treatment process ended up in our water supply.

Do you know which fruit contains the most microplastics?

Do you know which vegetable contains the most microplastics?

I googled it: Apples and Pears, Broccoli and Carrots, according to Greenpeace from research conducted by the University of Catania, Italy, in 2020.

While we may have solutions for treating wastewater in high-income countries, the same can not be said for middle to low-income countries; our civilization's supply chain is global. You can buy fruits and vegetables from everywhere now. The same goes for many meats, fish, and seafood; every country can import and export goods and services to consumers who buy them without concern because they trust their food is safe.

This trust now ends up in our bodies. Microplastics and forever chemicals are now found in our bodies, domesticated animals, and wildlife. The medical profession has found these substances in our feces. Microplastics are also found in our brain, heart, and liver organs. They have been found in our blood and breast milk. The World Health Organization has determined that microplastics and forever chemicals in our bodies are a matter of concern.

When people become aware, they complain to their leaders, which is similar to what happened in the dark ages, and it takes a long time for leaders to act. Some countries have the resources and technology to implement solutions, but others do not. The one area where all of this comes together is in our ocean.

Planet Earth is 71% ocean. The name for our planet should have been Planet Ocean. We are still a blue planet from space, although, according to the latest research, our ocean is turning green.

I have always been a fan of Jacque Cousteau, who invented the aqualung. He is, by many, considered the godfather of scuba diving. His explorations into the underwater world captivated me when watching his documentaries. Watching him and his crew sail around the world on his vessel, the Calypso became my dream, and it is still on my bucket list.

While living in Africa, I became fascinated with the sea, but I lived 505 kilometers away in a little African village, so all I had were his documentaries. Only when I lived on the Southern African Coast many years later did I discover the Ocean and become a surfer. Surfing became my passion. I even skipped school sometimes so I could go surfing with my friends when the swell was up. It was here where my love affair with the ocean began.

I became hooked when our geography teacher brought us on a school trip to a secluded beach west of the city to dive for rock lobsters. Rock lobsters are now protected in the same area, but back then, you had to be blind not to see them.

The plan was to have a dinner barbeque on the beach and eat the delicious fresh lobsters we had caught straight from the Ocean in the afternoon. Each of us was given a mesh bag to put the lobster in while we dived down to about 5 meters with our snorkel gear where, on a sea mount, we could take the lobster from their hiding places. The quota for each classmate was to collect at least one lobster. If you had plenty of air, you could catch up to three. Quite a few of the kids failed repeatedly. On my second dive, my geography teacher, an experienced scuba diver, pulled me to his side and pointed into the blue. In the distance, I could see a dark object moving closer and closer to our position. I was still holding my breath comfortably. The shape became clearer, and I saw a shark swimming towards us. It turned to the left about three meters from us. By that time, my lungs were screaming for air. My teacher noticed and passed his regulator to me so I could breathe. This technique in scuba diving is called buddy breathing, and from all my years of diving, this was the only time I had to do this. The shark circled us three times. It was about four meters in length. You could tell from its eyes that it was checking us out before finally swimming off. What surprised me the most was that I was not scared. Sure, my heart rate was up, which happens when you run out of air. I was fascinated by observing this magnificent animal in its natural habitat.

Back on the beach, my teacher asked me if I knew what type of shark it was. I did not. He asked me if I'd seen any markings, and I told him I saw vertical stripes along the side of his body. It was a Tiger shark. It was then that I realized I was home; I wanted to live near the Ocean for the rest of my life and discover the underwater world, like Jacque Cousteau.

Life took over; I had to move back to Europe with my parents due to boycotts, and it wasn't until 1994, while living in the Caribbean, that I achieved my open water dive certificate from PADI. I became an absolute scuba diving maniac. We went diving almost every weekend, even when I was still hungover from Friday night parties. I threw up many times underwater. As a result, my instructor, ex-addict, and a circle leader at Narcotics Anonymous took me and my friends to some of the best diving locations around the island. We saw all kinds of fish, turtles, and lovely corals, and on occasion, we encountered bull sharks, considered one of the more dangerous predators in the ocean. They were magnificent to observe. It only increased my fascination with these species. Over the years, I dove with lemon, tiger, and bull sharks in the Caribbean, and in 1998, I realized that within four years, I saw familiar dive spots disappear as we could no longer observe beautiful corals; the turtles were no longer there, and the sharks had gone. We had to go to protected areas to see stingrays. I was so disappointed.

I stopped diving altogether because we moved to Europe. I stopped diving because I believed there was nothing left to see; everything was dead. In four years and over 400+ dives, I saw coral ecosystems die. I did not even know what ecosystems were back then.

The ocean has changed. For over three hundred years, we have used the ocean as a free-for-all, take-what-you-can nature and dumping ground. The saying; don't shit where you eat obviously does not apply to us and our ocean. Fertilizer and polluted wastewater effluent flow from agricultural lands, cities, and industry producing all sorts of byproducts that are dumped into our rivers that flow into the ocean, creating dead zones like what we see off the coast from the Mississippi, Amazon, Orinoco, Rio Negro, Mekong, Nile, Ganges, and many other rivers. We are dumping radioactive wastewater from Fukushima's destroyed power plant into the ocean. We like to believe that we can dilute our pollution because our ocean is so vast. Now, the Ocean is in critical condition. Fifty percent of our plankton is dead, and the death rate is increasing by 1 to 2% per year. We fish for krill, a critical food source for whales in Antarctica, to be used as fish feed in salmon aquaculture and oil supplements, amongst other things.

We need Phytoplankton to sequester CO2. CO2 is highly absorbent in water and, as such, changes the Alkalinity of our water. Ocean PH, as it's called, is decreasing and currently sits at around 8.01. If it reaches a pH of 7.95, the ocean dies, as many species that need carbonate substances will die and wreak havoc on marine life and food webs. We continue to overfish in many parts of our Ocean. 90% of our global fish stock is severely depleted thanks to overfishing and illegal fishing. Our chemical waste is killing our reef ecosystems, which sustain 25% of all marine life; we are destroying our mangrove forests, which support 40% of marine life. Without a healthy ocean, we will not survive.

What we have dumped in our ocean over the last 100 years has created a new ecosystem: the Plastisphere. This ecosystem has all the characteristics of a natural ecosystem, complete with living organisms like bacteria, parasites, predators, and competitors, with one major difference. These plastispheres contain microplastic. These ecosystems have been found in the great Pacific garbage patch and sargassum blooms that wash up on Caribbean and Florida beaches. Even rocks containing plastic have been found in Trinidade in Brazil. Plasticosis is a disease found in seabirds. Birds' digestive tracts have been found full of scarring from eating plastic. The plastic they digest also damages the tubular glands in the first part of their stomach, preventing them from digesting their food.

According to the IUCN, we humans dump 14 million tons of plastic in our ocean each year. I'm convinced this is grossly underreported as in Indonesia alone, at least 5 Million tons of plastic waste is dumped in the ocean each year, and together with China and the Philippines, it makes up almost 40% of all plastic waste entering our ocean globally according to the World Bank.

Cleaning the ocean of what we have thrown into it will cost trillions of dollars. The substances we have dumped into the ocean over the last 100 years will still be there 400 years from now and even longer when you consider forever chemicals.

Water, our precious resource from where life began, has become a sewage system because it's highly efficient, and besides, you can't drink seawater, so who cares, right?

Today, I go diving with a mesh bag. Not because I want to catch a lobster. I need it now to collect plastics from a coral reef. In less than fifty years, from healthy reefs to plastic reefs. We humans need fresh water, so let us focus.

Rivers.

Do you know how much it costs to clean a river of all Pollution?

My grandfather used to tell me stories of catching loads of Salmon from the River Rhine. But when I was young, there were none left. In fact, the River Rhine was one of the dirtiest, most polluted rivers in the world.

More than 50 Billion Euros has been spent cleaning up the River Rhine.

Those 50+ Billion Euros were spent on;

1. Cleaning up the river; dredging the muck and the pollution out of the river.

2. Improving Water treatment plants.

3. Preventing Agriculture and heavy industry from discarding waste and pollutants directly into the river

4. Improve Waste collection and management facilities

5. Public awareness and education.

6. Waste and Pollution Regulations.

Many industries left and moved their operations to countries with no or lack of regulations.

Image of the River Rhine from 1986 after the Sandoz Laboratories Accident.

Today, I look at all these wonderful organizations tackling plastic waste pollution: Seven Clean Seas, The Ocean Clean-up, Sungai Watch, 4ocean PBC, Sea Shepherd Global Ocean Risk and Resilience Action Alliance, Ocean Integrity Group, Systemiq Ltd, and so many more passionate organizations with great people that are cleaning up our rivers and beaches. I applaud all, but we are not solving the problem.

The Ocean Clean-up conducted research, which was commissioned by the UN, indicates that 80% of Plastic waste comes from 1000 rivers. If it costs 50 billion Euros and more than 30 years to clean the river Rhine, how much would it cost to clean all 999 rivers? At the moment, The Ocean Clean Up, which means well, relies on donors so they can deploy more barriers in rivers to collect plastic waste. This means that as long as the tap is open, pollution will continue to flow down the river, kill its biodiversity along the way, and finally kill what is left in our ocean. But that's only plastic; the Ocean Clean-up does not remove nano and micro-plastic and chemicals from rivers. So what are we cleaning?

Two more rivers have been cleaned, and we have Lee Kuan Yew to thank. He was the founding father of the Republic of Singapore, a country known affectionately as the Garden City and unaffectionally as a Fine City.

"It should be a way of life to keep the water clean, to keep every stream, every culvert, every rivulet and river free from pollution. In ten years let us have fishing in the Singapore River and fishing in the Kallang River. It can be done."

Lee Kuan Yew 26 February 1977.

Picture: Singapore River 1977.

The Singapore government spent $300 Million Singapore dollars to clean up the Singapore and Kalang river between 1977 and 1987.

You might be interested to learn how this tiny country did it. Singapore at that time was still considered a fast-growing country well on its way to gaining developed status. Or what should be called a high-income country today. They did not have many resources, but thanks to Lee Kuan Yew, much effort was put into cleaning up this river. I use this example as a case study that can be applied anywhere with the proper will and resources. So how did they do it?

First, they started by relocating 27,000 Squatter families to government-built housing. They moved all cottage industries, 3600 backyard industries, mostly food processing factories, and 430 motor repair shops away from the river to government-built facilities. They moved 610 pig farms and 480 duck farms to designated farming zones. 4900 street hawkers who plied their trade

Image: Singapore River Clean Up 1977-87

on the river banks were moved to hawker centers, some of which are still in operation today. 390 fruit and vegetable wholesalers were moved to specially designed market areas with easy access for the population who by then were living in HDBs apartments building and riverine activities involving 770 bumboats and 64 boat yards were banned and closed down and moved to other tilling areas and polluting activities from boat yards including charcoal trading were phased out. 21000 premises were supplied with a sewage system, and wastewater treatment plants were upgraded. "Night Soil Bucket" was phased out in 1987. The river was dredged, and river waste was collected and disposed of safely. In 1987, the Singapore government launched an extensive education campaign to teach its population about the hazards of polluting nature. On the 30th of July 1979, Singapore opened its first waste incineration plant. Last but not least, the river banks and riverine nature were improved. Today, Singapore incinerates most of its waste in closed-loop plants. This means zero pollution: air, water, or on land. If this tiny country with limited resources back then could do it, why couldn't you? Where there is a will, there is a way, and a clean nature benefits prosperity and well-being.

All that took 10 years and required a lot of development, but it is no wonder today that Singapore is one of the world's cleanest, if not the cleanest country. In Europe, we are seeing attempts to clean up rivers. One of the latest is the river Seine, which is scheduled to be clean in 2024—total costs: 1.4 billion euros. Paris hopes to allow its residents to swim in the river for the first time in over a century.

The ASEAN region is one of the fastest-growing economic regions in the world, and we have a massive river pollution problem. Annually, organizations in this region collect over 100,000 tons of plastic waste from our rivers and beaches, but it's not enough.

Minister Susi Pudjiastuti from Indonesia declared, "Indonesia's seas will have more plastics than fish by 2030." She said this on October 28, 2018. Since then, 25 Million Tons of Plastic waste has been dumped into these seas and continues to rise. I was active in plastic clean-ups in Indonesia, where we worked with local fishermen to collect plastic waste from rivers and coastal areas. We collected tons of plastic; honestly, I felt good about myself because I had done something about it. The challenge, however, is that no one wants to pay for the clean-up, and what I mean by that is enough funding to permanently clean up the waste being dumped into the rivers and ocean and implement solutions that permanently prevent this waste from entering our water systems. That is why cleaning up plastic waste is not enough. The challenge is that most of these rivers contain microplastics, pesticides, and forever chemicals, many of which are banned elsewhere. All these rivers will need to go through a filtration system that removes these substances, and as of yet, I have not seen it deployed anywhere.

Another major concern and is considered a severe red flag for which there is no return, according to the Stockholm Resilience Centre, is our Biochemical flow, which contains two substances called nitrogen and phosphorous, which, according to the institute, has crossed the tipping zone of which there is no return. We are stuck with it, like plastic. We have used these substances for centuries in Industry and Agriculture. They have leached these chemicals in the form of pesticides into our nature and are now everywhere and causing havoc as these substances create algae blooms, resulting in dead zones in our ocean. Those in the Gulf of Mexico are good examples of how bad it can get. You may have heard about Algae blooms off the coast of Florida or Texas, but they are happening everywhere now. While I was writing this book, Reuters reported huge algae blooms in eastern Thailand off the coast of Chonburi, a city famous for its gemstone trade. Chonburi's coast is also renowned for its mussel farms. There are around 800 mussel farm plots, and 80% of them were affected, causing enormous losses for these farmers.

Agricultural and livestock farming run-off from the Amazon region feeds the ever-growing sargassum blooms in the Atlantic Ocean. With it comes Vibrio bacteria, which is a flesh-eating bacteria. Some of these Vibrio Bacteria species are lethal to humans, and 1 in 5 patients die once infected.

This Nitrogen and phosphorus, primarily when used in spraying crops, is absorbed into our atmosphere, carried thousands of kilometers away, and dumped via rain on our land and in our water. Causing additional damage, the first signs of which we are seeing as we see biodiversity decrease in both spheres.

The vast ocean has been an ideal dumping ground as our sewage system, combined with flows from our rivers, is creating a cesspool that is affecting the ocean's biodiversity. Our fish now contains the same material that we use in everyday life. 3.5 billion people depend on our ocean for their survival. The fish you eat is no longer the fish your grandparents had for dinner. Many fish now come with health warnings. Ask the Swedes who buy their fish from the Baltic Sea. The Baltic, South China, and Mediterranean are among the most polluted seas in the world.

Much of the fish we consume comes from anywhere in the world. Furthermore, the substances found in our fish, such as microplastics, forever chemicals, antibiotics, and pesticides, are also becoming an increasing focus of concern concerning food safety.

Since we have depleted global fish stocks in our ocean, we have moved to Aquaculture and now have fish and shellfish farms worldwide, a 300 Billion USD industry today. We need to keep feeding our population. Fish farms must use medicines, such as antibiotics and pesticides, to keep these fish healthy. One of the main concerns in fish farming is the presence of sea lice. Luckily, many pesticides and medicines are being banned thanks to the Stockholm Convention on Persistent Organic Pollutants treaty signed in 2001. Yet many remain in our nature and have been detected in fish we buy.

I discovered from my research that I should stop eating fish. I love sushi but have decided to cut back to once a month, even though it's my favorite food. The only fish I now eat besides Sushi is fish caught by local fishermen. I'm fortunate that some fishermen still sell their catch in local markets. As with everything that is depleting, these fishermen are becoming less and less, and most end up working in the tourism sector.

While this is not perfect, it's still better than eating fish that is processed or fed with fish feed. Fish feed composition stimulates the fish to mature much faster than in the wild. In addition, these fish are obese, meaning they contain a lot of fat. Fat contains pollutants because what a body doesn't need and can't excrete is stored as fat, like us. A good example is Silver Catfish, which comes from Vietnam and is sold worldwide as Panga. Most of these fish are farmed near the Mekong River, one of the most polluted rivers in the world.

Our rivers and sewage systems are all connected to our ocean. The ocean produces 50% of our breathable air, so every second breath you take comes from the ocean and the waste we dump there. We eat fish from the ocean, farmed and caught, a critical food resource for billions of people. Should we eat fish from a cesspool?

The challenge is that after thousands of years, we still haven't evolved enough as a species to manage our waste safely. We all poop regularly; depending on where you live, this poop gets treated based on available solutions. Once processed, it goes via our sewage systems to rivers and, in many cases, directly to our ocean. What we take from the ocean lands on our plates or faces—some substances like to remain in our bodies, causing all sorts of concerns. We poop again, and the whole cycle starts all over again.

I did not know this three years ago because my life was happy, and I did not care for what was happening beyond my borders. We need more projects to clean our water from pollutants from the source to where it ends up. Water is a critical resource for every living being on our planet.

Our Doom is the one to rule, to find them, to bring them all together, and in the darkness binds them.

We have found one, and it resides in water. There are more.

ATMOSPHERE

Iused to dig up worms using a farmer's rake from my dad's tool shed next to the stables where my parents kept their horses. I collected these worms so my friends and I could go fishing in a nearby river. We hardly ever caught fish. We had not the patience for it. What I still remember from those days is the smell of the soil. It was earthy, for lack of a better term. It was sweet, not sour. I also loved the smell of horse dung and still remember it as if it were yesterday. Mind you, I didn't care much for the smell of dog poop. I haven't smelled soil or manure since, and now I wonder if I can still smell rich, healthy soil or horse manure. It's funny how smells stay with you in memories; they are unlocked when you think of something, even sometimes when thinking of trivial, unimportant stuff. Did you know that each major city has its distinct, unique smell? You should try it when visiting your next city.

Can you still smell the favorite food that your mother used to cook for you? Humans have a sense of smell for a reason; it's not as good as dogs and other animals, but it's part of our senses. Even today, I see people smelling vegetables, fruits, meat, and fish in a traditional family-owned store or market. Smells tell us if something is bad or good, and we sometimes make our purchasing decisions based on what we smell. Some people are even convinced that we can recognize the smell of an object we see and hold for the first time as if it were imprinted in us. Some believe it resides in our subconscious or even our unconscious mind.

Humans like to complain of bad smells, which we've been doing for millennia. Remember when your grandfather farted at the dinner table? There are records of complaints of foul odor that go back to our earliest recorded histories. And yet, we have always considered the outside air pure and perfect. Taking some air is a common saying of old.

Our industrial revolution changed everything as we started burning more coal. Coal was a wonderful substance, and we've been using it for 3000 years when the Chinese used it to heat their homes. We used it in the metallurgy industry to make our bronze and steel weaponry agricultural and industrial tools. Coal was king until Prince Oil came along. Coal was used in the 1880s to generate electricity, and our civilization has been using coal ever since. Without coal, we would not be where we are today regarding prosperity and our doom.

London was the city that burned the most coal in 1800; it burned 1 million tons of coal per year with a population of around 1 million. So that's one metric ton for each person who lives in the city. The use of coal spread quickly to other cities and became the dominant source of fuel all over the United Kingdom. As a trading and manufacturing nation, the British Empire became the most dominant superpower the world had ever seen. The Spanish, Portuguese, French, Dutch, German, and Russian empires paled in comparison.

Smoke from coal in the 19th century was considered good as it was believed to be a repellent from organic diseases that came from waste. British citizens were happy with the smoke as they believed that smoke from coal burning was a powerful disinfectant. Despite centuries of coal mining and known sickness, especially to a miner's lungs, having been well established. But city dwellers were not coal miners, so what was there to worry about?

The invention of the steam engine, thanks to Thomas Newcomen and James Watt, allowed for animals and water energy to be replaced with machines, and industries were born. We could dig deeper for coal, mills started using steam engines, and everything from trains and steamships began using coal. A country's wealth was determined by how much coal you could mine. The volume decided how powerful you could be as a nation. England's economy was threatened in the twentieth century as they lost their lead in energy production to the United States.

Coal enabled factories to operate year-round as they no longer had to rely on nature, such as water supply during dry spells. Thanks to coal and its benefits, the population of London grew from 1 Million in 1800 to 5 million in 1900. They were burning close to 12 million tons of coal per year. Coal started to arrive in London as early as the 1280s. There have been sporadic complaints about coal smoke, but they were mere whispers. In the 1800s, most British cities were smoky. Still, it would take another fifty or so years before people started to complain in enough numbers that the perception of coal smoke being benevolent changed to that of it being a problem. Research commenced to analyze the content of this smoke, and it became a regular topic in newspapers and magazines. The so-called smoke abatement activists were born. They had enough of the grime this smoke created even when insufficient research in the public domain confirmed that coal smoke was detrimental to human health. There was, however, a study conducted in the army during WW1 where they measured the height of recruits. To their astonishment, they found that recruits from heavily polluted cities in the midlands were shorter than recruits from rural areas. Did smoke from coal used in households and industry have anything to do with it? They thought it might be one of the reasons.

By the 1900s, it became increasingly clear that smoke from coal burning was unhealthy and was a significant contributor to a city's air quality. However, it would take another 56 years before the Clean Air Act came into force—almost a hundred years since the smoke abatement movement started. Even writers in the 19th century, like William Morris and John Ruskin, wrote that Great Britain was losing its connection to nature and sacrificing it for progress, economic growth, and material gain. Even some linked the smoke to crime and civil unrest as poor people could not escape it, while the rich, all with connections and representations in parliament, could flee to their country estates. There was much resistance in the government, so they agreed to do more research. However, regulations to curb smoke emissions encountered significant and persistent resistance as the coal-fueled industry was the source of wealth, progress, and power of the British Empire. They feared it would threaten their dominance, especially concerning the rise of the United States.

So, smoke has been recognized as becoming increasingly unhealthy for humans in the past, as we've seen in Great Britain. What replaced coal was oil and, later, gas.

The Chinese first discovered oil in 600 B.C., but it wasn't until 1859 when Colonel Edwin Drake discovered oil in Pennsylvania. The discovery of the oil field in Spindletop, Texas, in 1901 started the oil boom and subsequent oil economy. Much has been written and published about the oil industry. Most of us who have done our research have read or watched something about it. We know that the industry has known for quite some time that the waste they create results in the warming of the atmosphere. Given our dependence on oil, this fact would be primarily ignored globally until the 2015 Paris Agreement, where it was agreed to make greenhouse gas emissions reductions legally binding for the first time to halt the increase in our average global temperature.

Oil, the wonder product of our age, has brought us enormous control over our world. We have much to be thankful for. It allowed us to make more products and connect people to better education, health, and communication through technological advances. We are genuinely global because of this source of energy. We would not have a mobile phone without this energy resource.

Today, many believe that the world is highly dependent on oil. Resistance to change from one energy source to another is not new. A good example of resistance to change was when people were asked to switch from coal to oil, even during the Great Smog of London in 1952. The smog was caused by a combination of factors, including coal smoke, fog, and cold weather. It killed an estimated 12,000 people and sickened hundreds of thousands more.

After the smog, the British government introduced several measures to reduce air pollution, including the Clean Air Act of 1956. The act banned the use of coal for heating in most homes and businesses in London and other major cities. Many people resisted the switch to oil. They were concerned about the cost of oil and used to the convenience of coal. Some people also believed that coal was a more reliable source of energy. The British government eventually convinced most people to switch to oil by offering subsidies and other incentives. However, it took several years for the switch to be completed.

Here are some other examples of resistance to the switch from coal to oil:

- Labor unions resisted the switch because it led to job losses in the coal industry.

- Coal companies resisted the switch because it threatened their profits.

- Some consumers resisted the switch because they were used to coal and did not want to change.

- Some policymakers resisted the switch because they believed coal was more critical to national security than oil.

This happened in more than the United Kingdom. It happened everywhere, where coal was the primary energy source for homes, agriculture, and industry. All this would sound familiar in the nature movement, but for those who are not, I'm here to inform you that this change process from one energy source to another is repeating itself.

We talk today about greenhouse gases, but only some of us honestly know what that means and how the greenhouse gas effect works. I hear arguments that CO_2 is only 0.4% of all greenhouse gasses, so how can it cause climate change?

The first greenhouse was built in 30 A.D. when the emperor Tiberius became sick and was ordered to eat one cucumber daily. People have known about greenhouses for over 2,000 years.

I was born in the Netherlands, a tiny country; when you try to find it on the globe, it is almost invisible and has a population of 17.53 million. It is also the world's second-largest exporter of agricultural products by value after the United States and the largest agricultural and food technology exporter. If it weren't for some bright kids from the University of Agriculture in Wageningen, Netherlands, I would have never known how to grow a weed called Skunk in a greenhouse or hydroponically. If you have ever been in a greenhouse farm, you will have noticed that the temperature inside is different from outside. That's because the heat generated by the plants is trapped inside the greenhouse by glass. Plants emit water vapor, the biggest contributor to the greenhouse effect in our atmosphere. This type of farming allows us to grow crops in winter, which we could not do before this invention. So, when I first read about greenhouse gases, I knew what that meant instantly.

Greenhouse gases are but one factor in greenhouse management. In greenhouse farming, CO2 is pumped into the greenhouse as fertilizer as it stimulates growth and increases crop yield. The more the crops grow, the more greenhouse gasses such as water vapor and CO2 are emitted, which causes the temperature to rise. Cultivating greenhouse crops such as peppers, lettuce, tomatoes, and cucumbers is highly specialized. You need the right balance between temperature, CO2 concentrations, and other gases, hours of direct sunlight, ventilation, water, soil, nutrients, leakage prevention, and a raft of different variables to maximize crop yield. Now it is mainly automated with software technology that manages all this for the farmer who can now sit on his butt and watch TV all day. These farms are enormous. Maintenance and health checks, soil, water, air, insect populations, and fertilizer systems are constantly needed. Besides, they also must manage their waste. So, these farmers have no time for TV.

All of us live in a greenhouse. The only difference is that we don't have a glass roof, software, or systems to manage the global greenhouse that we call Earth. At least not yet. So far, no fool of a geo-engineer has suggested creating escape valves in our atmosphere to cool our greenhouse temperature or release greenhouse gasses via spaceships. More CO2 is suitable for plants, as we have seen. According to NASA's research published since 2018 and other studies, our green vegetation has grown in density over the last decades thanks to our increase in carbon dioxide emissions. That's terrific news. The only problem is we can't control emissions. We can't balance the planet to ensure we have the right CO2 concentration, water vapor, soil health, fungi, insects, and mammals. We don't have a thermostat or an air conditioner remote control to regulate our ambient temperature. We can't even prevent our water from getting polluted.

Without the greenhouse effect, Earth's average temperature would be about -18 degrees Celsius (-0.4 degrees Fahrenheit). The greenhouse effect is essential for life on Earth. In 1900, the average global temperature was estimated to be somewhere around 13.73 Degrees Celsius, according to NOAA. This is derived from data collected from temperature readings logged on land and ships. Today, it is 15.3, an increase of 1.57 degrees Celsius. We have exceeded the COP 21 Paris Agreement for the first time in 2023. This can only mean that we have been pumping so much greenhouse gases into our atmosphere for over 123 years that our average global temperature has increased by 1.5 degrees. What comes next? We will see, as climate change is measured over 30 years, but if you ask me, this does not bode well because we can't regulate global temperature and water. We are starting to feel its effects. We've never had so many heatwaves and flooding events in history. Let me jog your memory and see if you can detect a trend.

- 1972: The Great Britain Heatwave
- 1976: Soviet heatwave that killed 23000 people
- 1980: Iraq drought caused widespread famine
- 1983: China Floods causing 24000 deaths
- 1998: The El Niño Southern Oscillation (ENSO) event caused worldwide heatwaves, flooding, and droughts.
- 2003: A heatwave in Europe killed over 70,000 people.
- 2010: The Russian heat wave caused over 55,000 deaths.
- 2012: The United States experienced a series of significant floods.
- 2013: The Philippines was hit by typhoons, causing widespread flooding and damage.
- 2016: The United States experienced a record-breaking heatwave.
- 2017: Hurricane Harvey caused widespread flooding in Texas and Louisiana.
- 2018: The Amazon rainforest experienced a significant drought.
- 2020: The Black Summer bushfires in Australia caused widespread damage.
- 2021: Hurricanes in the USA, Flooding in China, extreme winter USA, flooding in Germany
- 2022: Floods in Pakistan affecting 33 million people
- 2023: Extreme freezing in Afghanistan (-28C), Floods in California, Warm winter in Europe, Floods in Brazil, India, Hong Kong, Slovenia, China, USA, Malaysia, South Korea, and Libya, Wildfires in Canada, Heatwaves in USA and Europe.

For over 50 years, we have had many extreme weather events, but I think 2023 looks like it's the worst yet. You could argue that they are all isolated incidents, as the weather where I live is not the same as where you live unless you are my neighbor. The point is that these weather events are increasing and repeating in higher frequencies, becoming more widespread and with increased intensity simultaneously.

Many cities today have air pollution issues that can be found on any continent. According to IQ Air, only 58 cities out of 100 major cities in the world have "good" air quality. You can even download an app that tells you the air quality in your area. Sadly, according to the World Health Organization, around 6.7 million people die of air pollution-related illnesses yearly. That's much more than the 12,000 people that died in 1952 of smog in London. We still don't have a global Clean Air Act.

Our air includes not only greenhouse gases but also includes smaller particles such as microplastics. We know that microplastics are in our air because we have found them in rainwater. The purest form of water on our planet comes from rainwater. Another particle that is of significant concern is soot. Soot comes from burning carbon, particularly plants, trees, and our other favorite, coal. Soot is dark brown or black particles that, thanks to the wind streams in our atmosphere, can travel for thousands of kilometers and end up in places far away. Soot has been found in the Arctic and Antarctica, and it makes ice turn black and transforms it from a heat-repellent surface to a heat-absorbent surface, which causes ice to melt. Much of our agricultural waste in many countries worldwide is still burnt because there is no value associated with this waste. Add to that the enormous forest fires we have witnessed in Canada, Chili, Greece, and other areas, and you can imagine how much soot, also known as combusted carbon, it creates. This burning creates soot that travels to the poles and lands in our ocean. Soot is carbon, which, if you add enough of it, will decrease the alkalinity of water, as we've discussed in Chapter Water.

All the waste we find today in our air eventually drops towards land and water and is absorbed again into our air, so our waste is all connected in one enormous planetary sphere. Our global fixation on air, in particular, our atmosphere, from talking about climate change and climate action and a little bit about biodiversity loss seems to me at least to indicate that we don't take our whole planet, the greenhouse we live in seriously enough. Perhaps the information, the stories, and the arguments are not sinking in. Besides, since climate change is measured over a 30-year period, it is no wonder that people say there is still time. The process of Earth's spheres' degradation is slow, and questions are being asked about either slowing it down or re-engineering it to reverse it.

One question is yet to be answered: How can we reduce our current level of CO_2 concentration in the Atmosphere from 416.45 ppm (Source: NOAA Sep 2023) to 278 ppm (CO_2 Concentration in 1750)? We are still only talking about reducing our emissions. We are not talking about eliminating our emissions unless you are an activist. The good news is that the research suggests that our biodiversity can absorb our greenhouse gases.

The narrative of Climate Change and Climate action serves us well. It helps drown and silence the voices of many scientists. It is now also big business and not always for the right reasons. Furthermore, the dominant focus on climate change almost drowns out the noise about the use of our water and our land. Scientists that focus on pollution, or those that focus on plastics, forever chemicals, and pesticides polluting our air, water, land, and our bodies, are receiving little attention. It drowns out the voices who seek change at a personal and systems level. Last but not least, it drowns out why this is happening. What is the root cause? We create waste and pollute nature on all of earth's systems.

Many are designing a future for us, requiring us to think and act differently. Others are saying that we do not need to change. Those voices are heard everywhere, depending on where or who you are with. Activists are screaming so loud it feels like your ears are glued to the church bells of Notre Dame. Sadly, not much is sinking in. Especially on the global stage, and now we know why. We are not greenhouse farmers. You don't control a greenhouse by focusing on temperature and how much gas you pump into it. The world needs to start thinking more like a greenhouse farmer.

Lost in translation.

Scientists and economists use jargon and terminology that is specific to their field. It is natural as all professions have this trait. When a research report comes out, you will find many terms used that those not specialized in that field need help understanding. These reports end up on the desks of politicians, businesses, not-for-profit organizations, and consultants interested in this research. They will try to understand the meaning, which then gets translated to suit their needs. Finally, the public is informed and, depending on who you listen to or where the translation comes from, forms your understanding. People today tend to be informed by other people and the media that is in line with what they believe to be the truth or what they are convinced they know and how it matches their lifestyle, goals, and ambitions.

For example, the term carbon tunnel vision has been used far and wide in natural space, and this vision is considered dangerous now by many in this field. For those of you who have never heard of it, the community inside the nature space is focused too much on human-caused CO_2 emissions and is forgetting about the why.

It also works the other way. The climate change and climate action narrative are manipulative. For the most part, we are still instinctive beings tied to our personal and societal belief systems. I'll try to explain why we are chained to our beliefs through communication and specifically reporting human-caused CO2 emissions from scientists to politicians and businesses, not for profits and from those to the public.

CO2 emissions in our atmosphere are measured in parts per million, not metric tons. It's how scientists commonly measure concentrations of a substance in another substance. We currently live in an atmosphere with a CO2 concentration of 417 ppm. (source NOAA) That means what governments, businesses, and not-for-profit organizations will ask. For example, scientists could say it's terrible because the concentration at the start of the Industrial Revolution (1750) was 278 ppm. As the scientist's research clearly indicates, the scientist would add that this is due to human-caused CO2 emissions.

Government, businesses, and not-for-profits will ask, is this safe? Well, for humans, it is; for our global average temperature, it is not. When CO2 concentration reaches 40000 ppm, you will most likely die. 417 vs. 40000 is huge, so there is nothing to worry about, right? How about temperature? Temperatures will rise, and this will affect our climate. How? If the global average temperature keeps increasing, we will likely experience more extreme weather events, which requires more research. Will this affect the food and water supply? Two critical resources for any nation. The answer is yes. This will highly likely affect land, villages, cities, and even countries. We should remember that scientists will never say "with 100% certainty", so when a scientist says highly likely, you should get worried. What is the impact on humans related to higher average temperature?

Well, not much. Humans can live from -32 degrees Celsius to +45 degrees Celsius if we have heating and cooling habitats nearby. That doesn't help, so scientists explain that humans can live comfortably in an ambient temperature of around 25 degrees Celsius. This means that the temperature around us for which we don't need clothes for our bodies can produce heat from eating food and drinking liquids and cool us down through sweating. Our global average temperature is 17.2 degrees Celsius, so there is nothing to worry about; we need to add clothes and energy to stay warm. When the ambient temperature reaches a human body temperature of 36.7 degrees Celsius, we are in trouble unless we find a cool place. Those of us who have experienced heat waves would know all about that. People forget we are talking about global average temperature, not ambient temperature. I live in a country where the average yearly ambient temperature swings between 29 – 37 degrees Celsius in a year. This is nowhere near 17.2 degrees, and this place would be uncomfortable without air-conditioning.

Depending on where they are, governments have to figure out how best to communicate all this climate research to the public. That's why we now discuss greenhouse gas emission reduction in percentages and weight. We understand weight in kilograms and pounds. Metric tons get a little more complicated because many of us would find it hard to imagine what a metric ton of CO2 gas would look like, apart from the fact that it is heavy.

What narrative, i.e., story, would a government tell people like you and me so we can understand without causing a panic? Politicians are highly aware of how their voter base and opposition think. They have polls and, in some cases, spies. For businesses, especially those that emit CO2, they will and have said things like.

1. They discovered something we already knew in the 1960s and 70s.

2. It is not critical, so we can delay because humans are not at risk based on the data.

3. Besides, what does highly likely mean? For us, it means that it's not inevitable.

4. Uncertainty is good for us.

5. Besides, we are so big they will never allow us to fail, for the world economy will collapse. Remember the financial crisis of 2008?

They get additional help from public relations firms and lobbyists to ensure that governments develop a good story that protects our shareholders and stakeholders so we can operate as best as we can in the current economic climate. Let us also ensure that we keep the world's attention on greenhouse gas emissions and not the cause. Let us also show support for our customers by informing them how we calculate emissions and reduce them. We need to keep people happy.

British Petroleum came up with Carbon Footprint for a particular reason. To push the responsibility to the public and other businesses that depend on fossil fuel. They invented the carbon footprint calculator. This calculator has evolved and is being applied in many different forms for the public and businesses so they can now report their emissions. This is brilliant because what you can measure, you can manage, and we have plenty of time. Not-for-profits will ring the alarm bells and cause fear in their audience to get more donations. This may sound harsh, but it is not far from the truth.

Lost in translation has been going on for centuries, even millennia, and it's good for business. Maintaining the climate change narrative is a distraction as the primary cause of our changing world is rooted deeply in society. It is rooted deeply within our current individual beliefs and behavior. Part of it is instinctive and primal, which, over the last 300 years, has been exploited and camouflaged by terms like GDP, free markets, wealth creation, economic development, economic growth, and living standards. Society does not change willingly until the time comes when there is no other option.

We are fast approaching a period in the not-too-distant future when we realize that the air we breathe is affecting our personal health, caused by our behavior that will result in something similar to what happened in the dark ages. No, it won't be a deadly pathogen from nature that is airborne like SARS-COVID-19. It will be the substances that we have produced since the early 20th century and now reside in our bodies in large enough quantities, causing the medical community to raise their concerns.

When we use history as a guide, we should by now be aware that our actions ultimately result in dire consequences. We may wish to disguise, or we may wish to expose our doom as much as we can. Eventually, the world will have to decide. Do we wish to keep the climate change narrative going, or should we change the narrative to something that everyone understands and, more importantly, each of us, our community, and society as a whole can manage? Health may be the answer.

Our Doom is the one to rule, to find them, to bring them all together, and in the darkness binds them.

We have found the second one, and it lives in the air. There are more.

LITHOSPHERE

In Africa we lived in an old colonial house. It even had a tree in the pantry where our clothes were being washed and where we had our freezer. It was a large tree, around a meter in circumference and at least 40 meters high. The ceiling and roof were built around it. The roof was not water-tight, so when it rained, the water would flow down its trunk into the soil, which its roots could absorb. I loved that house, made of huge grey stones carved out of a nearby quarry and a red-colored iron corrugated roof. Our bedrooms were huge, in which we played football and basketball despite my mother's complaints about the noise. We had a huge living and dining room, and all across the front of the house, we had a veranda overlooking our immense garden. We had three gardens: one in front, a second further down, and one on the side. All in all, you could fit two football fields into our garden.

Beyond the garden, you would go into the bush, thick, lush greenery with trees and bushes, and a thick bamboo forest leading to the river below. I ventured there often looking for snakes. I didn't know anything about snakes back then, as I never bothered to venture into the school library to read up about them until I had to care for them. For me, this was paradise. I felt like Sir John Livingstone, the famous missionary explorer of Africa, who, I might add, hated slavery.

I caught many snakes, and quite a few times with the bites to prove it. I let them go because I did not know how to keep them alive in a cage. What I did do was keep rabbits. I don't know if you have ever heard of the term "breeding like rabbits," but boy, they breed fast. Soon, I had so many rabbits that I started to panic. I tried to give them to students at my school, but not enough of them would adopt one. It did, however, make me popular with the girls. I was left with only one choice: to release them into the wild. Soon, the bush area and bamboo forest down to the river bank were teeming with white, red-eyed rabbits, and I thought the problem was solved.

Well, not quite. Little did I know, but these lovely, innocent rabbits attracted predators. First came the Owls. Their incessant wooing drove me up the wall at night. Then came the wild cats, the wild dogs, more snakes, especially pythons, and even a leopard. The villagers from the coffee plantation next door started to complain. These wild animals ventured into their village, looking for more food. This is logical if you are a cat or a dog, as it takes a lot of energy to catch a bunny versus digging for food scraps in waste patches close to the village. So, I had to stop breeding rabbits. I had disturbed the balance. With my foolishness, I had introduced an invasive species into nature. I did, however, solve the village rat problem.

Humans don't have a good scorecard for balance and sharing, especially regarding land and water use. We will soon reach 9 Billion if all goes well, and the only species that have kept up with us are rats and the domesticated animals we need for sustenance. As for the rest of our animals, as the chart shows below, we have greatly pushed our weight around since the Industrial Revolution.

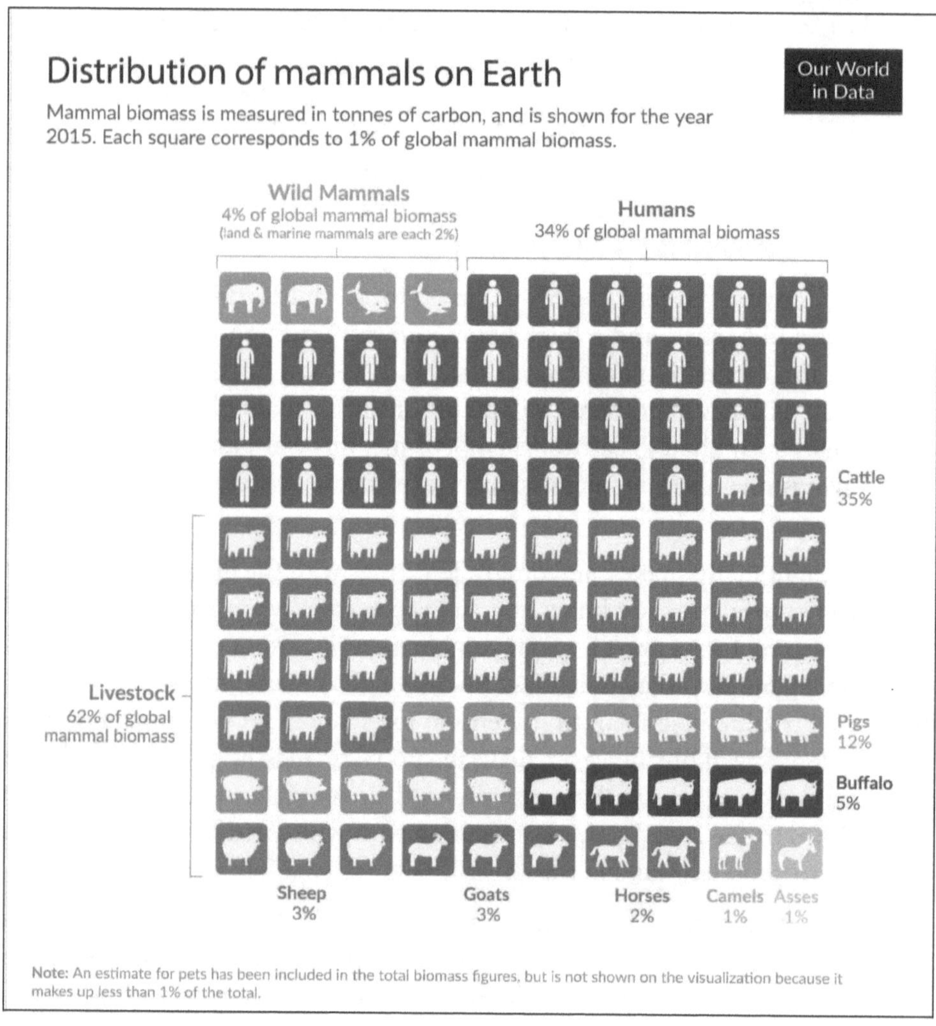

Interestingly, Rats are not featured here even though they are in their billions. They don't weigh much, as they weigh between 41 grams and 500 grams. Rats are a part of us because they love the way we live. Rats live in every city, village, and hamlet.

One of the main reasons we have so many rats is because of our food. Humans have become experts on food production as we use 4.8 billion hectares to grow food for a world population of 8 Billion. Our world data shows we use approximately 3.1 billion hectares for livestock farming alone.

That's pretty impressive, considering we used 1.1 billion hectares for 770 million people at the beginning of the Industrial Age. We have become super efficient even though we've taken a lot of land away from our fellow species. If you were a wolf, you would probably agree that humans are an invasive species, like those white, fluffy, red-eyed bunnies. The only difference is these bunnies, we call humans, can kill everything.

We have made enormous progress in increasing crop yields and keeping our crops healthy. One unique substance we have used to help us achieve this enormous progress is pesticides. Pesticides are substances that, as their name implies, kill pests. In other words, species that harm our crops. We have many pesticides available to us. We first started using pesticides around 4500 years ago in Mesopotamia, and they used sulfur dusting to protect their crops. In the 15th century, we used arsenic, mercury, and lead. Now, that's scary as these substances are nasty for you. In the 17th century, we used nicotine sulfate extracted from tobacco leaves; in the 19th century, we used extracts from chrysanthemums and rotenone from the roots of tropical vegetables.

There are many types of pesticides;

Herbicides slow down the growth of weeds or, at best, kill them.

Insecticides kill insects.

Fungicides kill fungi that slow down crop growth or kill crops.

Molluscicides for snails, rodenticides for mice and rats, nematicides for worms, and even bird repellents and fumigants that disinfect soils.

Until the 1950s, arsenic-based pesticides were dominant—a reason why so many aquifers are contaminated with it today. I'm happy I wasn't around then. It was Paul Hermann Müller who, in 1948, received the Nobel Prize in Physiology or Medicine for his 1939 discovery of a pesticide that we know as DDT. It was an effective insecticide and helped control malaria and yellow fever, which were still prevalent in many parts of the world then.

Chlorinates such as DDT were dominant until they were finally banned in 1972 in the USA and the 70's in Europe. However, chlorinate-based pesticides are still not banned everywhere. They are controlled, yes, but not banned. Many different types have emerged since then and are deemed safe, although few have been tested for human safety. Many pesticides are used in Asian rice farming, European greenhouses, and farms worldwide.

A legend in the nature movement called Rachel Carson, who wrote a book called Silent Spring, published in September 1962, was the first activist to draw attention to the harmful effects of pesticides, especially DDT. DDT was suspected of causing harm to both animals and humans. It wasn't until 2001 that it was confirmed that DDT caused congenital disabilities, low birth weight, and premature births in the USA. Poor Paul Hermann Muller discovered a product that caused unintended consequences. DDT was replaced in the U.S. by organophosphates and carbamates by 1975. Since then, pyrethrin, nitrogen-based compounds, carboxylic acids such as 2,4-dichlorophenoxyacetic acid, and glyphosate have become dominant.

Roundup is a pesticide used worldwide and contains Glyphosate from Monsanto. This company also sells genetically modified seeds for monoculture. Monsanto is now owned by Bayer, the famous aspirin company and the largest seller of pesticides in the world. They persist that these pesticides are needed to feed a growing population, hopefully without unintended consequences. In 2023, The European Union extended the use of roundup for another 10 years despite fierce opposition from nature groups.

While reading all this material on pesticides, I realized that humans like to shoot first and ask questions later. We are more comfortable with killing things than figuring out how we can come up with solutions that would aid our need to grow food without harming nature. Is this instinctive, or have we become conditioned that way? Is this still a part of our evolution that we must master?

Almost everyone has residues of pesticides in their bodies today, and how harmful or unharmful they are is still a matter that is being studied today. What is clear, however, is that time and time again, any substance harmful to our natural ecosystems ultimately harms us. It is also no wonder that insecticides and rodenticides (rat poison) used in our households are used in attempted suicide. (Please seek help if you are suffering from suicidal thoughts.)

We have plenty of examples of unintended consequences from our past.

There is much debate about glyphosate. When consumed in high enough quantities, it can kill you. Roundup is the name of the herbicide that contains glyphosate. Glyphosate is also an antibiotic from which GMO-produced seeds made by Monsanto are immune. Research indicates that this pesticide can cause neurological damage, and when tested on rats, yes, they are still with us, have shown that this pesticide is harmful to its liver and kidneys and thus harmful to animals like DDT. Glyphosate is predominately used in the early stages of crop growth. Crops are meant for livestock, not crops directly meant for human consumption.

Glyphosate likes to attach itself to soil and embeds itself in plants; hence, farmers use this herbicide as early as possible, way before a crop like corn or cotton can be harvested. It takes between 3 and 19 weeks for Glyphosate to break down. That's between 21 and 133 days. Corn is harvested 75 to 85 days after planting. So does this mean that harvested corn contains Glyphosate? We've learned from the use of pesticides that it harms our nature; it are dispersed in water and animal waste, which often ends up in our waterways and oceans, where it destroys marine life such as plankton. It takes approximately 90 days to float from St. Louis to the Gulf of Mexico. That leaves 43 days for Glyphosate to break down in the gulf. Well, Glyphosate does not break down in water; it persists. Poor fish, yes, glyphosate has been found in fish and affects their brain, according to research from January 2021.

You are what you eat, my mother once told me. She also told me always to finish my plate. Not a scrap should remain. This habit of ensuring we finished our plate came from our ancestors and was widely adopted in allied countries during World War 1 and World War 2. Finishing your plate has become part of our culture and has spread to many parts of the world. An interesting fact before WW2 was that most Americans did not consume enough calories, so the Standard American Diet was invented to fatten the population. Finishing your plate was critical. However, not everywhere. There are still cultures where leaving some food on your plate is polite. If you didn't, they would keep serving you until you exploded. I would venture a guess, but billions of people still leave food on their plates. All this food ends up as waste.

I've heard that finishing your plate causes obesity. In 2023, approximately 1 billion people globally are obese. That's 12.5% of the global population, 650 million adults, 340 million adolescents, and 39 million children, which is increasing, according to the World Health Organization. The countries with the highest obesity rates as a percentage of the population are from high to low: Pacific Island Nations, Kuwait, USA, Jordan, Saudi Arabia, Qatar, Libya, Turkey, Egypt, and Lebanon. Interestingly, the saying "finish your plate" is not a thing in Arab cultures. In Arab cultures, people like to meet over a meal. It is traditional to do business while having a delicious meal. I can only say that maybe they are having too many meetings to close a deal. It is important to understand cultures, for it is in cultures where we find beliefs. They may not always be a cause, but surprisingly, much of our behavior comes from our ancestors.

We also still have around 828 million people who regularly go to bed hungry. Mainly and still mostly in Africa, which we still need to address even after live aid in July 1985. We sent around 150 million dollars in aid, and then we all went home and talked about the fantastic performance of Queen, which is what most people now remember about Live Aid. 10% of the world's population goes hungry regularly. Despite our advanced technologies and social and economic advances, we don't share food resources well. Even worse is that according to the United Nations Food and Agriculture Organization, we waste between 34% to 40% of the food we and our domesticated animals consume.

That's a hell of a lot of wasted food, which poses a challenge for the future as the world population is forecasted to grow to 9.1 billion by 2050. This means that we require a 60% increase in food availability to feed the world population, according to the UNFAO. Does this mean that we will have 10% of our global population, which is close to a Billion people going to bed hungry regularly? Is this acceptable?

The good news is that our global population is aging thanks to decreasing fertility rates. We know that food consumption starts to fall once you hit 30 years old, and by the time you reach 50, your food intake energy requirement needs would have dropped by a third from peak levels in your twenties. So, understanding our food needs in an aging world needs to be examined to determine how much more we need to produce and how food would be distributed. Not all regions will have similar aging trends, especially in different countries. In aging countries, we would need less food per person than, for example, in countries with a younger population.

There will also be many more obese people, so maybe we could balance this. It's unlikely, but perhaps food for thought; pun most definitely intended.

We throw away food scraps every day,

Mother, "Linda, finish your plate."

Linda said, "Ahh, but I'm full and don't like broccoli."

Oops, the broccoli goes into the trash bin. Now, some of us have an organic trash bin and an inorganic trash bin, but as I've mentioned in the previous chapter, in which container do I now throw Linda's uneaten Broccoli?

Are we, as consumers, to blame for our food waste? Well, partly because we shop for food from family-owned grocery stores and local markets to giant supermarkets. We are even incentivized to buy a lot of food with discounts and special offers like buy two and get one free. You buy three apples instead of 2. In addition, you look at the fresh produce, and if lettuce has some brown edges, you leave it and pick one that doesn't. The same goes for fruit, as no one likes to buy an apple with a dent. The same can be said for processed foods in cans. Who buys a can with a dent in it?

Thanks to incentives, many of us bring home too much food that goes into the storage room or cupboards in our kitchen or the refrigerator and stays there until used for breakfast, lunch, or dinner. But not all the food is consumed; some even go bad in the fridge or reach an expiry date. Even meat in the freezer that has exceeded the expiration date is thrown away. So voila, it ends up in the trash, and you have to flip a coin or draw straws to decide which poor soul has to carry out the garbage for collection in the morning. The supermarket, well, despite all the incentives, still ends up with food that is not sold. That poor dented apple now has a brown-colored spot, and yep, all that goes into the dumpster behind the supermarket. You should check what is dumped there. Even items that have yet to reach their expiry date are dumped. In some locations, this organic waste is collected and used for compost, which can be used for communal gardens, parks, and even for your plants on the balcony. It's recycled, but unfortunately, this is not global, and many people live in high-rise apartments who do not have green fingers or even a desire to test their greenness.

1405 million tons of food is thrown away annually, and of that, 64% of the total Food waste is from households (569 Metric Tons), food service (244 Metric Tons), and retail (118 Metric Tons).

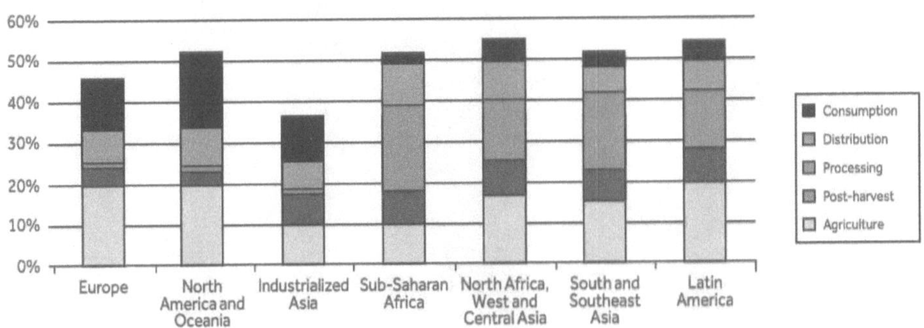

Figure 1. Percentage of the initial production lost or wasted at different stages of the FSC for fruits and vegetables in different regions. "Agriculture" indicates losses occurring during harvest operation and subsequent sorting and grading. "Post-harvest" indicates losses occurring during handling, transportation and storage immediately after harvest and before processing.

Source: UNFOA

However, food waste is not equal everywhere, so we must dig deeper to understand where our food is wasted within the entire supply chain from farm to table.

Since Fruits and Vegetables have the most waste at 45%, we use this as an example.

While we, as activists in wealthy countries or those with higher Incomes, try to make people aware of their consumer waste, we must also be aware that food waste is not equal globally. Food processing is a significant issue for regions like Africa, Southeast Asia, and Latin America. Is this due to High-Income countries' quality requirements or poor technology infrastructure?

In addition, we have a chart of the global level of obesity below. Of course, obesity and fruits and vegetables are not compatible bedfellows as eating fruits and vegetables is supposed to be good for you and help reduce obesity. Many times in society, we like to emphasize that eating fruits and vegetables is better for your health. However, it does show that overconsumption of food is a cause of food waste, and, in equal measure, food waste from agriculture is driven by quality standards, regulations, and expectations of quality from processors, distribution retailers, and consumers. It's a huge problem and getting even more challenging because our food is not what it was a hundred years ago.

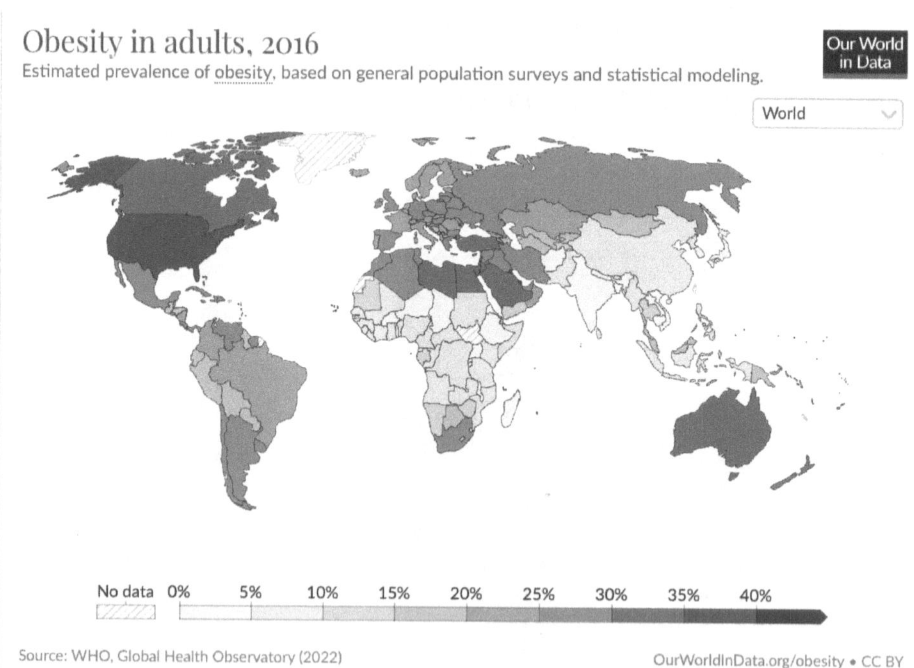

How much energy you consume and how much energy you use regulates your weight. More energy intake vs. less energy output equals weight gain. It's that simple and lies at the core of all weight loss diets, which is a massive market in countries with, wait for it, the highest levels of obesity. So I guess people prefer to be obese instead of slim as advertised by all these weight loss before and after programs. Why is that? It is not because of our consumerism alone, although it plays a role thanks to fast food, instant meals, and unhealthy food preparation. It is also a gene issue, as some people are more prone to weight gain than others. However, we humans fail to grasp what a balanced diet should be. This is a challenge for nutritionists as every person is different, and while most are good at their job, it is still tricky. Besides, who has a nutritionist? It could help to know exactly how much food we should buy and consume without gaining weight. We haven't figured that out yet, so our food waste problem persists.

We also consume a lot of meat. When I worked in South America for a bit, I used to love going to churrascaria restaurants and eating various cuts of the most delicious meat on the planet. In Australia, it was hard to avoid a Saturday or Sunday barbeque in the summer and even sometimes in the winter. South Americans, Americans, Australians, and even South Koreans love their meat and, for the most part, are proud of it, too. It is expected. There is little or no room for Vegans in some communities, well, almost, as this is slowly changing.

Since we have all this data, we now understand that we have a problem. We can apply, and what can be measured can be managed. But we have a bigger problem that is now coming out of more and more research papers. There is a substance in our food that does not belong there. But before we explain the alien substance in our food, I would like to know where all this food waste ends up.

In households, food services, and retail, our food waste ends up in our sewage system if it is small enough, or we throw it in the trash, which in some countries goes into the organic trash bin like what we see in many Northern European countries. In others, there is one bin for all our trash.

But as I mentioned earlier, there is something evil in our food today that can no longer be ignored, and no, this evil did not come from Hell. It is an evil we have invented, produced, and used for over a hundred years. These substances are called forever chemicals and plastic; they are everywhere, and we love eating and drinking them, too.

How did this come to pass?

By the middle of the 19th century, some animal-derived materials had become increasingly scarce in the wake of industrialized goods production. Elephants were facing extinction if demand for their ivory, used in items from piano keys to billiard balls, continued. The same fate awaited some turtle species, whose shell was harnessed for combs. Plastic saved the Elephant just in time, but we have the Elephant and Walrus to thank for the lovely Ivory keys on which pianists played Mozart, Bach, and many other composers. However, they used keys made of wood.

Inventors attempted to tackle nature and economic problems with many patents for new semi-synthetic materials based on natural substances such as cork, blood, and milk. One of the earliest was cellulose nitrate—cotton fibers dissolved in nitric and sulphuric acids and mixed with vegetable oil.

Its inventor, the Birmingham-born artisan-cum-chemist Alexander Parkes, patented this new material in 1862 as Parkesine. Considered the first manufactured plastic, it was a cheap substitute for ivory or tortoiseshell. Parkes himself didn't enjoy commercial success, such is what happens to most inventors, but his invention was taken up and developed by others, including his former factory manager Daniel Spill and the businessman John Wesley Hyatt, the latter of whom founded the Celluloid Manufacturing Company in the United States.

This new plastic made items like combs and billiard balls affordable to many more people, democratizing consumer goods and culture. Undoubtedly, celluloid's most remarkable cultural application was cinema film. Sunglasses were another fashionable product that became popular in the 1920s.

The 20th century saw a revolution in plastic production: the advent of entirely synthetic plastics. Belgian chemist and clever marketeer Leo Baekeland pioneered the first fully synthetic plastic in 1907. He beat his Scottish rival, James Swinburne, to the patent office by one day. His invention, which he would christen Bakelite, combined two chemicals, formaldehyde and phenol, under heat and pressure.

Bakelite sparked a consumer boom in affordable yet highly desirable products. Its dark brown, wood-like appearance could be easily mass-produced, making it ideal for bringing new design trends such as Art Deco to the masses. Some products became 20th-century icons: the Purma camera, the GPO telephone, and the Ekco AD36 radio. Bakelite, which contains around 5% Asbestos, is still used today, for example, in the production of light switches.

Leo Baekeland was a fascinating fellow. While working in the United States, he also developed photographic paper. His company, Nepera, was sold to Eastman Kodak Co., which dominated the pre-digital photography era.

I would also like to introduce Roy J Plunkett, a gentleman you may have never heard of, who, in 1938, worked as a chemical engineer for Dupont and discovered a substance called polytetrafluoroethylene (PTFE). The discovery was accidental, a fluke. PTFE is a chemical considered the most slippery material in existence, making it one of the most versatile materials invented. Many industries use and have used this chemical, including aerospace, communications, electronics, industrial processes, architecture, and house appliances.

Since its registration in 1945, Teflon, as it was renamed because who wants to buy polytetrafluoroethylene, has become a familiar brand, recognized worldwide for the superior non-stick properties associated with its use, such as in

- Coating on cookware.
- Soil and stain repellent for fabrics and textile products such as furniture, carpets, wallpaper, raincoats, and umbrellas.
- Superior coating in harsh manufacturing environments and industrial products such as personal protection clothing.

The first Teflon products were sold commercially under the trademark starting in 1946.

Roy J. Plunkett was inducted into the Plastics Hall of Fame in 1973, a year after the Clean Water Act was enacted in 1972. In 1985, he was inducted into the Inventor's Hall of Fame next to Louis Pasteur, Alfred Nobel, Gideon Zundback, who invented the zipper, and many others.

Source: The history of Teflon www.teflon.com

I don't believe Roy was a bad or evil man; he was doing his job as a chemical engineer. He certainly did not know how dangerous his invention was for humanity. Unfortunately, this is part of unintended consequences. Teflon also contains perfluorooctanoic acid (PFOA, also called C8), one of over 18000 forever chemicals in existence today. This Teflon is now banned in the USA (2014), UK (2005), and EU (2008).

Today, 97% to 99% of Americans have forever chemicals in their body. I could not find data for other parts of the world, although chemicals have been found in 17000 European locations.

My mother loved Teflon pans, and so did I as a student in the late 80s and early 90s. Before you throw away your non-stick frying pan, please remember that since 2014, it has been considered safe, although there are still quite a few chemicals in there that we are not sure of in terms of effects on our health, so there is that.

When you look at the timeline of Teflon being sold worldwide since 1946 and the evolution of wastewater treatment, we see that it is logical that most people today have contaminants in their bodies that initially came from the result of our manufacturing and consumption activities.

The first PFAS filtration system was implemented in 2021 in Orange County. So that's 75 years or, in other words, close to the average lifespan of an American, which is 77 Years, and we have passed it on to our current GenZ population like our chickens are passing on their ingested microplastics to their eggs.

Which food contains the most forever chemicals?

Well, the US Food and Drug Administration (FDA) conducted extensive testing and found that 74% of all seafood caught in rivers and in the ocean, including aquaculture, contained forever chemicals (PFAS), of which clams, cod, crab, pollock, salmon, shrimp, tilapia and tuna showed the highest concentrations.

Now, wait a minute. Has Forever Chemicals been found in Tuna? These fish are pelagic, meaning their habitat is below the continental shelf, and can be found everywhere in our ocean, both in tropical and temperate waters. Maybe they ingest forever chemicals from what they eat, which is fish like herring, squid, and crustaceans, or when they breathe through their gills, which means PFAS is present in our Ocean far from shore.

What about Meat products? The FDA has confirmed that PFAS is also found in meat sold in Supermarkets and even in Chocolate cake, which showed that PFAS found in the tested cake was 275 times higher than the federal guidelines of what is deemed safe. How about fruits and vegetables? The answer is yes, and the same is true for cereals.

Recently, the FDA has downplayed the threat of forever chemicals, and I wonder why. We certainly don't want to scare the global population as the USA has the safest food system in the world, or so they claim. We also don't see people dying in mass numbers, so all is good.

Food is a global trade, so what can be found in the USA can be found everywhere. The USA is the biggest exporter of food by value in the world. Products that contain PFAS and materials made of plastic can be found everywhere. Does 97 – 99% of the global population have forever chemicals in their blood?

The other evil that lurks within us is microplastics.

As shown in the previous chapter, plastics are found in our fruits and vegetables. Is this also true for meat and marine animals?

Unfortunately, micro and nano plastics have been found in beef, pork, and chicken; 80% of meat and dairy products, and even eggs, contain micro-plastics. A chicken passes her ingested microplastics to her eggs and chicks before her head is chopped off.

Even in the Netherlands, which incinerates almost all of its collected waste, beef and pork samples contain surprisingly high micro-plastic levels. If you watch nature documentaries from forty years ago, you will notice that plastic pollution was never mentioned, but today, all cover the subject. People active in plastic waste pollution clean-ups are now calling our host planet Plastic.

Microplastics and Forever chemicals are everywhere. They are present on all continents and spread widely into our ocean.

It gets worse as microplastics have been detected inside our bodies from stool samples. What is even more worrying is that microplastics have been found in our blood, organs, and lungs. Our body absorbs micro and nano plastics through our skin, breathing it in, eating it, and drinking it daily.

Have microplastics in our bodies been linked to illnesses and health complications?

Most research on the effects of forever chemicals, pesticides, and microplastics on our health is emerging. Studies show alarming results as they are now linked to several health effects. According to the European Environment Agency, when it comes to forever chemicals, these substances can lead to cancer, DNA damage, organ dysfunction, metabolic disorder, neurotoxicity, reproductive and developmental toxicity" and chronic diseases. (Source: ACS Publications; Article Potential Health Impact of Microplastics: A Review of Environmental Distribution, Human Exposure, and Toxic Effects, August 10, 2023)

Another recent study published on 8 September 2023, Risk Factors for Parkinson's Disease, conducted by several neurologists in the Netherlands, shows that Parkinson's disease has increased by 30%. One of the leading causes is linked to pollution, mainly from pesticides. It was already well known that greenhouse and regular farmers had a higher risk of Parkinson's than others. This research also established that it no longer affects people over 60. The youngest patient diagnosed with Parkinson's is only 13 years old, and more and more people in their twenties, thirties, and forties are diagnosed with the disease.

Another paper, a Pre-press paper called Parkinson's Disease is predominantly environmental, was published on January 9th, 2024, which confirms the same. Because of advances in neuroimaging, researchers are now better equipped with diagnostic capabilities. The paper suggests that it's the fastest-growing disease worldwide and grossly underdiagnosed in the Netherlands (12%), Beijing (48% and Rural Bolivia (100%). The paper claims that one of the primary sources of chemicals that cause Parkinson's disease is Paraquat. Paraquat is a herbicide widely used to kill weeds and several grass species. It was first used in Agriculture in 1962 and is still used today. Its unintended consequences are only now surfacing, and there is increasing debate over its continued use.

While still in the early stages of research, we know that plastics contain 13,000 chemicals, of which 7,000 have been screened. Of these 7000 chemicals, 3200 are of significant concern according to UNEP, which translates into something like, "holy crap," when you are not a cautious organization or a scientist. You certainly try your best not to piss people off. The primary concern does not sound so bad.

These chemicals affect both men and women as they could pass these chemicals on to their newborns through breast milk, which has already been found to contain microplastics and could cause neurodevelopmental and neurobehavioral-related disorders. In Men, it has a detrimental effect on fertility as it disrupts your endocrine function, meaning your hormone production cycle, as it reduces testosterone levels and sperm count. And for both men and women, these chemicals contribute to Alzheimer's and Parkinson's disease.

These are all worrying signs and much research has to continue. Still, thanks to the waste we generate, we are experiencing the consequences of our advancement and progress as a global civilization.

Side story: Did you know 1.6 million breast implant surgeries were performed in 2021 globally? Breast implants are made of silicone, which is a type of plastic. The breast implant market is forecasted to grow by 7% annually from 2.5 billion to 3.7 billion US dollars between 2022 and 2028. That is a lot of plastic that will voluntarily enter your body, but don't worry; this material is perfectly safe as it has been tested to have no adverse effects on women and their offspring. But, apologies for there is always a but. These implants are not removed when we die, and unless we are cremated, these implants end up being buried in the earth. The first breast implant was performed in 1962, so one could argue that quite a few cemeteries, and one in particular near Hollywood, would quite possibly have quite a few silicone breasts buried there, and since this material does not degrade, it will remain there as a waste pollutant for centuries as the material has been perfected so it cannot harm the wearer and as such could be considered a forever material. Is this relevant to our metacrisis? No, but it does illustrate our attitude towards nature, which shows that even when we die, we create unnecessary waste. We could have removed the implants before burial and safely disposed of them, similar to our medical waste disposal regulations.

The effects of forever chemicals and micro and nano plastics on our health or deteriorating health have already begun and are steadily increasing, and it all started around the 1950s.

Population growth or decline?

In many high-income countries, fertility rates are declining, and worldwide fertility rates are declining as fewer children per woman are conceived and brought to term. The vast majority claim this to be the result of economic growth; we are becoming wealthier, but at the same time, raising a child is becoming increasingly more expensive. In the past, I mean the 1950s and further towards 1760, the start of the Industrial Age, having many children was considered an advantage. Yes, the child mortality rate was high due to a lack of medical knowledge and experience, but overall, even up till 1950, women carried, on average, five children during their lifetime.

Ask any woman today in any country if they want five kids. What do you think they will answer? So based on economic growth criteria and effect on fertility, i.e., how many average births per woman is set to decrease. At the same time, the rest of us get older thanks to our health care and medicine providers. So, we are aging as a species.

According to the United Nations, our world population will increase to 10.4 billion by 2086, which will start to decline to 10.3 billion in 2100. Wow, that's a lot of people, and it's pretty crowded if you ask me. As our domesticated animals need to keep up with our overall food production, we will have 9 Billion rats.

What I found surprising is that fertility rates are not decreasing in humans, thanks to economic growth, as many claim. According to various online studies, Livestock fertility rates are also declining, particularly in dairy cattle. Is this due to economic growth, or is something else at play? I mean, cows don't drive cars, have mobile phones, go on holidays, or wear fast fashion.

Recent research shows signs that something else is happening with our fertility rate. I recently read several articles that state that average sperm concentrations have dropped by 51.6 percent, and total sperm counts dropped by 62.3 percent in the last 50 years. But don't worry; as long as you have 40 million sperm per millimeter of semen, you're okay.

For every man, a healthy sex life is still far and wide an aspect of masculinity that defines us. In our relationships, we are expected to perform our duty as equal sexual partners. But when your ability to perform starts to deteriorate, especially when you are still below 40, you risk increased tension in your relationship, possibly resulting in a breakup. How does this frustration manifest itself in public life and how you behave in society? Does it affect your work, your profession, and how you choose to entertain yourself? Do you start hiding from the truth and seeking continued drug access to make you hard? I would suspect that lower testosterone levels would have a societal effect in a male-dominated world. I would recommend some studies in this field to see if decreasing fertility has a societal impact.

We now know that micro and nano plastics and forever chemicals can affect hormonal functions. It decreases testosterone and, as such, reduces sperm count and, in some cases, causes erectile dysfunction (ED). I would assume that the more of these substances we consume, we will make matters worse for ourselves. But is this the case?

According to various medical research, which we can access through Google search, we can read that 8% of males between ages 20 to 29 suffer from ED, and 11% of males suffer from ED between ages 30-39, and it's increasing. Why should this increase? Are we not healthier than our ancestors? Do we not live healthier lives? Do we not eat more nutritious food? How many gyms do you pass when driving through your city?

When our sperm count continues to decrease, erectile dysfunction continues to increase, and testosterone continues to fall, is it too much of a stretch of our imagination to consider that our global population will decline sooner? What if our livestock fertility keeps declining? How will we be able to feed our projected growing population? Not to worry, animal sperm banks to the rescue.

The soil that gives birth no more is defined by how we use our land; it's a vast area with many components worth discussing. However, to cast our doom into extinction, we will continue our focus and avoid getting lost in the woods.

According to the World Bank, we produce 2.1 billion tons of solid municipal waste globally, conservatively 33% of which is mismanaged considering nature and human health impact. Industrial waste: 7.6 billion metric tons (Source: World Bank)

Personal waste is not distributed equally within our global population, ranging from 0.11 kg to 4.54 Kilograms per person daily. Waste disposal is also not distributed equally. While the Netherlands and Singapore incinerate almost 100% of waste, countries like India and Southeast Asia still throw their waste into open landfills. Waste generation is expected to grow, as per the chart below.

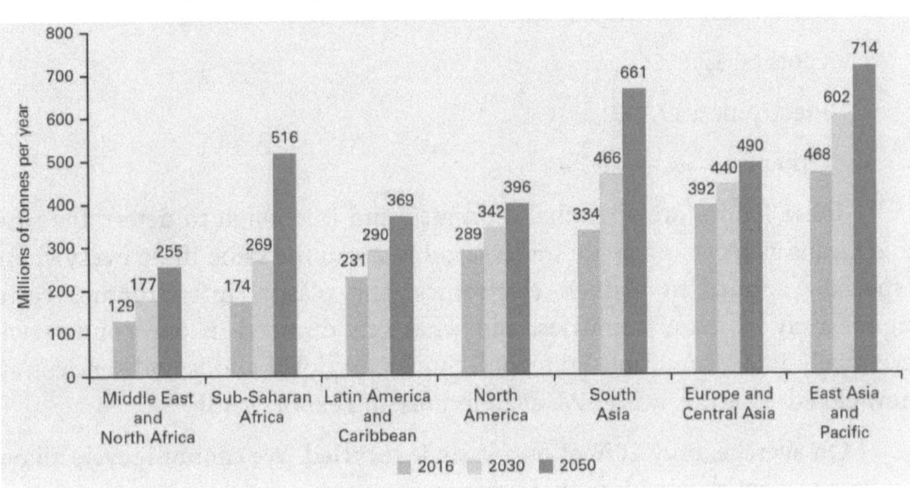

Projected waste generation, by region (millions of tonnes/year)

Waste is dumped in landfills, correction, trash mountains in many African countries, Latin America, and South and South East Asia. This organic waste rots and releases a lovely greenhouse gas called methane, so as per the chart above, the more trash we produce, the more methane is produced. In addition, please welcome back our rats, who are jumping up with joy at all the waste they are supplied with daily.

Our solid waste is no longer only organic. It consists of more than the food we throw away. Everything we use in our house, at work, at school, and everything in between eventually ends up in the trash. Some of it is recycled, meaning it goes through a process where the recycled material can be reused. There are three types of recycling: up, re-use, and downcycling. There is also mechanical and chemical recycling; depending on the material to be recycled determines the end state. Recycling is a hot topic of discussion these days, but recycling has been around for a long time and is not a recent development.

In 1031 A.D., the first evidence of recycling was recorded. The Japanese shredded their old documents and records and remade them into new sheets of paper, selling them through family-owned shops nationwide.

Current global waste recycling percentages based on 2021 data.

- Organic – Composting: 6%

- Paper: 58.5%

- Glass: 44.7%

- Plastic: 11.2%

- Wood: 58.9%

- Metal: 70.4%

- Clothes: 12.8%

- Electronics: 17.4%

- Others: 15.5%

These figures are all global estimates, and it is tough to determine what this means as recycling is not understood to mean the same thing everywhere, especially applied to textiles, electronics, and plastic. Infrastructure varies significantly in many countries, and what gets dumped in one country will eventually impact multiple countries. Since our global goods and services are now global, so is our waste. We even import and export it still.

On average, only 20% of our waste is recycled. We cannot recycle all our waste, so we must consider other options.

We need to address our waste. We have no choice, and our health depends on it.

"Is there any hope, I ask you? There never was much hope, only a fool's hope, or so I have been told."

We are a resilient species. We can take a lot of poison.

Our Doom is the one to rule, to find them, to bring them all together, and in the darkness binds them.

We have found the third, and it lives in soil.

TIME

Our newfound knowledge of the doom we carry weighs heavily on our hearts, minds, and bodies, causing fear, sadness, despair, depression, and anxiety. Some who have tried to warn others have been arrested, attacked, and even murdered. But the journey continues, for there is much yet to learn and many answers to be found.

"At least for a while, we must endure. The road must be trod, but it will be very hard. And neither strength nor wisdom will carry us far upon it. This quest may be attempted by the weak with as much hope as the strong. Yet such is often the course of deeds that move the wheels of the world: small hands do them because they must, while the eyes of the great are elsewhere.

Quote: from Lord of the Ring. JRR Tolkien.

When I went scuba diving with my friends in the Caribbean, we stayed underwater for at least 90 minutes at an average depth of 22 meters with a single 12-liter tank. We sometimes ventured to depths of 50 meters or more to look at a wreck or follow a manta. You should not go deeper than 18 meters as an open-water diver. That's the rule. When you have your advanced open-water dive certificate, you may dive to a depth of 30 meters. None of us back then were advanced; we were irresponsible cowboys.

The deeper you go, the more air you breathe, thanks to water pressure increasing as you descend. When we went deep diving, as we used to call it, our air would last less than 50 minutes. One of the funny experiences was that when you go deeper, your brain starts to slow down, and sometimes you become drunk or feel like you've had too much ecstasy. It's called nitrogen narcosis. We used to joke about it all the time. Under nitrogen narcosis, you could be a fish and start breathing water. You also have the unpleasant experience of the bends when the trapped nitrogen gas bubbles try to escape your body. It is a harrowing experience when you drink beers with your friends clustered around a campfire on the beach after diving all day. As a diver, you learn to manage your depth.

Managing your time and depth was essential to maximize your air consumption. None of us wanted to be the first to signal that air was running low. I cannot recall how often I surfaced with almost no air, but it was a lot. To control air consumption, you had to learn how to breathe underwater in a way that doesn't suck your tank dry. Air consumption and pressure were the two factors that provided you with time. The more experienced you become, the better you can predict how much time you could spend underwater.

So when we say we have insufficient time, we mean we are doing too much and under more pressure. When diving, we like to see corals and beautiful, even dangerous fish, and we get distracted by all the beautiful colors and the wonders of the underwater world. Thanks to our dive computers today, we are told that when we are too deep, we must do a safety stop and decompress. Our tank gauge tells us when we are low on air. We are saved and can come up to breathe the beautiful free air once again. Technology is a wonderful thing, but it can't change time.

The resistance to fundamental change is still very persistent. Plenty of politicians, business leaders, community leaders, and even some scientists and individuals claim that our metacrisis is a hoax. Some still say that fighting climate change is more harmful than doing nothing. I also observed a shift in focus from avoidance to adaptation and mitigation as the effects of climate change become more visible. Some segments of the global population believe they can insulate themselves from the worst effects of our metacrisis. These segments prefer to provide costly handouts to the vulnerable.

Perhaps these esteemed and respected leaders and experts are correct, but what about the rest of civilization? What about us simple folk who would rather stay within our borders and prefer others to handle our global problems? We know that the vulnerable amongst us will suffer the most, potentially resulting in significant loss of life while the wealthy endure.

Can we keep dumping waste into our ocean, waterways, lands, and air? Not much has changed in humanity's awareness and knowledge since a hundred years ago when the British Empire dominated the world. Or even from the days of the Roman Empire or the Middle Ages when the black death was upon us. Despite our evolution and incredible progress, we still don't get it. We know how empires fell, not by conquest but through mismanagement and a lack of attention to the core fundamental issues causing their demise. Our collective history from South and North America, Africa, Asia, Europe, and the Middle East should have taught us enough so that we know what to do.

We have forgotten for none now live who remember it, and our trove of information and knowledge is so vast that we now need help from artificial intelligence to assist us.

We do not care much about our waste because humanity's survival never depended on it. We choose to forget bad, personal, and embarrassing experiences and bury them deep within our subconscious and unconscious mind. Waste was considered harmless until it wasn't. Talking about climate change is convenient as it's abstract for most people, as the climate is measured over a minimum period of thirty years to detect changes. Who remembers what they ate twenty years ago? Despite our knowledge that greenhouse gas emissions change our climate, we are happy to continue to fund millions and millions of dollars into research that confirms what we already know. We don't "feel" climate instantly unless we travel from a temperate to a tropical or arctic climate.

Our global industries and superpowers are in love with the terms climate change and carbon footprint. It allows us to talk about consumerism and that we, the consumer, must change so that others don't have to. Tension is increasing every year, and billions of dollars are spent maintaining the narrative on both sides that are reducing human-caused Greenhouse Gas emissions. Let's face it: this is another type of human waste we like to flush down the toilet is the way to go.

Climate Change has become a massive money-making machine. It is spawning more industries, from management consulting and accounting services offering ESG advisory and outsourced reporting services to not-for-profit organizations that want people to donate more so they can also take climate action. To software companies designing software to make it easy for companies to complete their ESG and Sustainability reports and ever-increasing compliance deadlines. Manufacturers create fantastic machines and solutions that can capture carbon, reduce carbon emissions, and return it to where it once came. Even the oil and gas industry has jumped on the opportunity to explore Hydrogen gas so they can start drilling it and offer it as green hydrogen. Add to that the voluntary carbon credit market and climate change is now a massive industry worth trillions of dollars while we still add more waste and dump it on our planet.

Climate change is good for business as long as we keep changing the climate and seek ways to manage it. Many people live under Cassandra's curse, and one more serious influence, which I will introduce later. The same thinking that got us here persists, which leads me to conclude that we are not taking our health and that of our planet seriously enough.

If we were serious about sustainability, all men who regularly shave would by now be using a Straight Razor. These razors used to be passed down from generation to generation. All these men would save electricity from electric razors and plastic from disposable razors. That's a lot of carbon dioxide and plastic waste avoided. Take shoes. Would you rather buy a pair of shoes worth

$150,= per pair that lasts three years, or a pair of shoes worth $50,= that lasts six months?

Few stories describe our planetary abundance because we, as a species, have never bothered to see it as unique. We care about scarcity and fight over it. We envy rich people because they have more, and we want to be like them. We don't value abundance because it's there for the taking. We only care and act when someone tries to take it from us, which means we fear conflict and try to protect ourselves with weapons. Finally, we don't want to be left alone and need to be connected with our toys.

We as a civilization have never tried to live in harmony with nature, I mean, not really. We dug up the ground during the Agricultural age and grew crops until the earth became infertile, and we moved on to the next piece of land. From 10000 BC till about 6000 BC, this was the practice. In the Middle East, they started crop rotation 6000 years ago. The Chinese, Greeks, and Romans started using crop rotation 3000 years ago. It was later widely adopted in the Middle Ages and became standard practice in the 17th and 18th centuries. We could take land away from our fellow species and use it for our purposes until it yielded crops no more. Crop rotation was likely adopted because they ran out of arable land as demand for cereals, vegetables, and fruits increased. Changing the types of crops grown on a single piece of land helped the soil recover and restored soil health when left alone for a while. The use of fertilizer, mostly livestock manure and our feces, helped improve crop yields even more.

Today, we have massive farms producing crops sprayed with mainly nitrogen, phosphorous, and potassium-based fertilizers, which help our crops grow even faster. This is all to ensure that we can meet the demands of our growing global population. We can't afford to take more land from our fellow species because we have realized that the planet's biodiversity is needed to solve our metacrisis. With a lack of available land, we are evolving food production to other forms of growing our food, such as vertical farming.

We have cleared massive tracks of forests. Over 6000 years, we cut down more than 50 percent of central and northern Europe's forests for lumber and agriculture. The Romans fought the Gauls in a forest, not on an open field. Julius Caesar finally defeated Vercingetorix, Chieftain of the Gallic tribe of the Averni, after a long-fought resistance from behind a fortress made from trees from the surrounding forest. Another famous battle was the Battle of Teuroburg Forest, where three legions, that's around 15000 men, led by Publius Quinctilius Varus, were defeated by the Germanic tribes in 9AD who used the cover of the forest to defeat the Romans.

There are many examples of descriptions of travels through Europe's forests. They were dangerous places, especially for road travelers who highwaymen could ambush. That is why the Templar nights were of help as they invented the letter of credit, where a traveler from Paris could deposit his money at the Templar's temple and receive a credit note written in special code. The traveler's unique "signature" would travel to Marseille and collect his money at the Templar Knight's Temple when he arrived there safely. The Templar Order invented banking; today, you can experience the same when you visit an ATM anywhere in the world. It is, therefore, no wonder that people back then happily cut down our forests so our kind wouldn't attack us despite the Templar knights.

We have lost most of our forests globally, half of which were cut down between 8000 BC and 1900, and in the last 300 years, we lost around 1.5 billion hectares of forest globally, equivalent to 1.5 times the size of the United States. Now, we need forests more than ever for climate action to cool our planet back to safe economic conditions.

Big game hunters in the 19th century were famous and revered. Hunting big game was a favorite pastime of royals and the rich and famous in the twentieth century. Who remembers Queen Elizabeth 2nd and her husband going on a Tiger hunt hosted by the Maharaja of Jaipur in 1961? Do you remember Bror Blixen, a Swedish baron who hosted the Prince of Wales and Ernest Hemingway on hunting safaris in Kenya? How about Lady Grizel Winifred Louisa Cochrane, daughter of Countess Dundonald, who hunted and killed hippopotamus, wildebeest, leopard, rhinoceros, waterbuck, and Cape buffalo? Her hunts were extensively covered in popular magazines and newspaper articles,

In the early twentieth century, big game hunting epitomized humanity's control over nature, while people living in English cities were suffocating under thick clouds of smoke from coal burning in the late 19th and early 20th centuries.

We often quote Charles Darwin's "Survival of the Fittest." Ever since he wrote it, he has been misunderstood. Even Charles Darwin explained that it means that organisms that are better adapted to their nature have the best chance of survival. Evolution is all about fitting in and the ability to adapt. Yet the belief that the strongest will survive persists today. Beliefs are hard to change.

We have no experience or knowledge of living in harmony with nature and have never felt the emotions that emerge from this experience. We left the harmony era when the agricultural age began. We went from Animism to a Plural God belief system. If we had done the process in harmony with nature, we would have changed long ago. For most of our evolution, we have seen nature as something that must be tamed and domesticated. We discard what we don't need or is deemed old and out of fashion, and we buy or acquire new and move on. This applies to all people. People work in and for companies, so it is no wonder companies act the same. Our emotions have shied away from the essence of life, and we pursue artifice, growth, and wealth to keep us happy.

We have been killing for centuries, yet when speaking about it with people like yourselves, I keep hearing, "But we didn't know any better back then." This reminds me of what Germans used to say after World War 2: "Wir haben es nicht gewusst," which claimed that the vast majority of the German people did not know about concentration camps. Even Nazi leadership had to acknowledge that what they did was atrocious, but their excuse was that they lived in a system where Adolf Hitler held all the power. I hope by now that you understand that we did and do know that we have known this collectively for thousands and thousands of years. And so I ask you again.

What is the correct baseline for a particular species? How many of each species should there be in any given area? How many trees, plants, elephants, dung beetles, tuna, nudibranchs, vampire squid, sharks, tigers, ants, mosquitos, bees, flies, and rats should there be? What is the baseline?

What is Humanity's "baseline"? How many of us should there be?

We have forgotten, or we have buried it deep within us. There is a way to unlock what has been buried so deep, fortified with our beliefs and instincts, so we can prosper as a civilization and restore our planetary health. We succeeded as a species because of our planet; our planet is our friend; without it, we would not be where we are today. How much pressure can it take? We have created a great doom, which is starting to devour us.

We have created the monster that is eating us alive. Our world is on the road towards Doom, but not to cast our doom into its fires; we are on the road to throw ourselves in it. It will be up to us folk and those who come after us who must complete this task that lies before us. We first have to go through the mirror of ourselves and discover who we can become as a species that is better than the previous version of ourselves. To do that, we have to look into the mirror as therein lies opportunity.

Do you want to look in the mirror?

The less we consume and with less pressure, the more time we have.

Our Doom is the one to rule, to find them, to bring them all together and in the darkness binds them.

We have found four, and it lives in time. There is, however, one more.

ERASED

Have you ever seen drawings of Caras Galadhon? It is described in the Lord of the Rings and can be briefly seen in the movie. Sometimes, it reminds me of Singapore's Gardens by the Bay. Its inspiration came from Singapore's national flower, the Orchid. It expresses its beauty, but what makes it unique is that it mimics the functions of the orchid through its sophisticated architecture for managing energy, water, and waste.

Metaphorically, the mirror we look into is a silver bowl. It becomes a mirror once filled with pure crystal-clear water devoid of pollutants. It can only be used when the full moon is at its highest in the sky.

"Will you take a look and tell me what you see?"

"What will I see?"

"Even the wisest cannot tell, for the mirror shows us many things."

"Things that were, things that are, and some things that have not yet come to pass."

You can look in the mirror. At first, you would only see your face, tired with signs of anxiety and despair. Gradually, you see scenes of wide-open grass plains, with rivers flowing through huge forests. This water came from mountains and lakes and flowed pure and clear towards the Ocean. Upon a closer look, you see massive herds of Bison, millions of them. Sixty million bison roamed the vast prairies of America back in 1800. You see hordes of elephants, millions of them. There were 25 million Elephants in the 16th century. You see whales, which counted well over a million. The land was lush and green, and there was no human in sight, as there were only an estimated 300 million people in the year 0 of the Christian calendar. The scene changes, and you notice people tilling the land and growing crops.

You see sheep, horses, cattle, pigs, and sheep in enclosures, some cattle pulling plows which they tore through the earth. You noticed people fishing with sticks in rivers and ponds full of fish. The sky was clear, sunny, and blue. Your face turned from anxiety to happiness as the scene reminded you of what once was long ago, and, in an instant, it was gone. Soon, dark scenes emerged of black and white smoke coming from tall chimneys, houses covered with soot, and people coughing and wearing handkerchiefs over their mouths. You saw soldiers on the battlefield with lots of explosions and people dying. Animals are dying in burning forests, rivers black and empty of fish, oceans full of brown, green, and red sludge. People are wearing masks and falling sick. Empty streets in a red glow of heat and smoke, mass migrations of people moving away from coastal cities. Construction of massive domes that could house cities where people could live in fresh air, grow crops, and raise livestock. The dome's roof is covered in solar panels, and thousands of hectares of wind farms mostly idle outside the dome. Huge factories outside the city domes burn waste and convert the foul air into clean, breathable air, pumped into the dome, where the air is recycled and purified. Huge factories that purify polluted water and pump it into the city. Inside the dome, land was tilled and recycled with natural nutrient additives.

Mycelium is the new gold. Outside the dome, you saw cemeteries everywhere and huge mounds or mausoleums where cremated bodies found their final resting place. The world population has shrunk to a few billion. Outside the domes, the world was a barren wasteland, the oceans still green and brown with plastic-filled sludge, mountains, and hills showing rocks with plastic protruding of all shapes and colors, and all land and marine life long extinct. Plastics, chemical pesticides, and forever chemicals are banned. We eat food that no longer contains pollutants from our waste. Everything is recycled, we no longer extract, we live in manageable communities where we teach our children the importance of nature and what it means to be regenerative, and history lessons are focused on what once was, about abundance and how our ancestors almost made us extinct. We hope to return to the outside world one day. We have spaceships launching regularly to outer space to find a habitable planet. We no longer talk about GDP, economic growth, and profit. These things are managed by A.I. We conserve our medicines because it's hard to make new ones; we can no longer treat the sick, so only strong, healthy people can stay. Fertility is extremely low, and every birth of an animal, bird, fish, or human is celebrated as a miracle. Creating waste was punished as Zero Waste became law. You would be expelled from the city dome and left to fend for yourself in this wasteland where few of us can survive.

Then it was gone, and you could see your face again. It was not a happy face, but it again changed to fear.

"I know what it is you saw, for it is also in my mind."

"It is what will come to pass if you should fail."

"The movement is fractured, it has already begun. They will try to cover up our doom, you know of whom I speak."

Adapted from Lord of the Rings JRR Tolkien.

My dream when I was twelve was not to become a millionaire. My dream was to work and live on every continent in as many countries as possible and be free to move anywhere whenever I wanted. In 1979, we had no idea what a digital nomad was. We knew nothing about the Internet, mobile phones, and electric cars. Nomads were Bedouins who lived in the Arabian desert. Digital Nomads didn't exist. Yet it was my dream, and it became a reality as I've worked and lived on every continent except Antarctica. No sales jobs on the South Pole, trust me. Being in sales helped me work and live wherever I wanted.

The most valuable lesson in all my years is that dreams can come true. However, your actual reality differs from when you first dreamed of it. Now I have a new dream, and that is to spend whatever time is given to me to provide a path for me, you, and others towards a new world where our next generation does not have to end up in domed dystopian cities but can live in beautiful thriving regenerative towns and villages surrounded by nature.

Many, in the quiet corners of the world, are building a new future, and from what I have seen, it is possible to build cities that look like giant forests surrounded by lush greenery and wild animals. Without the map app on your phone and road signs, you would probably not even get to the city, for you will hardly see it. I can imagine villages that look like the surrounding landscape. I can imagine that the water from our rain is captured on our roofs, filtered, and stored. I can imagine all our organic waste being composted. I can imagine a crystal clear blue river without pollution. It is already happening slowly. You need to look for them as they are hard to find. But we have yet to turn off the tap, engine, and hunger, and we need to figure out what to do with our technology and governance.

I look outside. I see the capital's skyline with its skyscrapers and congested arteries stuffed with cars and a dome of brown smog choking the city's inhabitants, and I wonder if it is all too late and I'm hallucinating. We have a choice: extend our suffering and worsen it or extend our survival and seek to prosper in harmony. I cannot predict what the future will bring. It is a journey we all must take, one step at a time. We can ignore all this and focus on the latest and greatest technology and clean up as best we can with the tap open, or can we change? To achieve change, we have to continue on the road toward our doom and show you how to cast it into extinction. I do not know if we shall succeed, for there is much doubt in my mind.

I ask you again, would you look in the mirror for a second time?

This time, I warn you that it will not show events and scenes from the past and present and what has not yet come to pass. It will show what is in your mind. It would expose your conscious, subconscious, and unconscious. You may not like what you see, for some parts are hidden deep, well camouflaged, and perhaps best left in peace. Will you look to see your beliefs and myths?

You hesitate but are curious, and you cannot resist the temptation. You want to see for yourself. Don't say I did not warn you.

You love Scarcity.

Scarcity in our society is celebrated, we love it, and it draws enormous crowds, in the millions and even billions. The number 1 sport in the world, Football, also known as soccer, draws 5 billion people who watch it regularly. What is the one goal that is the most elusive for most nations that have a national football team? To win the World Cup. Winning the World Cup is rare, and we humans flock in our billions to watch who will obtain that elusive prize every four years. The global football market is worth US$ 3.2 Billion.

Celebrating scarcity is all around us. We even celebrate scarcity with Champagne. Champagne can only be called champagne from the Champagne region in France. It's called sparkling wine everywhere, and the price is reflected in this difference.

When I worked in the Caribbean as a Jewelry salesperson, I sold scarcity daily, camouflaged as exclusivity, caring, and love.

Here is an example that went something like this:

A customer walks in and asks: "Do you sell Rolex?"

Me: "No, Sir, but we do have a range of other exclusive watches. May I show you our latest addition, an 18kt Gold Patek Philippe Chronograph with a beautiful Crocodile leather strap?"

Customer: "Yes, please, and what can you tell me about the watch?"

After a lengthy explanation, the customer reverts to wanting a Rolex watch instead after I mention that the Patek Philippe costs US$80,000. An 18kt Gold Rolex at that time would cost half that.

I asked him: "How many of your family and friends own a Rolex?"

Customer: "Almost everyone."

Me: "So you would like to compare your Rolex to theirs?"

The customer looks at the watch again, now neatly fastened around his wrist.

Me: "May I ask what you do for a living?"

The customer: "I'm the CEO and Founder of a Hamburger Restaurant Chain."

Me: "Wow, incredible, so you are unique. There is no better way for a man to show his loved ones that you are special than with a rare and unique timepiece that defines you as a person. Patek Philippe watches were meant to be worn for the purpose of passing it on to future generations."

The customer: "OK, thank you. Do you accept American Express?"

It did not quite happen like that, as he had to sleep on it, so he passed by the next day to give his Amex.

I used it daily, selling Watches, Diamonds, Emeralds, Rubies, and even Amethyst gold jewelry. Making something scarce, real, or perceived increases desirability, and desires can be manipulated to achieve objectives.

No matter your business, scarcity sells, even when selling to other businesses. When you make something scarce, it can be anything, even a small part of a product or solution. People are imprinted with the belief that scarcity equals value. Selling Optical/IP integrated networks that supply data to your phones and computers is no different than selling a diamond ring. It's an investment for the buyer to win one over. If it exceeds the buyer's requirements, it's a sale. Selling scarcity is easy, and we do it every day.

When I worked in the gemstone and jewelry industry, I often felt a slight feeling of guilt—not paralyzing, just a tiny bit of guilt—for I knew that I was selling products that came out of the ground and from animals that belong in the wild and not in a zoo or, worse, a crocodile farm where they were bred for their skin. Early on, I learned how minerals were mined, including diamonds that had been in the earth for millions of years.

I knew about conflict diamonds way before the movie Blood Diamond came out. By the way, a side note, but T.I.A, as mentioned in the movie, also meant This is Asia, which we gemstone dealers used to describe when a gem deal turned sour in Chonburi, Thailand. Conflict has always surrounded the diamond and gemstone industry, and they want to keep this quiet, even today. I knew because I bought and sold rough gemstones worldwide while working for a Gemstone trading and cutting firm in Idar Oberstein, Germany, in the early 90s. I knew, yet I sold diamonds, emeralds, rubies, and tourmalines daily. Because it paid the bills and could pay for all the luxuries I could afford, it must be tough for people who work in the fossil fuel industry, chemical industry, industrial livestock, and crop farming. Combined, these industries employ over a billion people, or in other words, almost a 3ʳᵈ of the global workforce of 3.4 billion. I can't help but wonder why it must be hard for those employees to accept the harm the companies they work for are causing. I spoke to a few of them, and I can confirm that they are aware and hope that things will change. The challenge is not awareness. The challenge is how can we change.

We love the scarcity systems we humans have created, and they have served us well and not so well at the same time. It has helped to subjugate other groups of our same species, from when we were small bands of hunter-gatherers to when we became empires who conquered tribes all the way up to World War 2, where one nation was faster than another to create a weapon that would end the war and enter a new world order where a push on a button could destroy the planet an all who live on it.

We love scarcity, for it gives us power and control, and we can abuse it. For example, Russia blocked grain exports from Ukraine when they invaded, which nearly caused a food crisis. It increases the value of a commodity by making it scarce either artificially, such as with diamonds, or through national policy or adverse actions between groups of people. We do this in business and in our society every day. In most nations, if not all, energy, food, and water security are top of mind.

Scarcity increases value. Abundance reduces value, or so we now believe so deeply within ourselves. Let's start with freedom of speech, which long ago was considered valuable because not everyone was permitted to speak. "Permission to speak, sir" still exists today. Not long ago, women were not allowed to speak at dinner tables about affairs considered a man's domain, such as business or politics. In democratic countries, the freedom of speech holds little value as it's a given, which is good. In totalitarian countries, freedom of speech is restricted, so it has a high value. Time is of enormous value in sectors where time is of the essence, like in business. Other parts of our global civilization view time differently, and one could argue that time is not valued the same everywhere. This presents a problem when faced with multiple crises. We are now trying to put a price on nature to protect it. We even have financial instruments now that put a price on Nature's ability to deal with the climate crises. Nature, once so abundant, is becoming scarce. Hence, its value increases. Humanity has become conditioned this way while we have enough resources to share among us all if we don't waste so much of it.

The best example I could find is a spice called Nutmeg, which once came from only three little islands in the Banda Sea called Banda Neira, Hatta, and Rhun. This spice was not found anywhere else in the world and was highly valued for its medicinal purposes. This spice was so valuable that it was worth more than its weight in gold in the 17ᵗʰ century. It was so valuable that one of the smallest Islands, Rhun, occupied by the British, was traded for Manhattan, then called New Amsterdam, occupied by the Dutch. Today, nutmeg can be found in every supermarket worldwide and costs a pittance of what it once was. We have the English to thank for that because they stole some of the nutmeg seeds and decided to plant them in India, and hence, the spread of this lovely spice began. This was done not because they wanted to share. They wanted to break the Dutch monopoly on nutmeg and mace at that time.

While scarcity is celebrated, we love to break it because scarcity creates envy. Why can't we have what they have? Have you ever wondered why sushi became so popular outside of Japan? Or how fast fashion became so prevalent, not to mention supermarkets and especially convenience stores.

When something holds value, we treasure it. When it loses value, we take it for granted and throw it away. Take computers. Who would use a Commodore 64 today? Where have they all gone? Consumerism today can be classified as consuming out of fear, and marketers and entrepreneurs specialize in tapping into these emotions to create false fear. No one wants to be left behind because how would that look? It takes an enormous amount of effort to break free from these buying habits that can risk losing relationships with loved ones, family, or friends.

Even products that are available in abundance, like fashion, try to insert scarcity in their marketing and sales campaigns. How often do we hear statements like;

- The latest collection is out and selling fast.

- Hurry, only a few pieces left.

- Discount only last till the end of this week.

Consumer bias is a real thing and influences our purchase behavior in several ways. There are many different types of consumer bias, but some of the most common include:

- Anchoring bias: This is the tendency to rely too heavily on the first piece of information we receive when deciding. For example, if we are told that a product is worth $100, we may be more likely to buy it, even if it is worth less.

- Availability bias: This tendency tends to give more weight to readily available information. For example, if we see many positive reviews of a product online, we may be more likely to buy it, even if there are also negative reviews.

- Confirmation bias is the tendency to seek information confirming our beliefs and disregard information that contradicts them. For example, suppose we are already convinced that a particular product is the best. In that case, we may be more likely to look for reviews supporting this belief and ignore studies criticizing it.

- Framing bias: This is the tendency to be influenced by how information is presented to us. For example, if we are told that a product is on sale for a limited time, we may be more likely to buy it, even if the discount is insignificant.

- Herd mentality: This is the tendency to follow the crowd. For example, if we see that many people are buying a particular product, we may be more likely to buy it ourselves, even if we have not done our research.

They can also lead us to make decisions not in our best interests, such as buying products that are harmful to our health and nature. Consumers do not change their buying behavior even when presented with the facts. There are many reasons, and I suspect more research is being conducted on this topic, especially in the context of greenwashing and how to get people to buy more sustainable products.

So, if resources are becoming less available, and land and water resources are stressing biodiversity, why are we not making products that were made to last? It was not long ago when craftsmanship and durable products were the norm. People expected to buy goods that would last forever back then. But with the rise of mass production capabilities, we stopped buying products built to last in the mid-20th century. Mass production allowed manufacturers to produce goods more quickly and cheaply, but it also led to a decline in quality. On the other hand, consumerism encouraged people to buy more things, even if they didn't need them.

There are several reasons why we stopped buying products that were built to last:

- Cost: Mass-produced goods are cheaper than high-quality, durable goods. This is because mass-produced goods are made from less expensive materials like plastic. Manufacturing technology became more efficient as it replaced expensive labor.

- Convenience: Mass-produced goods are also more convenient to buy. They are available in various stores and can be purchased quickly and easily. Single items wrapped in plastic packaging in supermarkets, for example.

- Social pressure: Consumerism encourages people to buy new things all the time. This can lead to social pressure to buy new products, even if we don't need them.

- Planned obsolescence: Some manufacturers intentionally design their products to have a short lifespan. This is known as planned obsolescence. Planned obsolescence can be achieved by using low-quality materials, making it challenging to repair products, or releasing new models of products frequently. The average lifetime of a mobile phone is two to three years before an upgrade is needed. To name one example.

All this has led to increased waste, pollution, and damage to nature. It has also made us more vulnerable to consumer debt.

In less than eighty years, we have erased the belief that durable products are better than less durable products. Now, we anxiously await the next version of our phone. I'm old enough to remember when I received a toy as a present, and if the toy had "made in China" printed on it as opposed to "made in Germany," I instinctively knew that the product made in China was cheaper and of lesser quality than the toy made in Germany. This instinct has now largely disappeared as if it was erased from our minds.

Our Doom is the one to rule, to find them, to bring them all together, and in the darkness binds them.

We have found the last one, which lives in what we have erased. Do you know what our doom is?

SPHERES

The technology sphere is the most important sphere to understand. No one else created our technology sphere, and it's all around us 24 x 7 nonstop, from toilets to sewage infrastructure, from steam engines to carbon capture, from Lego blocks to spacecraft, from pills to clothes, from fertilizers to frying pans, from genetically modified wheat to a sandwich with peanut butter to an apple pie. You name it. Our technology is all around us. We can't live without it. We are now totally reliant on technology. I would venture a guess that without our technology, we would be suffering from withdrawal symptoms in less than a minute.

"Mummie, where is the bread?" Sweet Jolene asks.

"Sorry dear, what is bread?" Mum replies.

"Seriously?"

"Yes, dear, I don't know; I think it must have been the AI that erased my knowledge of bread."

"Why?"

"Why? Why, why, why, why must you always ask why? Ask the AI, why don't you? It will know."

Making technology and harnessing our energy sources are our superpowers. It makes us superorganisms that can control the world. As long as there is energy and enough resources, we will build into infinity in an endless pursuit of…hmm…pursuit of what? To develop tools to meet and solve our challenges and venture into space, of course. I love technology, don't get me wrong. I couldn't live without it, and I successfully sold speed on Lucifer's steed for over two decades - 3G, 4G, 5G. How many Gs do you want? Apologies. How many Gs do you want on your phone?

We build technology and change our nature so fast that we are the slowest species to learn how to walk. We must sit and crawl around to imprint this world before we even dare walk, let alone run. We might be run over by a silent electric car if we do. Our progress is thanks to our capacity to develop technology with cheaper and cheaper energy. The spear helped us to hunt animals bigger than ourselves. The plow gave us agriculture. The wheel allowed us to transport heavy goods, and sewers gave us the means to keep our noses clean. The printing press gave us literacy for the masses, which led to democracy and the end of feudalism. Mobile phones and the internet have given us access to information at lightning speed, and now we have AI. Incredible feats of progress that can not be disputed. It has brought us from the hunter-gatherer age to the agricultural and industrial ages to the digital age.

History is rife with warnings about humanity's relationship with technology. You can find these warnings in religious texts and many folk stories and myths. It is unsurprising that a sphere called a ring symbolizes humanity's relationship with technology. You can find rings of power in Greek mythology, Nordic mythology, Arthurian Novels and in Eastern myths. A ring symbolizes binding, like when a couple gets married and exchanges wedding rings. We bind ourselves to technology too. These rings have the power to symbolize that technology gives us power, but power corrupts, so there is a dark side to this power that the wearer must endure as it consumes the wearer when the wearer desires more and more of the power of technology. The ring can make you invisible when driving a car or flying on a private jet. It makes you invisible when using a computer. You can portray yourself as a completely different being online.

It's, therefore, sad to now sit here in the middle of the Age of Consequences and having to deal with all the shit we did with technology as a result. We are moving into an era where people's development and use of technology and energy directly impact our planet's health and our own. Many books have been written about climate change, ecosystem collapse, and even the collapse of our civilization. Why has no one ever analyzed the root cause of the unintended consequences that created the wastesphere before? The root cause is our relationship with technology and lack of understanding of its potential risks with the use and disposal of technology.

We like to break all the waste or pollution into little pieces and tackle them individually because we can't comprehend the scale of it all. Burning oil produces carbon dioxide, plastic bags create microplastics, computers create e-waste and I could go on and list the waste of all our technologies. Have we failed to understand our thought and behavioral processes? We must know by now that everything is connected to us in how we think, talk, and act.

No matter where you live, the village, city, or country you call home, and what you do and believe, we are all connected with our technology sphere. Technologies' by-products, use, and disposal have resulted in the wastesphere and have infected all of humanity and all life, like one massive plaque—slow-emerging cancer that is growing and for which there is currently no cure. The wastesphere is the manifestation of our doom.

I hereby introduce you to the Wastesphere or, if you prefer Latin, the Vastumsphere.

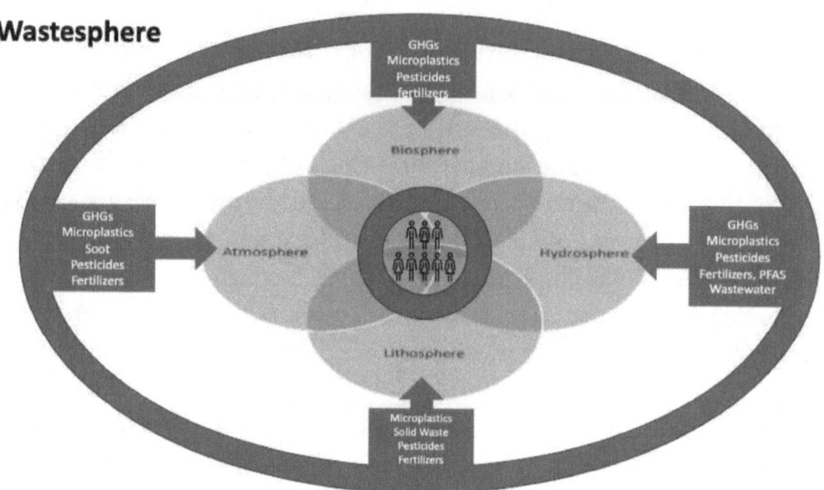

Why do we still have COPs on Climate, and another one on Biodiversity, another on Plastics, another on chemicals, and another on human health? Do we know what is causing all this? Do I need to keep explaining and whining? Why don't we go over to those people and kindly ask them to stop what they are doing? Yes, that's what a child would ask, and what do you answer? Uhhh, well, it's complicated. No, It's not. We choose to make it complicated.

Guess what? All that waste is now in our bodies, causing all manner of harm. Our wastesphere is causing a health crisis of which we have seen nothing yet. It all came about thanks to our technology sphere's design, manufacturing, implementation, use, and disposal. To understand the Wastesphere, you must understand the technology sphere. Without the Technology sphere, you would not have a wastesphere. Without our technology and waste sphere, you wouldn't have a health crisis, but before we go there, let's stay with externalities and forget what's brewing inside of us. Waste is defined as follows.

Something that humanity has produced and discarded, which causes harm to our planet and ourselves, is released into the air, water, and land. Most of humanity's emissions into our atmosphere (gases), on our land (Municipal,

Humanity bears the sole responsibility for creating the Wastesphere. The term planetary boundaries would be more familiar, but from my perspective, it does not sufficiently attribute the nine planetary boundaries to the technology sphere, at least not explicitly. The planetary boundaries lack the deeper psychological and philosophical aspects of our predicament. I do not use the word predicament lightly. Its use provokes the feeling of embarrassment, which certainly exists, and it also refers to predicated, which evokes a feeling of inevitability. Both are defeatists in nature, so can embarrassment conjure up positive action? A collective action that enables us to focus on the deeper, more fundamental cause of our wicked problems?

The Wastesphere that surrounds the biosphere causes damage to our Atmosphere, Hydrosphere, Geosphere, and Cryosphere. The Wastesphere is a sphere that everyone can understand as we all participate in; it surrounds us and is now within us, and we maintain it and feed it, and if we don't get rid of it, it will cause our total demise and that of our livable planet. The planet will survive without us, but our legacy will remain as evidence of how we have treated it as a single species. We all want to leave a positive legacy behind when we die. Would you prefer your gift to be that of having created a beautiful house, or would you prefer to leave this world behind as a trash mountain?

It is the Wastesphere that we need to make extinct, not all species. Our waste problem is a global emergency. The amount of greenhouse gases, plastics, chemicals, fertilizers, forever chemicals, and burnt carbon (soot) on our planet and within our bodies is reaching tipping points that, once crossed, will become irreversible. Bye-bye, evolution. As history shows us, we humans like to control things. With each development and evolution, we have progressed as a species that now dominates all we do on our planet. We lack humanity's ability to control and eliminate the waste sphere. It is our blind spot, the embarrassing part of us, that we prefer to avoid, like an alcoholic who denies that he is one. The final frontier is that we now wish to control and manipulate the five earth spheres. We can't. However, we can prevent our wastesphere and make it extinct. As much as we like, we cannot make our waste completely extinct. We need resources to survive, and with their use comes waste. We can make it functionally extinct, meaning that it loses its function to harm and, hence, no longer is of consequence.

Addressing our doom in the context of waste would mean that no one gets a free pass, and each of us is accountable. The cost is enormous. We all, as an entire population, contribute to waste creation. It can no longer be a case of whether it is their fault or they are not doing enough. It's not a question of Global North vs. Global South or China against the USA, Or us versus the corporations, and it's not about you vs. I. We, no matter where you live, what you do, how rich or poor you are. It doesn't matter. You have a responsibility to eliminate waste from your life. It is up to you to help others do the same. It is up to you where you work. It is up to you where you govern.

What we waste in our Hydrosphere, rivers, lakes, oceans, and on our ice sheets, such as forever chemicals, micro and nano plastics, rubber tire particles, soot, and pesticides, not to mention the amount of industrial waste and agricultural nutrient run-off and finally, our lithosphere where we store most of our waste in landfills and our wastewater. How we pollute our world with what we discard because of poor, underinvested waste management infrastructure in all countries, which results in waste being dumped in ecosystems, all need to be addressed under a single banner with a single purpose. Waste is all connected now. We and our planet are integrated with it. Waste is global, and like the earth is a sphere, so is our waste.

Circular pollution.

In 2022, many European countries, including the UK, exported pesticides banned in their own country. The recipients, such as Egypt, Cameroon, Algeria, and Colombia, use these pesticides and export their crops to the countries they received the pesticides from.

Egypt exports potatoes, cotton, and fresh fruits,

Cameroon exports Cocoa and Bananas,

Algeria exports sorghum, millet, corn, rye, and rice,

Colombia, Coffee, avocados, limes, pineapples, oranges, cocoa, and tangerines.

All these countries export these crops to Europe. I call this circular pollution.

"Would you like a slice of Lime in your Gin Tonic?"

"How about some rice pudding?"

In addition, the top 10 global agrochemical companies have manufacturing facilities worldwide. What they may not sell in one country, they might be allowed to sell in another. Remember, your food no longer comes from your backyard.

The same can be said for micro-plastic beads used in cosmetics and personal care products, which have been banned in many countries but not all. Even in Europe, reducing these beads was voluntary except in countries like Ireland, France, and Italy that have enacted bans. Yet many products still contain micro-plastic beads or different types of micro-plastics that bypass the definition of a micro-plastic bead, as each jurisdiction has a different definition. They have started using bioplastics, which sounds good; however, bioplastics do not break down in nature and our bodies due to plasticizer chemicals, which must be removed after the bioplastic has been decomposed in special composting facilities. Even in Indonesia, where micro-plastic beads have been banned, we still find body scrub products with micro-plastics. Microplastics are still used in many products, and once we discard them via trash disposal or our bodies, they still pollute nature and cause harm.

Circular pollution continues because we don't manage waste from a global perspective. Regional regulation does not solve the issue. Opportunity works both ways; it can benefit us or hurt us. Through an equal collaborative global effort focused on eliminating waste from the Atmosphere, Lithosphere, and Hydrosphere and, finally, if possible, removing the harmful waste from our bodies and preventing the next generations from breathing, eating, and drinking these toxic substances, we will be able to solve our crisis. Of course, becoming regenerative is an essential part. We should work to continue to implement regeneration on land, in our ocean, and in our economy and how we use it, restoring biodiversity through ecosystem restoration and protection. We should work on regenerating our Hydrosphere, Atmosphere, and Lithosphere. All three spheres are equally important. Each should have an equal voice. All are focused on delivering an outcome for humanity to live healthy lives in harmony with its host, who has given us so much. It is high time we returned the favor.

What is as critical is that we must avoid unintended consequences as much as possible. We must design and discover substances that are pro-life and pro-planetary health, and if they fail, the litmus test should never see the light of day. Urgent need for testing the 80% of chemicals out there that have yet to undergo human and nature's safety tests must be done. Yes, I've read it will take centuries, but if we don't remove them as much as we can before they keep causing harmful effects, we should do so.

Waste has finally embraced our planet and is everywhere, from pole to pole, from the highest mountain to the deepest part of our Ocean, and even resides within us. Its power has finally been unleashed.

Water that once was,

Air that was fair,

Soil brings birth no more,

Time, once so abundant for You and I, used up,

Erased all memory from whence we came.

The great evil that was once part of the shadows and far from our minds has exposed itself to the masses and is using all its might to make you believe that only his view exists and will dominate our path.

Nature does not care where you start or finish, but the one thing that nature does not tolerate is waste. It does not care how nature looks. It does not care; it is and makes what does not belong extinct.

You should not waste your time debating right and wrong in a domain that affects us all.

Some people would claim that waste is not equal, and others would argue that some are more equal than others, like in the book Animal Farm by George Orwell. It is also true that Waste is not created equally in each country and hence requires a local focus. For all these arguments, I propose to view our challenges from the perspective of the biosphere and its land and marine ecosystems instead of our human-centric approach. In my view, this is the first step, as it is a problem we understand, and we know what to do about it. All it takes is recognition and the will. The issue is, however, tied to the current conviction that we need to address it from our current system's perspective: Economic growth to cater to a growing population that seeks to increase living standards.

We shall get there, whether by folly, luck, or pure grit. We will get there, for we must.

Do not cry for aid, for none will come. We have been forsaken by those who can aid us, who are busy in their towers divining and consolidating power to take what they deem is theirs and protect their own at all costs until the end. The resistance is strong as there is much profit in it.

Do not cry for aid, for none will come; it will be up to us, the small hands that turn the wheels of the world, who must complete the task before us.

To stay true to purpose, we will need both visible and obvious tools and invisible, which are not so obvious.

Dare to dream of a reformed Council.

Almost all national leaders attend COPs. The WHO covers health issues, the UNEP covers solid waste, the UNFAO covers food, etc. There is only one COP that has the power to focus our attention on what matters. We need to hold them to account. There is only one recommendation.

Reducing GHG is not a solution that would eliminate our wastesphere. It is only part of the problem and does little to prevent a health crisis. The consequences of focusing on GHG at COPs pose the risks of negotiating tradeoffs between Temperature rise, Biodiversity protection, and restoration, pollution clean-ups and prevention, access to fresh water and food, and our health issues due to chemical pollution, inequality, and national responsibility. All are global concerns. We don't need horse traders. We need spherical action.

It seems doable. However, energy demand is projected to increase by 47% or as expressed in a CAGR of 1.3% till 2050 on the following conditions:

- Population growth: from 8 billion to 9.1 billion by 2050

- Economic growth: 3.3% per year, which means that the world economy would have doubled in 27 years with an expected GDP of 200 Trillion USD

- Rising Living Standards: More consumption, higher energy demand.

By 2050, based on the most optimistic forecasts, renewables will make up 44% while the general consensus, according to Statistica, is that renewables will be 32% while the rest is split between coal (13.5%), oil (20.2%), and gas (23.8%), nuclear (3.6%) and hydro (6.3%) Meaning fossil fuels would be 57.5 % of total energy consumption.

We are not only dealing with Climate change. We also have three other foundations to worry about, in case you have forgotten. Air, Land, and Water are as important. All 3 elements of our foundation come together under one banner called waste.

Three key fundamental contributions cause our waste:

1. Population and growth

2. Economic growth

3. Increased consumption due to rising living standards.

We will not have a home if we don't restore our foundation. The wastesphere is another way of explaining the planetary boundaries. This is true, but I have found that explaining the waste sphere to people who are unaware or perhaps partially aware is less complex than explaining our planetary boundaries.

Once people understand our waste, I.e., the Pollution crisis, we can gradually guide them toward more complex issues.

Those issues surfaced after I realized we do not have the institutions or leadership to solve our waste crisis. We have to dig deeper and find the root cause, and we need to consider our fellow species in terms of the potential risks we face. This means we need to address not the Ecological crisis but also socio-economic and psychological crises. In other words, our metacrisis. The metacrisis is a set of multiple crises ranging from pollution to socio-economic to health and governance. The Metacrisis requires a fundamental change in thinking to address it. Few people know its scope as it requires a novel approach, a different kind of imagination, and courage to tackle.

HEALTH

Before we can change, we must heal; we need to recover from what we have exposed within us and for what we have caused. We cannot build a better future if we don't evolve ourselves. We need to confront our deepest fears that brought about our crisis. We need to bring it to the surface. What lies beneath must come forth so we can embrace it and change how we behave, think, and talk. I have already discussed the physical health problems we face thanks to our wastesphere. On top of them, we also have another disease that is hovering over us and is likely to become the disease of the 21st century if we don't address it on a global scale.

There are three main healing requirements that we need to address. It is a disease that I would like to call The Lack of Relationship Disease (LRD)

1. The Lack of relationship with Nature.

2. The Lack of Relationship with Society.

3. The Lack of Relationship with Mind and Body.

1. The Lack of relationship with Nature.

What is the difference between something you like and something you love?

The answer may surprise you, but liking or loving something is complicated. You can like and even love something you see, like a movie. The terms are also used interchangeably, for a man may say he likes his girlfriend while he, in fact, dearly loves her emotionally, but amongst his buddies, he prefers not to show that part of himself. However, both terms can be answered regarding behavior, and I found a simple answer.

When you like a flower, you pluck it. When you love a flower, you give it water.

Love also means that it contains an element of sacrifice. You sacrifice some of your time and water for the flower's benefit. Love includes discipline as you need to repeat time and water for the flower, and lastly, it includes constraint not to pluck it and give it to someone you love.

It's a beautiful sunny day with clear blue skies, and you have decided to take your family out for a picnic. You find a beautiful field with a great view and a perfect spot under an Oak that has been there for 600 years, providing plenty of shade. You set up the picnic and start eating the sandwiches prepared this morning, and a fly comes and sits on the other half of your sandwich, which is still on your plate. What do you do?

Most likely, you would swoosh it away from your sandwich. That's what most people would do. Or you think you are fast enough to kill it, which some people do. Now I ask you. Does that fly have as much right to be there as you?

If you love all things in nature, the answer would be yes.

Now apply that to all living things, and you would quickly become aware that all species have a right to exist, grow, prosper, and die in peace so that nature can process and use it again for birth and life. It's the circle of life, and we are integrated with it.

I understand flies can be a nuisance, especially if they are in your house. Fly swatters sell super fast when spring comes. What attracts flies? Waste, of course, as they love garbage. Love works both ways. Although I'm unsure if flies love waste, I hope you understand my meaning.

No garbage equals fewer flies, so before you buy a swatter or insecticide, you should first try to live in nature with no garbage or exposed food leftovers. Once you know what attracts a specific type of species you prefer not to have around you, and you love nature, you will first try to do something about the cause instead of killing it. You don't kill your partner when she eats your cookie, so why would you kill that fly sitting on your half-eaten chocolate cake?

While writing this book, I came across an article about wolves that were once nearly extinct in Europe and have managed to rebound and, in some regions, live within a healthy ecosystem. However, some farmers have complained that there are so many wolves now that it threatens their livestock, which is meant for food for us. The European Union agrees that farmers can use whatever means to protect their livestock from these wolves. So, they kill them, which is the easy thing to do. Finding solutions that prevent wolves from attacking livestock on farms as a first option has not been considered because it is more expensive than buying a bullet. As Chris Rock once said, "They should make bullets cost US5000 = each". Maybe then people would think twice before shooting each other or a wild animal.

Wolves and humans are not friends, at least not in the natural sense. Relationships between people and wolves have existed in the past. Our pet dogs came from wolves and other wild dog species. We domesticated them.

Wolves do not like humans and, as such, will avoid us as much as possible. So why would they venture onto a farm? Well, again, the answer is surprisingly simple. There is not enough natural prey within their ecosystem. So, instead of killing them, you may wish to consider increasing the population of their prey or, in the worst case, moving them to areas where plenty of prey exists. Killing them should not be the first option.

These are simple examples of complex situations. Still, when you experience events when you are confronted with something unpleasant by another species that you cause, you should first find out why this is happening. You will realize that when you analyze the issue from the perspective of the other species, you may find answers that are more in line with how nature behaves versus having to wake up your colonizer instinct to kill first and ask questions later.

In Singapore, people complain to the government about bird noise. Complaining citizens regard chirping birds as noise pollution and request the government to take care of it. This happens every year, especially when migratory birds like the Daurian Starlings come to visit the Garden City for a brief period. Countless local news articles have reported on this over the years. If we are to become part of nature again and love our fellow species, we still need a lot of education and regain experience of what it feels like to be surrounded by nature.

Another example that is close to my heart is shark attacks. It all started with the Matawan man-eater, a great white shark that killed 3 and 5 people in 1916 near the Jersey Shore. This event gave all sharks a whole different meaning that is still prevalent today. This event served as inspiration for the movie Jaws. Ever since the movie, humans have been afraid of sharks, no matter what kind. Deadly shark attacks, especially those committed by a great white, make front-page news and are prominently broadcast on all major global networks.

There are over 500 species of shark in our ocean today, of which only a few are considered dangerous and are in the rank of aggressiveness: 1) Oceanic Whitetip, 2) Bull Shark, 3) Tiger shark, 4) Great white. The great white is the most feared and the least aggressive towards humans in this group. Thanks to the movie MEG, people believe that the Megalodon still exists. Even Scuba divers fear the great white while they know better. This fear, directly linked to our primal instinct of self-preservation, is an excellent example of how humans react and behave towards a threat from our nature that others have imprinted in us.

When you swim in the ocean near a beach and know there may be sharks, you also know you are taking a risk. You hope there will be no sharks. We kill a hundred million of them every year for no reason other than to profit from their fins for shark fin soup and squalene, which is used in the cosmetics industry for sunscreens, anti-aging creams, lotions, hair conditioners, deodorants, eye shadows, lip balms, lipstick, and face cleansers.

You continue to swim happily in their habitat. Sharks are the apex predator, meaning they are at the top of their food chain. They also form part of the ocean's medical faculty. They keep the ocean clean of ailing fish to prevent diseases from spreading and damaging their ecosystem. All 500-plus species of sharks play a vital role in the ocean. So when you are in their territory and accidentally get bitten by a shark, you should consider where you are, and that shark that bit you has as much right to be there as you, who chose to ignore the risk. All shark attacks are accidental as humans are not part of their food chain; we have never been since the dawn of man. Sharks have been around for 400 million years vs. our 400,000 years. Will they eat us if we are thrown in the water? Because we are not considered part of their ecosystem, eliminating that "waste" is required. Humans like to hunt them for sport because it's a cool, manly activity—Man vs. Beast. Not dissimilar from what we observed in the early 20th century, and still, even today, "hunters" go on safaris in Africa to shoot wild animals. Why? Because it lifts their egos, they can display their trophies on the wall back home. We are the only species that hunt for fun. We love to watch sharks on TV, and it triggers our fear. We love watching scary movies. That's why Shark Week is so popular. "It's must-see TV."

Ask yourself this question whenever you encounter a species, be it a frog, fish, butterfly, flower, tree, cockroach, or the favorite animal you don't like, the rat. Do they have a right to be there? If the answer is no, which may be true when you see a cockroach or a rat in your house, consider the following. First, have some respect and find out why it is there instead of killing it. Fix the cause of why they are there. All species should have rights.

Unfortunately, words alone do not create awareness or understanding. Any teacher knows that. It takes practice, which means you need to experience the event. We should experience what we learn and become emotionally attached to it to feel it. Over time, this becomes an instinct that will find its way toward our three primal instincts and replace those primal myths and metaphors harmful to us and our planet.

We will not change our ways unless we become emotionally attached to all our species. This task is enormous, for as we have seen in previous chapters, it can take thousands of years to change a person's beliefs, which are kept company by our myths and metaphors deep in our unconscious mind. Our unconscious mind includes things we can visualize but not explain unless made conscious through association or acute crisis.

If we become emotionally attached to a flower, housefly, cockroach, or shark as much as we are attached to our cat or dog, then only then will we change our beliefs and myths about our other species.

When your dog that has been with you for 12 years passes away, you are sad, and tears will flow. When your goldfish dies after two years, you buy a new one and, if you are respectful, will bury it or, worse, throw it in the trash. I've yet to see anybody weep for a goldfish. But a goldfish is as much an animal as your dog, but okay, your goldfish won't give you her fin.

We need to learn to become emotionally attached to our species, all of them. We need to experience what it is like to be with and surrounded by all species. Watching a butterfly visiting your garden would be a good start. People worldwide need to experience this within their bioregion, of which there are 185, but more on this later.

Please don't sit in a cage with a snake. Keeping animals in captivity for the purpose of entertainment or "education" lies at the core of how we view nature. I still regret that I once kept snakes in captivity.

To surround yourself with nature in Australia could be challenging as there are many deadly poisonous animals out there, so be careful where you venture. Start with your garden or go to a park.

Teachers will have to be taught. This alone is a massive global effort in addition to preventing waste. Becoming emotionally attached to nature and all its species is not easy. I see it in young children under the age of 5. For some reason, I cannot explain why they like to throw stones at dogs, cats, birds, and even fish in a pond. Why do they do that? It's doubtful they got it from their parents. Perhaps they saw other older boys and girls do it. But even if that were true, why did they do it? Even when these kids have been corrected by their parents to stop. They keep doing it until they are told again to stop. Is it for amusement? Is it something primal that triggers this behavior? Perhaps evolutionary psychology can answer that, for it may be that our primal instinct of self-preservation has evolved to killing animals for fun, similar to those high-income "hunters" today who like to be like Ernest Hemingway.

I've lived around nature most of my life, have always been close to animals, and have never really been scared. Well, there was the one time when I was 10 when a big baboon thought I wanted to steal one of his wives. Monkeys are generally not aggressive unless you threaten their group, at least not in Africa. I recently had a close encounter with a Macaque in Puncak, a beautiful area in the hills south of Jakarta. The macaque is a common monkey found in Indonesia.

He definitely showed aggressiveness towards me, which surprised me. I quickly learned why. It had acquired threatening behavior because he had learned that by drawing his teeth, people ran away, often screaming and leaving their food behind. I did not move. I could see the puzzled look on his face. He even came closer threateningly, his shoulders low to the ground as he approached me. I did not move, and the macaque did not know what to do, so after a few moments, He turned around and decided to climb a tree. Then, one of the hotel staff members came with an airgun to chase it away. The macaque jumped from tree to tree until he was back in the forest outside the border of the resort. These monkeys have been there for generations. The resort we stayed at had been there for ten years, and guess what? The monkeys are still there, and yet they are regarded as pests.

Lack of a Healthy Relationship with Society, Mind and Body.

"It is no measure of health to be well adjusted to a profoundly sick society." Krishnamurti.

The pressures to manage your relationship within this society, mind and body, are increasingly stressful in today's hurry-hurry material economy with its infinite number of rat races. Combining that with the prevalence of nihilism and loss of meaning, we could argue that our society is sick. I would even go as far as to say that at least 30% of our urban society suffers from a lack of healthy societal interaction. How does this manifest itself under one issue? Mental Health and the statistics don't lie.

- Millennials (born 1981-1996): This generation, burdened by immense financial pressures, job market uncertainties, and rising living costs, experiences 32% higher rates of anxiety and 20% higher rates of depression compared to older generations. Additionally, the "always-on" digital culture fuels feelings of social isolation and comparison, exacerbating these problems.

  These statistics are supported by the medications that are used to treat these issues. 21.7% of Millenials aged 26-34 reported using any mental health medication

- Generation Z (born 1997-2012): Entering adulthood amidst climate change and pollution, economic turmoil, and social unrest, Gen Z grapples with 25% higher rates of self-harm and 30% higher rates of suicidal ideation, raising alarming concerns about their long-term mental well-being. 14.3% of them aged 12-17 are on some mental health medication and this percentage is increasing.

- Generation X (born 1964 - 1980) Shows statistics that are markedly lower than the other generations, which is interesting. Within this generation, we see a 16% to 20% higher rate of Anxiety and a 10% - 15% higher rate of depression. While Surprisingly, 20.7% of Gen Xers aged between 45 - 54 are on Mental Health medication.

- Baby Boomers (born 1946-1964): While facing age-related concerns like retirement and healthcare transitions, this generation also experiences the impact of rapid technological advancements and changing social norms. Studies suggest they are more prone to 28% higher rates of loneliness and 15% higher rates of depression, highlighting the need for intergenerational support systems. 17.7% of boomers aged 56 - 74 are on mental health medication

Sources:

- City Living and Mental Well-being - Psychiatry.org: https://www.psychiatry.org/patients-families/depression

- How the city affects mental health - Centre for Urban Design and Mental Health: https://thrivingcenterofpsych.com/blog/mental-health-effects-of-living-in-a-city/

- Cities and Mental Health - PMC - NCBI: https://www.ncbi.nlm.nih.gov/pmc/articles/PMC3230535/

I suspect that the above statistics are underreported for three reasons. One reason is that there is still a huge stigma associated with mental health issues. The other reason is that these medicines are relatively easy to obtain because you can order them online or using messaging apps. What is also not included in the above is the use of narcotics because it is not counted as medicine. Last but not least, it's difficult to find data from Asia, Africa, and South America. I know what you may be thinking. Maybe it's not so bad globally if we add all continents. That may be so, but I would venture to guess that in a dominant macho society like South America, mental issues are stigmatized, like in Asia, where it is considered shameful, and in Africa, a concern that is generally not regarded as most pressing and therefore ranks low on the scale of health risks—just my opinion.

What does this tell us is that from a metacrisis perspective we can see that there are four main causes.

- Urban stressors: Noise pollution, traffic congestion, lack of green spaces, and fast-paced nature contribute to chronic stress, a significant risk factor for mental health issues.

- Social isolation: Despite high population density, cities can foster feelings of loneliness and detachment due to anonymity and transient social connections.

- Socioeconomic disparities: Poverty, unemployment, and limited access to healthcare disproportionately impact marginalized communities, exacerbating mental health burdens.

- Digital age pressures: The constant connectivity and social media comparison culture contribute to anxiety, depression, and distorted self-image, particularly among younger generations.

DEGRADATION

As I sip the juice from a cool coconut and gaze at the ocean, I realize how vast this body of water is. I could swim from Bali to New York if I wanted to and not see land the entire way. I could make it if I did not need to eat and drink. I might have to wait till 2029 so that all the fish are gone so I won't be mistakenly attacked by a shark.

Global GDP in 2022 was approximately 100 trillion USD. Global debt to GDP now stands at about 235 trillion. This translates to $29,375 of average debt for each person globally versus GDP per person of just $12,000. Government debt-to-GDP leverage grew aggressively by 76% to 102% from 2007 to 2022. (Source: IMF)

Now, I ask you a simple question. What do people do when they are in debt? They buy less to pay off their debts. They stop buying things. They stretch their purchases of food, clothes, and luxuries. They use their car, phones, and other consumer products for as long as possible.

When you apply reducing debt to a national level, they need to cut costs and look for more efficient means of operating to pay back this debt plus interest. Governments keep borrowing money and raising taxes. Together with tax revenue, develop a spending budget for defense, healthcare, education, infrastructure and maintenance, and incentives for economic growth and employment, to name a few. As a result, little money is left over for cleaning up our wastesphere, be it in the form of gases, liquids, or solids. A country's ability to manage waste depends on how wealthy it is. That's why many middle- and low-income countries have poor waste management; the money needed to invest in proper waste management is not there. Most waste management is privatized now, so the burden has shifted to the private sector, where the community pays waste collectors to bring the waste to a landfill that the government provides. Waste to Landfill is still the dominant method of waste disposal globally.

Whether you live in a high, middle, or low-income country, you will find that allocation of funds towards waste management, pollution clean-ups, and prevention takes a back seat to more pressing matters like employment and healthcare. This is why it is so difficult to finance eliminating waste in our air, water, and land. When waste increases, more money is needed to pay for the damages caused. By damages, I mean polluted rivers from landfill leakage, air pollution in cities caused by industrial emissions, and land pollution from open landfills and dumpsites to nitrogen runoffs that create dead zones in the ocean. Investments needed to improve water quality supply and sanitation or increase permanent and safe waste disposal are severely lacking.

Indonesia is a good case study. Indonesia ranks 2nd in the world after China in plastic waste pollution, and approximately 5 million tons of plastic waste makes its way from rivers into the ocean annually. 40 million tons of waste is deposited in nature, which does not include greenhouse gas emissions.

Billions in green infrastructure development financing are available, but only a tiny portion is allocated to waste management projects because they are not investable. Of the 185 billion USD available in 2021, 94% is allocated to energy and transport, 5.4% to water and sanitation, and 0.3% to Municipal Solid Waste management. (Source: World Bank). Private investment in water and sewage was 1%, and Municipal Solid Waste Management was 0.04% of the total private investment pie. Energy was 61%, transport was 36%, and IT was 1% of 52 Billion USD in 2021. Waste management is currently not investable because the risks outweigh the returns. These risks are:

- Poor governance and technical capacity

- The creditworthiness of capital providers

- Lack of legal special purpose vehicles to ringfence investors and borrowers

Returns

- High capex investment and low to negative profit margins

Currently, Indonesia uses door-to-door fee collection versus, for example, a waste tax, as seen in many other countries.

When you compare High, Middle, and Low-income countries, we see that Indonesia's local government budget on waste management is only 0.7% versus 11% in a low-income country, 19% in a middle-income country, and 4% in a high-income country. Monthly spending on waste management per household in Indonesia is 50% lower compared to a middle-income country and 30% lower than a lower-income country.

The conclusion is that approximately 5 billion dollars of capex investment is needed to set up waste systems to collect 80% of the waste produced annually and dispose of this waste in a way that does no further harm to nature.

When the United Nations issued the 17 Sustainable Development Goals, they assumed that most of the money would come from the private sector. I have some experience in this at a micro level when consulting for a green tech company. This company offered a marketplace where companies could buy impact units for ecosystem restoration projects, plastic removal projects, and social justice projects. For example, a unit of impact could be one mangrove tree planted, 1kg of plastic removed from a river or beach, or one person per course.

The product they delivered to their clients was a dashboard where they could access the impact of their purchases depending on what they bought. For example, a company could buy a hundred mangrove trees planted in a degraded forest. Upon the purchase, the not-for-profit organization under the startup's curation would plant the mangrove saplings and upload the evidence via the app that was provided to them by the start-up. The customer would be provided with the information that shows how their purchase contributed to CO2 removal, how much marine biodiversity is created, and other benefits such as contribution to the local economy and mitigating against the risks of flooding, which is what mangrove forests provide. The same applies when you buy a hundred kilos of plastic waste. The money received would pay for the removal of plastic from a beach, and the customer would be provided with an online report detailing the benefits.

I liked this approach because the core purpose of a business is to serve the people so they can improve their lives. That's why I moved to the ICT sector in 1999. To help people get access to information via the internet. Internet access helps people acquire knowledge that helps them in their lives. I was unaware of the negative downsides until I watched the Social Dilemma documentary. I was not naïve; businesses focus on revenue, profits, and shareholder value. But in essence, I still believed back then that the purpose of a company should be to serve humanity.

Selling units of impact to companies to restore nature and remove pollution was perfect. Well, not so fast, for I learned very quickly that companies were not prepared to invest in ecosystem restoration or waste removal services. We even showed evidence that when a company did, their revenue would increase because consumers were more motivated to buy an item from a company that supported these projects financially.

The feedback often was that they had already allocated their corporate social responsibility (CSR) budget to other projects. Another interesting feedback was that they could not tie this service to their ESG reports because we did not sell carbon credits, which they needed to offset their emissions. Lastly, paying for these services was not tax deductible because we were a for-profit company.

Despite all our efforts to provide customer references and case studies illustrating the return on investment results and potential, the net result was that companies were more comfortable buying plastic and carbon credits as offsets so they could balance out their emissions but not eliminate them. Fortunately, the green tech start-up that I supported did manage to get through to quite a few companies who did buy services from them, and as a result, thousands of kilos of plastic have been removed from rivers and beaches. Coral reefs are being restored, millions of mangrove trees have been planted, and hundreds of women and children are getting an education they had no access to before.

It showed me that perverse incentives were also present in the sustainability and regenerative space. Buy a T-shirt made with cotton, plastic, or synthetic material, and we will plant a tree if you opt-in. This is an excellent example of perverse incentives. It's a convincing case illustrating a lack of understanding of 2nd and 3rd-level causal effects. While planting a tree is good, the incentive is not to become nature-positive as a business but to sell more clothes and claim that you are sustainable. We generate 92 million tons of textile waste annually, roughly 80 - 100 billion garments. 8 to 10 pieces per person per year are thrown away. Only 20% of what is produced is recycled. Recycling is more costly than disposal, so circularity is economically challenging. This textile waste, often containing petrochemicals such as polymers, ends up in our nature as micro and nano plastics that pollute our air and water. To produce 1 T-shirt requires 2700 liters of water, so by default, you are depriving water from that tree, but since it's planted on the opposite side of the planet, we ignore the impact.

Furthermore, global companies are not interested in these projects to remove waste permanently from nature. They are at least trying to reduce their waste but not clean up the waste they have already created. This is mainly because companies argue that it's the consumer's or government's responsibility to dispose of their products responsibly. A classic case of conflict mistake theory where the producer claims deniable responsibility. They try to use less water and keep contributing to not-for-profits that plant millions of trees for them to get a tax break. Some companies are buying up large pieces of African land to plant trees to generate carbon credits to offset their emissions.

Many companies today, primarily global and regional companies, proudly list the various SDGs that they support in their annual reports. However, according to the United Nations, the financing gap for the SGDs is currently 3.9 Trillion dollars, or 3.9% of GDP, and as we shall see later, the SDGs are presently not on track to reach their goals.

Economists can no longer ignore the laws of physics and ecology and the natural resource base on which society and the existence of an economy depend, according to Nicolae Georgescu, a well-respected but pessimistic economist who explained that natural resources degrade over time through economic activity and that earth's carrying capacity to sustain human populations and consumption levels would ultimately decrease and lead to our extinction if we do not change our behavior.

From what I remember from high school, the first law of thermodynamics says it is impossible to create something from nothing. All products we produce result from transforming natural raw materials using energy. Thermodynamics is part of physical science that deals with the relations between heat and other forms of energy, such as mechanical, electrical, or chemical energy, and, by extension, the relationships between all forms of energy.

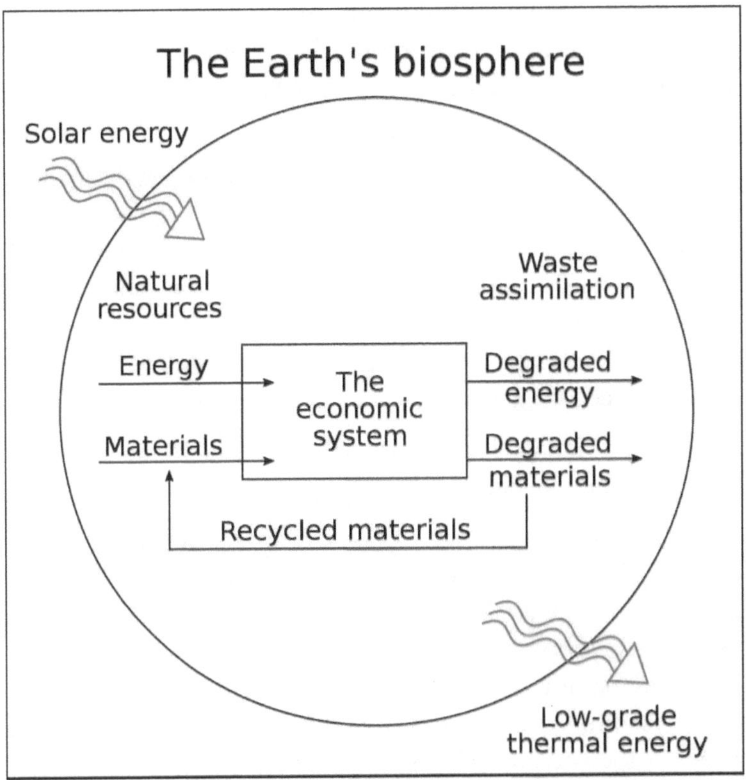

All human-made products break down, wear out, and eventually fall apart, returning to nature as waste. The extraction of raw materials from nature and the return of disordered waste is known as throughput. Maintaining existing stocks in the face of gradual decline requires continuous throughput flows, creating even more waste. This physical throughput is essential to nearly all economic processes, including electronic and digital transactions, which depend on some combination of power in the form of electricity or food and tools in the form of paper, pens, computers, or phones, all of which depend on throughput.

The simplest laws of physics and mathematics tell us that the exponential growth of any physical subsystem of a finite system is impossible. Since all economic production consumes raw materials and generates waste, the economy is a physical system. If this is so, then our current economic system, which is capitalism, focussed on infinite growth and profit, is not sustainable when waste becomes so prevalent that it threatens the people who participate in it, which is, after all, all of planetary Life.

Herman Daly has pointed out that anyone who thinks they understand money probably has not studied it enough. I'm quick to admit that I do not understand the role of money in the complicated ecological economy except as a value communication tool necessary for transactions. We now have important insights explaining why the current approach to money creation and circulation is incompatible with our global economy and how alternative systems are required.

Money functions as a lubricant that greases the gears of the economy. When economies grow, they require more money to chase more goods and services. When money becomes too scarce, the engine of economic growth can grind to a halt, typically causing severe misery. However, the rise in misery is not the result of a no-growth or de-growth economy but rather the result of poorly constructed economic institutions, particularly the monetary system, according to a few economists focussed on post-growth economic theory.

We will be extinct when our finite natural resources are entirely depleted, so Nicolae Georgescu may have had a valid point.

No wonder we live in a world fascinated by speed, especially in high-income societies. We are all out to get our piece of the pie with what is left before it is too late. We have no care for our planet, and we certainly don't give a damn about the next generations based on how we operate today. We have lost our connection to our natural ecosystems. Now, that is not entirely true. We do care. Our younger generation genuinely worries about the future and hopes that the people currently focussed on solving the metacrisis will find a way.

So what's the solution? We talk about systems change, but we cannot change our system if we don't clean up the waste we have created. It gets even more challenging when our foundation, SDG 15 Life on Land (Biodiversity), SDG 14 Life Underwater (Our Ocean), SDG 6 Water (Hydrosphere), SDG 13 (Climate Action), which all require financing are not investable assets of economic value that deliver healthy returns. Those who are convinced that Biodiversity, Ocean, Water, and Atmosphere are investable assets in our current economic system may soon find that this approach will inflict more harm than good, thanks to the perverse incentive structure of our systems.

Carbon Capture Technology is enjoying significant focus as it fits into our economic system—or privatizing water supply, which will likely become more lucrative due to increased scarcity. Investing in infrastructure to clean our rivers and oceans of plastic waste, pesticides, and forever chemicals and prevention is currently not financially attractive, but buying rainforests is. Last but not least, Investing in closing down landfills, or I should say, trash mountains, from our lands and prevention is also not an attractive proposition in our current economic system. If we cannot find a way to fix our foundation, how will we even achieve the other 13 Sustainability Goals?

I'm reminded of what Lord Elrond said at the council of Elrond.

"The Ring cannot be destroyed, Gimli, son of Glóin, by *any craft* that *we* here *possess*. The Ring was made in the fires of Mount Doom. Only *there* can *it* be destroyed."

Lord of the Rings by JRR Tolkien.

Change the word ring with metacrisis. The scene that follows the above quote exposes something fundamental and critical. When you think about that scene, you can see it all around us today. An evil influence that is unspoken in global discourse. Only a few know its name and recognize its influence. Many follow it, and they don't even know it.

Economists who focus on climate don't always have their economic models peer-reviewed by climatologists, which increases the risk that these models do not factor in events caused by our climate. They tend to focus more on temperature changes, overlooking critical variables like shifts in rainfall patterns, intensifying extreme weather events, rising sea levels, and socio-economic impacts, including conflicts and mass migrations. Add to that the causes and symptoms of the wastesphere, which is more than greenhouse gases, and I would venture a guess that these models are completely useless for the mid to long term.

Isabel Schnabel, a member of the European Central Bank's board, acknowledges that current economic models used by European banks may be downplaying the financial repercussions of climate change.

Risks are increasing year over year, and they are becoming a reality. The current focus on climate change, which is only 1 out of the 9 planetary boundaries that the Stockholm Resilience Centre focuses on, is increasing these risks. Whatever economic system we evolve towards will depend on how our Earth Systems will change.

The planet has been in an ecological recession since 1971, when we first started measuring Earth's capacity to resupply itself. Today, we read about overshoot day, slowly moving closer to the beginning of the year. In 2023, it was August 2nd. Global overshoot occurs when humanity's demand from nature exceeds the Earth's supply or regenerative capacity. Such an overshoot leads to a depletion of Earth's life-supporting natural capital and increases waste. At the global level, ecological deficit and overshoot are the same since there is no net import of resources to the planet from the universe. Local overshoot occurs when a local ecosystem is exploited more rapidly than it can restore itself.

Here are the following overshoot dates since 1970;

- 1979, November 1

- 1989, October 11

- 1999, October 4

- 2009, September 25

- 2019, July 22

There are signs that we are finally reaching a stage where we have stopped the decline. Since 2015, overshoot day has ranged between July 28 and August 8. The outlier was 2020, the height of the COVID-19 pandemic, when overshoot day retreated to August 22nd. An impressive 24-day improvement in one year because, for the most part, the world was in lockdown, giving nature a reprieve to restore itself. It is too soon to say if we are on a path towards regeneration. The critical question is whether we are plateauing or there is still the opportunity to restore the planet to 100% regenerative. We are at 1.7 Times the Earth's capacity to regenerate.

The chart below shows that Earth's overshoot day can also be measured on a country level.

A local economic system can be somewhat circular if we adopt a regional resource approach that can be replenished and waste is disposed of without causing further harm. This would be most challenging in countries where overshoot day is the furthest away from December 31st. Taking and using what can be replenished within their ecosystem would be difficult. They simply don't have the resources.

You only take and use what can be replenished without creating any waste that harms this balance. Globally, we have overcome many recessions, but the planetary's ecological recession is the one we have yet to recover from. I sometimes wonder if we can recover from this recession because, to do so, we would need to redefine wealth and tie it to ecological wealth, not geological wealth. We would need a new currency in a system where its accumulation is aligned with ecological wealth, not material wealth. A proposition is worthy of presenting to the council.

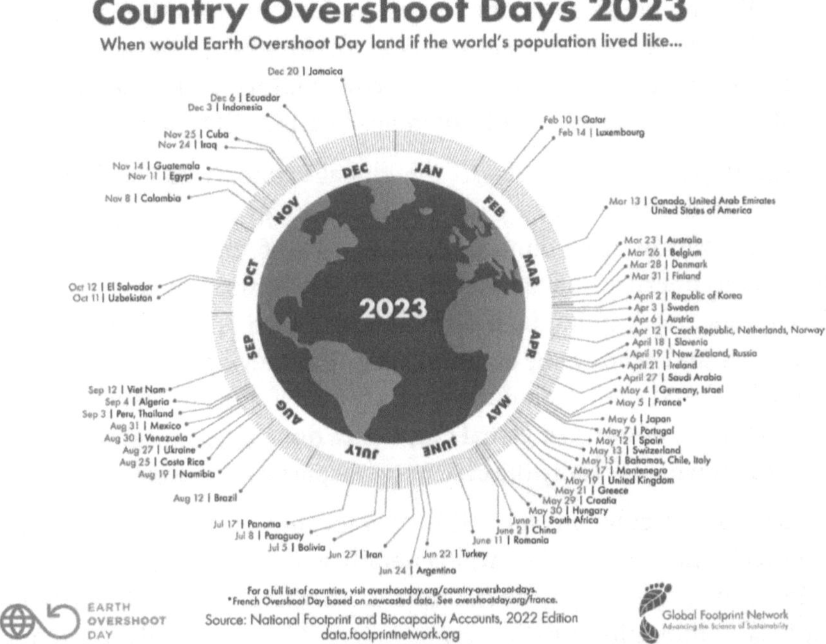

What is interesting and not talked about often enough is the following. We can quickly determine which companies contribute to our GHG emissions, biodiversity loss, and industrial and agricultural waste creation. Our technological advancement enables us to do so—particularly blockchain and A. I monitor systems.

The opportunity for significant change lies in the Small and Medium Enterprise sector.

Small and Medium Enterprises (SMEs) account for the vast majority of enterprises globally, with an estimated 90% of all businesses falling into this category. SMEs are defined differently in different countries but are generally considered businesses with fewer than 250 employees.

SMEs play a vital role in the economy, accounting for approximately 50% of global GDP and 60-70% of global employment. They are also a significant source of innovation and entrepreneurship.

Here is a breakdown of the percentage of SMEs by enterprise size:

- Micro-enterprises (fewer than 10 employees): 60%

- Small enterprises (10-49 employees): 20%

- Medium-sized enterprises (50-249 employees): 10%

SMEs are particularly important in low and middle-income growth economies, where they can account for up to 90% of businesses and 70% of employment. SMEs are also major contributors to the service industry, accounting for 60% or more of GDP in nearly all OECD countries.

The importance of SMEs to the global economy is widely recognized. According to a 2022 report by the World Bank, an estimated 99.6% of SMEs operate only within their country. Less than 0.4% of SMEs export their products or services to international markets. What these businesses contribute to waste and how much they pollute our air, water, and land is poorly understood, but what is clear and needs to be emphasized is that they have a direct relationship with the land and their community, which increases their responsibilities and accountability, a power that global corporates don't have unless they manage to control them which is sadly the case in many parts of the world.

Laws and regulations bind SMEs via locality, and if followed, depending on enforcement capacity, they will generally abide by them. They do not have sustainability managers and do not have to provide ESG reports. SMEs are part of the local community, usually serving their best interests, and do not care much for what happens outside their border despite their overall contribution to GDP. For them, GDP is mostly irrelevant. They fear recession and instability. Besides that, in most countries, their voices are mere whispers compared to the voices of large enterprises. Localization of a global crisis can provide opportunities for these businesses. Especially when they become aware of their impact and can implement programs that help tackle the situation. We need to give them the tools to do so.

Enter perverse incentives, and SMEs fall victim to the supplies of these global companies who would like to think that they can exert control. But what if SMEs locally, once aware and presented with inspiration, motivation, and incentives, allowed them to change what they procure? Better yet, they can refuse certain goods harmful to their nature and customers that global suppliers want them to buy or sell. This could have a huge positive ripple effect, resulting in a tsunami of natural positive change. The closer you are to what you cause, the better equipped you are to deal with it. Each has their part to play.

Another challenge that needs to be addressed but could produce a positive impact is smallholder farmers and artisanal fisheries. Both add up to over a billion people, 570 million smallholder farmers, and 500 million artisanal fishermen. Unfortunately, they are some of the poorest people in the world despite smallholder farmers producing 30% of the global food supply in crops and meat, and artisanal fisheries catch 40% of the world's fish. These two sectors are in decline, mainly due to economic pressure, especially in artisanal fishing, where catches are decreasing due to depleting fish stocks caused by heavily subsidized industrial fishing. Employment is still rising but predominately in aquaculture, i.e., fish farms, which is increasingly detrimental to humans and wildlife. Artisan fish farming is a sector that is not widely adopted. Industrial aquaculture dominates this sector. Localization may be an answer and, if implemented correctly, may support the restoration of our biodiversity and elimination of our waste. SMEs and artisanal food production, crops, meat, and fish are a scope worth investigating.

Undoubtedly, global companies wish to keep the status quo and would resist a localization strategy. There is, however, opportunity when you know where to look. They are prepared to spend a lot of money to ensure that we remain blind. In the context of our crisis, what should be our primary focus? Remember, it is the tiny hands that turn the wheels of the world. We need enough of them while the powerful look elsewhere.

The debate around systems change and circularity rages on. Still, the only circularity I see is our waste because what we waste ends in our food and becomes waste again, and the cycle continues. I am also convinced that our economic growth is no longer directly tied to assets. However, the last frontier, the bio and blue economy, is the latest asset class we want to exploit to maintain our growth narrative, which, let's face it, is funded by more debt. That massive global sword, called debt hangs over our heads that we need to feed to maintain the narrative that growth is good. Our increased debt is not sustainable, and as long as we maintain the debt sphere, we will increase our wastesphere.

Economic prosperity goals still dominate the world, but two more require urgent attention: social prosperity and ecological prosperity. Each has different goals, distribution, criteria, processes, and types of goods, and there is tension between each prosperity goal.

Economic Prosperity:

Goals: Efficiency, Productivity, Consumption

Distribution: Market Scarcity

Criteria: Prices

Process: Private transactions

Type of Goods: Private

When our economic growth includes climate change mitigation and adaptation, a blue and green economy, then, in essence, we are building a repair economy in a place where resources are finite and where scarcity still plays a dominant role tied to economic goals.

Social Prosperity:

Goals: Inclusive Society

Distribution: Redistribution

Criteria: Social inclusion, Honesty

Process: Political process

Type of Goods: Public goods.

We find this focus on prosperity in predominantly socialist democracies, sometimes called welfare states. It's purpose is that all its citizens can have a share in the wealth of the state often provided by means of free education and healthcare.

Ecological prosperity

Goal: Healthy liveable planet

Distribution: Regeneration

Criteria: Biosphere boundaries

Process: Public and Private collaboration on managing our commons.

Type of Goods: Global Commons

Ecological and Social prosperity is declining, and we are trying to reverse this by applying economic prosperity goals, distribution, criteria, and processes. However, these aspects are not aligned, and tension leads to the emergence of perverse incentives and a take-all-what-you-can process that may end in conflict. We should ask ourselves whether we should develop new prosperity metrics that align all three. This would apply to a state, a bioregion, and globally and should include well-being metrics that factor in all of our global spheres. Each state would be measured on the Health of Global Spheres. This is a proposal for the world to consider.

Global Spheres Prosperity

Goals: Durability of goods and services, Inclusive Society, Healthy Planet.

Distribution: Limitarialism. A system that provides individual and social freedoms to pursue goals inherent to today's aspirations but is aligned with well-being metrics that include two critical components of wisdom: constraint and sacrifice.

Criteria: Spherical health: Biosphere, Atmosphere, Hydrosphere, Lithosphere, Technology Sphere, and Waste Sphere. The health of the technology sphere and the reduction/elimination of the waste sphere are measured in how they contribute positively to our planetary spheres.

Process: Magisterium style of governance.

Type of Goods: Private, Public, and Commons

SCIENCE

Scientists have been part of our kind since the dawn of time. In our modern society, Aristotle is considered the first social scientist. However, the term predates him by 2000 years, so there were many before him. Ancient civilizations must have had them, but they did not keep written records, so we have no way of knowing. Some have passed into legend, like the wizard Merlin, the personification of various sources of pagan wisdom from the English Isles. He may well have been a druid, a priest of druidism, a religion practiced by the Celts. Druids had many duties, one of which was to provide medical services to his people.

We know that religious authorities from the 13th century until the 17th century didn't look too kindly on healers and women called midwives who helped mothers during childbirth. These women used herbal medicine to help heal wounds and soften the pain of an injury. Midwives used Belladonna, a weed, to ease women's pain while in labor, and Ergot, a type of fungus found on Rye, was used to alleviate migraines. However, the church did not approve as a woman's suffering from inflicted injuries was under God's purview to heal. I found this curious: if God was a healer and his representative was a priest, Shouldn't the priest be a healer as well?

But anyway, what is more shocking is that the church believed that women had to suffer severe pain during childbirth to account for Eve's original sin. She ate the forbidden fruit while strictly told by God not to. These midwives had learned the skill from their ancestors, who had used these herbs for ages. Using these herbs was a skill because Belladonna could kill if taken in large enough quantities. No one knows who was the first to discover this, but these herbal medicines were effective. The source of this knowledge now is part of myth and legend told by women with strong ties to nature, some of whom still live in the remaining jungles and on the plains in Africa. Even the Masai Mara used herbs to alleviate pain when I stayed with them. There was no aspirin for me.

These midwives and healers were prosecuted because these acts were considered abnormal and against God's will. Scholars found that the first Witch Trials started in the 13th century and continued well into the 17th century. They believe 40,000 to 60,000 women were prosecuted, and many were burnt at the stake. Not all these women were healers or midwives, of course. Others were convicted because they had a black mold on their skin, a sign of the Devil, or they had some deformity. Essentially, these women who healed and helped other women during childbirth were the forebearers of medical practice. Nature provided these medicines for them. We will never know how many expectant mothers and their babies died or were saved during these times. Using herbs to treat aches and pains was a science back then.

Scientists exist because we humans like to understand and prove how things work. Scientists want to experiment, test, and make things. In some ways, we are all scientists, but as with all of humanity, some have created something that can harm us, and others have invented things that protect us and keep us healthy. We revere scientists for their amazing discoveries that have contributed so much towards our well-being, both physically through technology and physiologically with medicine. In a way, scientists are like fools but intelligent and specialized. We have much to thank for what they have discovered. Some examples, which I found in The Lifesavers of Science Article published on 26 November 2020 on bbvaopenmind.com, are listed here.

Many scientists have saved millions of lives, such as Alexander Fleming (1881 – 1955)

Alexander Fleming was a Scottish medical doctor and microbiologist who discovered the world's first effective antibiotic substance, which he called Penicillin, in 1928. This antibiotic has been estimated to have saved over 200 million lives.

It gets better as Karl Landsteiner (1868 – 1943) and Richard Lewisohn (1857 – 1961) saved an estimated one billion lives through their discoveries. They discovered the different types of blood groups in humans and developed blood transfusion techniques.

Louis Pasteur (1822 – 1895)

He discovered that microorganisms were responsible for the contamination of drinks and that this did not happen when they were heat sterilized and kept in closed containers. In 1865, Pasteur patented this method, which we now know as pasteurization. But in addition to developing its industrial applications, the chemist also discovered that microbes were responsible for disease through infection. Until the nineteenth century, the public still believed that living things could arise spontaneously from nothing; for example, according to Aristotle, greenflies were born from dewdrops. The existence of microbes had begun to be assumed in the mid-sixteenth century. Still, it was not until the fermentation experiments that he could confirm that spontaneous generation did not exist and that all living things come from other living things.

Linn Enslow(1891–1957) and Abel Wolman (1892 – 1989).

Lack of access to clean water remains one of the leading causes of mortality in developing countries today. According to the United Nations, 3.575 million people die from contaminated water; 90% are children under five. However, these figures vary based on where you search online. Nonetheless, people should not die from drinking water.

Tap water was a health risk worldwide in the early twentieth century; most industrialized countries already used pipes to supply water, but often, the quality was poor, and the tap could serve as the entrance point for lethal infections such as cholera, typhoid, and dysentery. Even in countries like Indonesia, drinking water from the tap is still not considered safe.

In the late nineteenth century, water chlorination began to be experimented with as a sterilization method, but sometimes, the cure was worse than the illness since chlorine is toxic. Finding the correct quantity of chlorine to take advantage of its antiseptic properties without poisoning the populace seemed too risky a challenge until a sanitary engineer from the Department of Public Health of Maryland, USA, called Abel Wolman, set out to find the exact formula. To do this, he enlisted the help of the chemist Linn Enslow. Together, they designed, in 1919, a standardized method to chlorinate Baltimore's drinking water supply.

Although the authorities were initially reluctant to pour chlorine into their water pipes, Wolman and Enslow's system proved reliable and safe. Chlorination has been rated as one of the most significant public health advances of the last millennium, which ScienceHeroes.com estimates has saved 177 million lives worldwide.

Despite our heroes, well-respected scientists have clashed with authorities, some of whom were arrested, imprisoned, injured, and even killed. Some had their work destroyed.

Abu Bakr Al-Razi (865-925)

Muhammad ibn Zakariyā Rāzī, or Rhazes, was a medical pioneer from Baghdad. He was responsible for introducing Western teachings, rational thought, and the works of Hippocrates and Galen to the Arabic world. One of his books, Continens Liber, was a compendium of everything known about medicine. The book made him famous but offended an Imam who ordered the doctor to be beaten over the head with his manuscript, which caused him to go blind, preventing him from future practice.

Michael Servetus (1511-1553)

Servetus was a Spanish physician credited with discovering pulmonary circulation. He wrote a book outlining his discovery and ideas about reforming Christianity, which was deemed heretical. He escaped from Spain and the Catholic Inquisition but came up against the Protestant Inquisition in Switzerland, who held him in equal disregard. Under orders from John Calvin, Servetus was arrested, tortured, and burned at the stake on the shores of Lake Geneva. Copies of his book were thrown in for good measure.

Henri Oldenburg (1619-1677)

Oldenburg founded the Royal Society in London in 1662. He sought to publish high-quality scientific papers. To do this, he had to correspond with many foreigners across Europe, including the Netherlands and Italy. The sheer volume of his correspondence caught the attention of the authorities, who arrested him as a spy. He was held in the Tower of London for several months.

Antoine-Laurent Lavoisier (1743–1794)

He was a French aristocrat and a chemist who became a leading member of the pre-revolutionary French Academy of Science after discovering oxygen. Lavoisier opposed the election of Jean-Paul Marat to membership in the Academy. Years later, when Marat was a prominent leader of the French Revolution, he remembered Lavoisier. Lavoisier was arrested on trumped-up charges of financial irregularities and tried by a revolutionary tribunal chaired by Marat. Lavoisier was guillotined on the day his trial ended, and his body was buried in an unmarked grave.

Gerhard Domagk 1895-1964)

Gerhard Johannes Paul Domagk was a German pathologist and bacteriologist. He is credited with the discovery of sulfonamidochrysoidine as an antibiotic, for which he received the 1939 Nobel Prize in Physiology or Medicine. Because he was a Nazi critic, Carl von Ossietzky, had won the Nobel Peace Prize in 1935, Domagk was forced by the Nazi regime to refuse the prize. He was arrested and held by the Gestapo for a week. After the war, in 1947, he finally received his Nobel Prize, but not the associated cash prize, because too much time had elapsed.

Albert Einstein (1879-1955)

His work on the General Theory of Relativity and his pacifist politics roused violent animosity from right-wing members of German society. When Hitler came to power in January 1933, Einstein was in California and almost immediately deprived of his Berlin posts and his Prussian Academy of Sciences membership. His property was seized, and his books were burned in public. Einstein never returned to Germany and signed a letter to President Roosevelt alerting him that Germany might be developing an atomic weapon. He recommended that the US begin similar research.

You would have thought that by now, we respected scientists. But in the context of our metacrisis, we see the same happening again.

We now read that climate scientists have become a target. Luckily, as far as I know, none have been killed, but some have been arrested. For example, Peter Kalmus, a climate scientist and a data analyst at NASA, was arrested for handcuffing himself to the offices of JP Morgan. Most recently, while writing this part of the book, arrests were made in the Netherlands who blockaded the A12 highway. Some of those arrested were scientists. There is even a union of concerned scientists. It's an organization founded 50 years ago at MIT (Massachusetts Institute of Technology) with over 250 members. Scientist Rebellion is another organization; the membership total is not known. They have been active as they blocked local airports in 2022 to demonstrate urgent climate action.

It is alarming when Scientists who are specialists in their field go out in public to demonstrate that something is going on. When they also get arrested, it gets even more worrying.

As history shows us, there has always been resistance to science. Why? Is it ignorance, or is it something different?

The beliefs we so desperately but unconsciously cling to prevent us from accepting what science has produced and demonstrated to the world. Even today, some refuse antibiotics and trust God to heal them.

To show the extent of resistance to accepting the work of climate scientists, the Union of Concerned Scientists published a list of organizations in 2013 that work hard to undermine and deny that Climate Change exists, that Biodiversity Loss does not matter, and that pollution is an exaggeration.

These organizations are as follows;

1. American Enterprise Institute

2. Americans for Prosperity

3. American Legislative Exchange Council

4. Beacon Hill Institute at Suffolk University

5. Cato Institute

6. Competitive Enterprise Institute

7. Heartland Institute

8. Heritage Foundation

9. Institute for Energy Research

10. Manhattan Institute for Policy Research

I'm unsure if they still proclaim climate change is a hoax, but a quick scan confirmed what the Concerned Scientists have published. Many of these organizations have powerful sponsors from the business world and significant influence over politicians. Like the church did in the 13th to 17th centuries, politicians in the 18th, 19th, and 20th centuries and businesses in the 20th and 21st centuries still undermine the work of scientists. Especially those that threaten current world views and the status quo.

Climate Change is an easy target because people do not feel it; they only experience weather events that change year over year, and because most people have busy lives, they can't even remember what they had for dinner on September 19th unless it was their birthday. A rancher overlooking a white landscape in Montana may even say he is witnessing 6 inches of global warming in the middle of January.

Most of the world's population has some idea of what climate change means. The level of understanding varies region by region, education level, and access to information sources despite the Aarhus convention. The Aarhus Convention provides the legal rights for all citizens to have access to information about nature, to participate in decision-making concerning nature, and to have access to justice. It does not give you the right to justice, only access, to be precise. When I mention the Aarhus convention to my Asian acquaintances, they quickly ask me who this Aarhus is.

What do Climate Scientists do? Does the general press and media explain Climate Change and what Climate Scientists do well? This is important because the science of climatology is complicated. Scientists who study the climate are called climatologists, which is a more accurate term. I know you may be thinking Pothato – Potato, but this is important because not all climatologists are created equal. I'm not a climatologist, but if I were, I would probably cringe whenever I read or heard the word climate scientist. There are 11 types of climatologists.

1. Descriptive climatology. This field studies observable land and water variations of global climates over an average 30-year period, which helps define normative climate patterns.

2. Scientific climatology This topic focuses on the structures and forces of the world's climate and the root causes of climate fluctuations, including how these changes occurred across history.

3. Applied climatology Refers to identifying, interpreting, and studying relationships between the climate and physical, organic, and cultural nature. It involves identifying links between the climate, industry, humans, and agriculture.

4. Bioclimatology: This subfield studies the potential effects of climate on living organisms, including humans, animals, and plants.

5. Paleoclimatology: This involves studying the origins of global historical climates through evidence, such as ice cores and tree rings, to identify and understand current and future climate phenomena.

6. Paleotempestology: This studies ancient and historical geographic data on hurricane and cyclone activity to determine present and future frequency and intensity better.

7. Historical climatology: This studies the climate relating to human history and poses a hypothesis to predict future climate changes resulting from human activity.

8. Boundary layer climatology: This branch studies natural systems and phenomena that connect the Earth's surface to its lower atmosphere and predict its effects on climate.

9. Physical climatology: Physical climatology studies the properties of climate through earth-sun relationships, atmospheric elements, ground attributes, and general laws of physics.

10. Synoptic climatology: This is the study of atmospheric circulation, focusing on links between large-scale circulation, focusing on connections between large scale circulation trends, and differences in surface-weather patterns at regional and local levels

11. Hydro climatology: This topic investigates the relationship between the climate and water systems, such as lakes, streams, and groundwater, to understand its impact on water resources and large-scale climate fluctuations.

These 11 types are highly specialized fields, and I would like to know how a Hydroclimatologist would talk to a boundary layer climatologist or a palaeoclimatologist. It's like a brain surgeon talking to a heart surgeon; both would have general deep knowledge of the human anatomy, but would you ask a brain surgeon to do a heart transplant?

Climatology is a complicated field of collecting and analyzing data and trying to make sense of it all. Data analysis from each year, which has four seasons and is spread out over 30 years, could put a roof over our atmosphere by now. Now add to that 185 bioregions and 844 ecoregions each with their own climate patterns.

That is a lot of data requiring supercomputers to help these scientists understand it within their respective fields. Then, all that data needs to be correlated from 11 fields to one topic, climate change, and you quickly understand that climatology embodies a super high degree of complexity. Trying to explain this to non-climatologists is like trying to explain Einstein's theory of relativity to me.

So what do individuals or organizations that wish to maintain the narrative that climate change is a hoax do? They divide and conquer to prove that climate change is not accurate and spread disinformation. I always wonder, when someone says "what people say," who are they talking about? Me? This also happens within the scientific community, and it is standard. Scientists do not always agree with each other. They debate and argue like you and me. Even some change their perspectives. That's why scientific papers are peer-reviewed, i.e., reviewed by other scientists with the same specialty or at least have deep knowledge of a particular subject about the research. You wouldn't ask a brain surgeon to review a group of heart surgeons' research unless there was a connection between the brain and the heart that was relevant to the study. What makes it more complicated is when climatologists change to becoming climate skeptics. When this happens, some corners of our world will jump on it to prove to you that climate change is a hoax, feeding what is called confirmation bias. The same applies when people who believe climate change is real will automatically have their convictions confirmed when climatologists get arrested when they protest.

Confirmation bias is a tendency to interpret new evidence as confirmation of one's beliefs or theories. It is a widespread human behavior trait and prevents you from having an open mind. We choose what we like to believe in accordance with our way of life. It is no wonder that an energy sales executive would do everything he can to convince himself that what he does is right. It does not matter if you are in the oil, gas, coal, or renewable energy sector. The executive may not know the detailed causes of climate change, but when he hears it from an expert who confirms his belief, he automatically accepts it. Belief is not the same as knowing. When it comes to climate change, understanding is the hardest part of all. Only time will tell as climate change is measured over 30 years and must factor in all the findings and analyses from 11 different fields. One must first understand the complicatedness and, from there, understand what is happening in this field.

That is why climate change can be manipulated on both sides.

An excellent example of how skeptics convince themselves they are correct is by reading or hearing from other skeptics, especially climatologists. Judith Curry is such a scientist. She is a climatologist. Her research interests include hurricanes, remote sensing, atmospheric modeling, polar climates, air-sea interactions, climate models, and unmanned aerial vehicles for atmospheric research. Her core specialty is Hurricanes, which means she is a paleotempestologist interested in three, maybe four, other fields.

She published research indicating that hurricane intensity would increase due to global warming. Her research was challenged and concluded to be incorrect. So she repeated her analysis and found that the scientists were correct in concluding that there was insufficient proof to confirm that hurricane intensity would increase as the planet warms. I don't know about you, but Hurricane Otis, which slammed onto land close to Acapulco in October 2023, confirmed that Hurricanes were increasing in intensity, both in force and speed.

We now understand El Nino and La Nina a little better in public discourse. We know that both of these phenomena affect our climate worldwide. While El Nino causes temperatures to rise worldwide wide, it also reduces hurricane frequency in the Atlantic. While La Nina brings a cooling period but increases hurricane frequency in the Atlantic. Over the last seventy years, we've seen mean global temperatures rise, with 2023 being the hottest on record, with 2024 yet to be determined, but so far, we're on track to break them all. The trend remains persistent, and temperatures will continue to rise until the world reaches a period where our greenhouse gas emissions are close to zero and no longer threaten global warming. According to the latest research, this is still decades away, so we will likely see more extreme weather events. I think the science is clear, so let's focus our collective science capability on finding solutions.

Our world is complex, and we now have many wicked problems for which we lack solutions, such as;

How do we remove all the plastic in our bodies that has polluted our entire planet from Pole to Pole?

How do we remove the forever chemicals found in our bodies and all over our planet?

We don't have the science to clean it up. We live in strange times. Luck is a key component of how humanity has stumbled out of one crisis or another. Future historians may provide answers as to why we have been so foolish. Luck is not science, and maybe that's why Science is not a catch-all for our wicked problems. Perhaps it has to do with our understanding of the word solution, which is a technical term for solving a problem versus a nexus problem.

Compared to the first half of the 20th century, we have not made any substantial scientific advances. The calculator, computer, and the spark of AI were all invented during that period. We've optimized it. Perhaps because our world has become increasingly complex beyond our capacity to solve them, or we have become too reliant on machines to do the work. As such, we have become entirely reliant on machines, so we assimilate with them, reducing our capacity for imagination.

I sense a lack of imagination within the science community of the 21st century. This may be caused by the increasing need for more specialization, which reduces the scope of relational observance. I draw on this sense because when I compare past scientists, mathematicians, authors, and deep thinkers like Arthur Koestler, Alfred North Whitehead, David Bohm, Albert Einstein, Marie Curie, Stephen Hawking, and Carl Sagan, I perceive a lack of Philosophical thinking within the Climatologist community. I hope I'm wrong.

It is as if we have reduced science to numbers, percentages, letters, and units that we plug into machines that model a world divorced from life's complexity. I feel we are viewing a reality based on a machine's view that does not care and has no morals. I believe the scientists mentioned above struggled with their field of expertise in sense-making and perhaps were searching for relationality between things, their deeper meaning, and how it applies to our civilization.

I would like to propose a need for an additional quality for the sciences called wisdom. I'm not saying that wisdom is not present in the sciences. After all, experience and knowledge are key components of wisdom but wisdom is far more than that and includes the following attributes;

Sound judgment: involves making good decisions by considering all available information, potential consequences 1st to 4th order causal effects analysis, and different opposing perspectives.

Emotional intelligence: Wise people can manage their own emotions and understand the emotions of others. This allows for empathy, compassion, and effective communication.

Humility: A key part of wisdom is recognizing that you don't have all the answers and being open to learning from others.

Perspectival knowledge: The ability to see the bigger picture and understand how their actions fit into the larger context. The ability to consider the long-term consequences of their decisions.

Acceptance of uncertainty: Life is full of unknowns, and wise people can gracefully navigate this uncertainty. They can adapt to changing situations and learn from unexpected events.

Balance: Striking a balance between different values and priorities.

Does science competitiveness for funding, for example, strengthen or weaken the sciences?

Does commercialization in scientific fields elevate or degenerate the value of science?

Perhaps something to think about.

Albert Einstein once said: "I am enough of an artist to draw freely upon my imagination. Imagination is more important than knowledge. Knowledge is limited. Imagination encircles the world."

GOVERNANCE

The metacrisis affects every system humanity created: Politics, Economics, Society, and all businesses that operate on Earth. We will all need to transform to ensure we can manage our transition to a system constrained to our planet's limits.

There are many crises, but the biggest of them all and the most severe and destructive is:

THE GOVERNANCE CRISIS.

Our civilization has evolved since the agricultural revolution, becoming a bureaucratic dream. We have perfected the art of reductionism, where we can create a worldview that is familiar, certain, static, explicit, abstract, decontextualized, disembodied, categorized, general in nature, and reduced to its parts. We all desire the world to be predictable and controlled. This inanimate universe is presented in charts, maps, and reports. We have increasingly become more complicated while we debased complexity at the same time. Our minds are innately complex; we still don't know enough about it, so we embrace the complicated as the only relevant way for existence. This is the reality we believe to be the only truth.

What I mean by complicated is the computer mind, which is finite with a massive set of data and relationships between them. A Complex mind is where there is infinite data, an infinite number of relationships, and infinite processes for transformation. A Complex mind can be compared with Nature, which has emergent properties and is nonlinear, subtle, and fleeting. We used to know this, but it has been suppressed because our civilization needs to be governed in conformity with society and culture, where Nature can be manipulated to suit our needs and can be managed by bureaucrats. We now witness the consequences of this view.

A complicated mind cannot create something new that includes the emergent properties of nature. It is essentially trapped but excellent at grasping things. We developed complicated systems that are a substrate of the complex. Let us discuss Wheat as an example of what I mean. Wheat is found in the wild; it is part of a complex ecosystem that includes the rich characteristics of the soil, moisture content, fungi, bacteria, insects, and mammals. Each has emergent properties of its own, interdependent relationships, and infinite possibilities for transformation. We only want the wheat, so what we do is we take the relevant layer and territory and optimize it to yield more wheat. As part of that process, a finite number of characteristics are identified, which can be measured and controlled. We moved a plant from a complex natural system into a complicated system. This process has had enormous positive and negative implications for humanity's progress as agriculture was born from this ability, which is why we are so good at making any technology.

As we evolved, we became colonizers; we left our indigenous beliefs and wisdom behind and slowly increased our ability to manipulate our nature first and, later, other people, tribes, and civilizations. As a result, our spirituality has transitioned to the invisible, a force or set of forces where we can seek meaning, grace, mystery, and magic and embrace the sacred. Colonization is an action of manipulation. Our complicated mind thinks in finite systems, only extracts what is necessary for our understanding, and defines that as reality. We mentally set boundaries around what cannot be explained and have, by and large, discarded the complex. We then keep that complexity away from the complicated through control. We do this by producing pesticides to control wheat crop yields for example. That is why colonization is an embedded trait within us. It's in our psyche. We have all been colonized by using technology to manipulate our own internal nature in the name of progress. We need this mind; it's essential to meet our needs, but we must be aware that it's not the whole mind.

Education is another evolutionary process where our civilization is primarily focused on specialization as the primary focus. The more we specialize, the less we can retain an open, complex mind where emergent creation resides. Only those who challenge and question society, like artists and philosophers, present a mirror of the complicatedness of our culture while, on the flip side, trying to remind us of the complexity. They may have done this unknowingly, but I'm sure they sensed the existence of complexity. It is unsurprising that today, people feel like they are a cog in the machine.

The last time we witnessed a significant rebellion against "the cog in the machine" was the flower power movement. Today, we see the emergence of the climate movement. Still, it lacks the intensity of the late 60s and early 70s, which focussed on breaking old norms, values, and belief systems with a strong yearning for individualism. I would argue that this is due to the use of our technology. Our technology has become so pervasive in everyday life that we can no longer live without it. Some sociologists and psychologists today have even gone as far as saying that our society's need for technology borders on addiction and total dependence. I'm inclined to agree with about 80% of that, as most urban people wouldn't be able to survive in the wild when forced to.

To keep this system going, we must provide enormous energy that must be extracted from the Earth. Wind, Solar, and Waves are renewable sources of energy. To harness this renewable energy, we need to build complicated systems to convert it into electricity to supply the life force of the technology we now so depend on. To build these complicated systems, we must dig deep into the earth again to extract the raw materials. We are replacing one energy source with another, from wood to coal, oil to gas, hydro to iron, nickel, copper, iron, cobalt, and silica. At the same time, we continue to deplete our planet of gravel, sand, and clay needed to build the infrastructure to support our growing population. We keep repeating the same manipulative approach because our complicated minds tell us to, without understanding the complexities or, more accurately, the unintended consequences that will emerge. Wouldn't it be better to discuss energy use and how we can bring the amount of KWh in line with planetary boundaries? So far, I have yet to see any attempt to combine Energy, Technology, and planetary boundaries and set targets to align to living within our planet's boundaries.

The bureaucratic dream is no longer fit for purpose because we have reached the edge of its usefulness. By the edge, I mean our planetary boundaries and our capacity to govern effectively to solve global problems.

What can be measured can be managed is an age-old saying applied to all aspects of civilization. We are hard at work on managing everything we can measure. We are considering managing our atmosphere with geoengineering as if we are gods.

Our governance leaders are measured on Economic growth, Employment, Inflation, Budget surplus or deficit, Debt to GDP ratio, Healthcare, Education, Infrastructure, Public Safety, Nature quality, and security.

Based on the above, you can follow that through with how well your government serves your country's interests. How do we measure a politician's performance?

- Electoral or Government party performance: How well the politician performs in elections or appointments.

- Policy achievements: This is how successful the politician is in implementing their policies. This can be measured by the number of laws they pass, the amount of money they allocate to specific programs, or the impact of their policies on the economy or society.

- Public opinion: This is how the public views the politician's job performance. This can be measured by public opinion polls, media coverage, or social media posts censored or covered by freedom of speech.

- Integrity: This is how honest and trustworthy the politician is perceived. This can be measured by their record of corruption allegations, financial disclosures, or willingness to disclose conflicts of interest.

- Communication skills: How effectively the politician communicates with the public. This can be measured by things like their public speaking skills, ability to answer questions from the media, use of social media, or other channels and stages.

- Commitment to public service: This is how dedicated the politician is to serving the public good or their club. This can be measured by their voting record, attendance record, or willingness to work with people from different backgrounds and beliefs.

We all know this, yet I see many examples where this is no longer true. Ask yourself. Is there still a connection between elected officials and those who elected them? Sometimes, we are back in the dark ages, and our feudal lords decide our fate to suit their personal needs and that of their court. They are more worried about which Duke will likely politically kill them versus what the average man in the street needs. Integrity and commitment to public service have left the station for many politicians. This is the current sentiment based on what we view or read in the news, online searches, and social media.

We know that government policy is not shaped by our votes directly. Other governments try to implement policies that benefit all, not only those who voted for them. Either way, policies are influenced by businesses and nature organizations no matter what system of government you have.

The business world and nature organizations have significant influence in shaping government policy. Businesses have a lot of money and resources, which they can use to lobby politicians and influence legislation. On the other hand, nature organizations have a lot of public support, which they can use to pressure politicians and raise awareness on nature issues.

Businesses spend billions of dollars yearly on lobbying. We know this thanks to investigative reporting. Businesses do this to influence policies that affect their bottom line, such as taxes, regulations, and trade agreements. Not-for-profit organizations also lobby, but they have a much smaller budget. However, they are often effective at raising awareness of nature, social, and economic issues and pressuring politicians to take action. The top global NGOs spend significant resources ensuring they have a "seat at the table."

In recent years, there has been a growing debate about the influence of businesses and nature organizations on government policy. Some people argue that companies have too much power and are putting the profits of a few ahead of the needs of the many. Others argue that nature organizations are too extreme and that they are not realistic about the economic costs of restoring our planet.

Interweaving business interests and nature groups with politics and national policy development is complicated. There is no easy resolution, but it is a significant problem that needs to be addressed when faced with wicked global problems. Pollution is a global wicked problem we have known for decades and have not been able to deal with it effectively.

It is easy to criticize governments and lack governance, but it becomes challenging when you criticize your own governance. From an individual governance perspective, we are confronted with littering laws. Consumer littering is against the law in many countries, and the countries that have the steepest fines can be found in Singapore, Japan, Hong Kong, Europe, the United States, and many more. Some countries still do not have specific anti-littering regulations, and even peeing in public is not banned everywhere. For example, no particular law restricts people in many parts of the world from peeing in the bush or in a river, which would pollute nature with nano and microplastics and forever chemicals.

In the Whitelake River in the UK, the concentrations of MDMA quadrupled downstream a week after the Glastonbury Festival. I guess ecstatic fish were having the time of their life and sang, "I've never felt like this before." Interestingly, the Twelve Foot Rhyne, which is closest to the festival site, must have carried all that MDMA to the Whitelake River, which flows quite a distance away from the festival. What would the micro-plastic concentration be after the festival, or what is the impact on crops or livestock that use its waters? Perhaps the impact was insignificant or yet to be studied, and after digging a little deeper, no dancing cows were reported as part of the Whitelake River study.

I cannot speak for many countries, only what I've experienced while living in Singapore and Indonesia, both of which have anti-littering laws. They are neighbors. Singapore is considered one of the cleanest cities in the world, which is not surprising when you think that anti-littering, including peeing in public, is strictly enforced. Fines range from S$300 to over S$1000 when you are caught. Even tourists are aware and act accordingly, as signs everywhere show the fine for littering. Singapore is a Fine city; it's small, so enforcement is less complicated. But what I find surprising is that when Singaporean residents visit Indonesia, all this behavior is forgotten, not by all, but some happily trash the place. Excuses abound; there is a lack of trash bins, no one is watching, no signs, and whatever else they can come up with. The worst is a sheepish laugh once confronted with their crime. When you visit your neighbor, do you throw your waste into their home?

Behaviors change only when laws are strictly enforced, and steep fines serve as deterrents. Herein lies the challenge for most countries with anti-littering laws.

Indonesia is a prime example as they, too, have anti-littering laws, but peeing in the bush and into rivers is still allowed. The fine for littering in Indonesia is steep, IDR 500,000, which is high as the minimum monthly salary is around 4 million rupiah. However, littering persists because it's not strictly enforced, and the public is not continuously made aware of this law through media channels and education. Infrastructure is severely lacking, as many places don't have bins. I must add that local communities in their kampungs (villages) keep their houses and the surrounding nature clean. They collect organic and inorganic waste every day and, before sunset, burn that waste to repel insects, not knowing that the smoke contains harmful microparticles. Remember the Londoners in chapter Atmosphere? City dwellers, once they are outside their homes, consciously and even unconsciously, throw candy wrappers, plastic bags, and cigarette butts on the street and along the highways.

Regulations for Companies.

All businesses are impacted by laws that cover health safety and social and nature impact. The most significant difference is your jurisdiction(s) and which rules apply to your business. Each country is given the freedom to enact their laws. Companies are made up of people, so it is no surprise that businesses behave the same way. Businesses comply with the law if it is strictly enforced and where there is government, social, and media oversight and significant reputational risks. Where these laws are not enforced, and social and media oversight is restricted, we see businesses taking advantage to protect profits and their bottom line while keeping their reputation intact through political influence.

Furthermore, if businesses can find jurisdictions where laws are less strict or, worse, where laws are not strictly enforced or can be bought, we see them moving their business or parts of their business to those jurisdictions. Corruption is still a significant issue in many countries. The result is that they keep polluting or violating strictly enforced laws from where they once came.

We have enacted laws that hold companies accountable in their country of origin for unlawful practices conducted in other jurisdictions. But when it comes to waste responsibility, we see no evidence. The Union Carbide Corporation, responsible for the Bhopal disaster in India in 1984, was never prosecuted in the USA, where they are headquartered. Warren Anderson, the CEO at that time, never faced trial despite being indicted in India.

Europe is leading the world in legislation to protect the planet, so what do businesses do? They move their operations to countries where such legislation does not exist or lobby the legislative branches to dilute the proposed laws. Europe only covers 6.8% of Earth's total land area. We are dealing with a Global Wastesphere that impacts everything and everyone, and we only have the United Nations that manages global risks via the General Assembly and the Security Council. So far, no resolutions have been accepted by the Security Council that cover any of the risks we have covered here.

The United Nations has existed for almost eight decades and has, by and large, fulfilled its primary function: to prevent WW3. It has also done enormous good by building a collaborative, mutual consensus governance structure to solve world issues. Well, it used to. The SDGs are failing. The United Nations needs a collaborative, participatory, coordinated governance structure for our metacrisis.

Fix governance, and all the others will follow. Our global climate change conferences are failing because we wish to maintain our complicated mindset, which manifests in our continued conviction that we need to grow our energy demand regardless of whether it comes from fossil fuels or other minerals. Furthermore, climate change is only one of nine planetary boundaries. These nine planetary boundaries have one thing in common: pollution, which has created the wastesphere. Would we have made progress if our conferences had focused on pollution and planetary boundaries? Because pollution is hard to deny, it is something that we recognize and understand deeply.

As we have witnessed with COVID-19, our most significant risk is that we will be forced to endure draconian measures once metacrisis tipping points have been crossed. We are not prepared, and our growing health crisis is ignored as it is a slow-growing crisis that will affect at least 20 to 30% of our population. That's 3 billion people by 2050. To address our metacrisis, we require global coordination and cooperation. We are a global civilization, and we need to recognize at an individual level that we are all in it together as global residents.

NIHILISM AND MEANING

The further you venture into the vortex of the metacrisis, taking the steps that I have taken from water to our current civilization, the more we need to discuss its characteristics. I've argued that our governance structures are no longer sufficient to deal with the threats that we face. One thread that runs through our civilization, particularly our dominant Western culture, which, let's not forget, has penetrated most cultures in Asia, Africa, and South America, is nihilism and, in particular, a struggle with meaning. To understand the metacrisis, we need to discuss this trend.

Nihilism is a complicated philosophical stance that rejects widely accepted notions of meaning, value, and knowledge. It's more like a spectrum of thought than a single, unified belief system. Here's a breakdown of the key aspects:

Main themes:

- Meaninglessness: Nihilism implies that life, the universe, and everything in it lacks inherent meaning or purpose. This doesn't necessarily imply negativity but rather a neutral acknowledgment of the absence of predetermined significance.

- Rejection of values: Nihilists often question or deny traditional values, morals, and ethical frameworks. They argue that these systems are not objectively true but rather human constructs, potentially influenced by culture, power structures, or personal desires.

- Knowledge skepticism: Some forms of nihilism express doubts about the possibility of attaining true knowledge. They might argue that our understanding is limited by perception, language, and inherent biases, making absolute certainty elusive.

Different types of nihilism:

- Existential nihilism: Focuses on the individual's experience, arguing that each person is responsible for creating their own meaning and values in a meaningless world.

- Moral nihilism: Denies the existence of objective moral truths or principles, suggesting that all moral judgments are ultimately subjective and based on personal preferences or societal norms.

- Epistemological nihilism: Holds that true knowledge is impossible, or at least unattainable by humans. We can only ever have interpretations and perspectives and never fully grasp the true nature of reality.

- Metaphysical nihilism: Denies the existence of anything beyond the physical world, rejecting concepts like soul, spirit, or afterlife.

From a crisis perspective and how each is cascading from what is external, our pollution, to society's behavior and underlying attributes, we need to recognize the dark side before discussing what we can do to change.

The Chilling Effect of Nihilism: Navigating Meaninglessness, Moral Decay, and Skepticism in the Digital Age

Today's workforce appears listless and apathetic. We see this with GenZ almost begging senior management to reinforce their purpose and how it benefits society and the planet. Society is fractured by relativism, and collective action is hindered by distrust. This, unfortunately, is a potential future fueled by the subtle yet pervasive influence of nihilism. In today's hyper-connected, information-saturated world, nihilism's core tenets – meaninglessness, moral relativism, and information and knowledge skepticism – pose significant challenges to businesses, communities, and democracies.

Let's face it: a society and workplace that are bereft of meaning is a disengaged one. When employees see their tasks as pointless cogs in a meaningless machine, motivation plummets, innovation stagnates, and productivity suffers. Nihilism's allure, particularly among younger generations, can exacerbate this, leading to higher turnover and hampering efforts to build engaged, purpose-driven teams.

Morality: The erosion of objective values, championed by moral nihilism, presents a stark reality: without a shared moral compass, trust crumbles, cooperation falters, and ethical lines blur. This translates to an increased risk of misconduct, fraud, and unethical practices in business, ultimately damaging brand reputation and customer loyalty. For society, the erosion of values undermines social cohesion, breeding cynicism and fueling societal unrest.

Truth or Fiction? In an age of "fake news" and weaponized information, skepticism is crucial. However, with its radical doubt of all knowledge, nihilism goes too far. When individuals lose faith in truth, critical thinking is paralyzed, and manipulation flourishes. Conspiracy theories run rampant, hindering collaboration and impeding effective problem-solving, both within organizations and across broader societal challenges.

These aspects must be better understood, and academia is responsible for widening its audience in a language everyone can understand. We have lost much of our spirituality. This is evident in a surge of seeking spirituality online. There seems to be an undercurrent gushing through our civilization, desperate for a new spirituality. Stoicism seems to have become the new divine. At the same time, our churches are empty, and our mosques and Hindu and Buddhist temples are slowly losing the younger population, particularly in dense urban areas where the pursuit of wealth trumps spirituality. While religion is still vital, there is no denying that it is slowly eroding and countered by an increase in fundamentalism.

This brings me to another issue that we need to discuss briefly: the current meaning crisis that we need to explore to understand the context of the risks we face as a global civilization. The meaning of crisis is, at its core, the disconnect with our wisdom to meet our needs. We are beings of desires and temptation now unrestrained. We are now in a phase where we pursue them relentlessly, not realizing that this pursuit will outstrip or consume more than what we need. The way I can describe it in the most horrific manifestation is a heroin addiction. The initial euphoria of the experience leaves us wanting more. The more we take, the more our mind and body suffer, and the initial euphoric experience can no longer be obtained. Every user knows this intimately, but we find ourselves trapped to continue to use heroin until we either have an intervention or we die.

Exploring the Meaning Crisis and Its Impact

Imagine a world where the ground beneath your feet feels increasingly shaky, where familiar anchors of purpose and meaning drift further away. This isn't dystopian fiction; it's the essence of our meaning crisis, a growing phenomenon with profound implications for individuals, communities, and businesses.

While existential questions about life's purpose have always existed, the meaning crisis goes deeper. It's a pervasive sense of disconnect – from ourselves, each other, and the world around us. This disconnect stems from a complicated role in how our historical, cultural, and technological factors have shaped us. We then substitute this disconnect with things that manipulate us and to which we have become addicted to realize that these things can't provide the meaning we so desperately need. Add to that the fear of withdrawal symptoms, and the sphere of self-destruction intensifies.

Several vital themes underscore the meaning crisis:

- Eroding trust: Long-held institutions like religion and politics struggle for legitimacy, leaving individuals adrift without a moral compass.

- Individualism: While empowering, emphasizing self-fulfillment can lead to isolation and a fragmented sense of belonging.

- Technology: Our hyper-connected world can ironically fuel loneliness and information overload, further deepening the disconnect.

The ripple effect: The consequences of the meaning crisis are far-reaching, impacting individuals, communities, and even business performance:

- Mental health: Rising rates of anxiety, depression, neurodevelopmental health and despair point to the crisis' toll on individual well-being. Examples: Neurodevelopmental damage (See chapter Soil), also known as ADHD, currently affects 6 Million Children (9.8% of total) between the age of 2 - 17 in the United States.

- Social fragmentation: Declining trust and fractured communities hinder collaboration and exacerbate societal challenges. Polarization is a rising threat of dystopia, as seen in Europe and the USA. Especially in the USA, where the halls of government are almost paralyzed by their extreme division.

- Disengagement and apathy: Individuals become less invested in contributing to their communities and organizations without a sense of purpose. Some even go as far as escaping into small groups and building survivalist communities far removed from society.

- Susceptibility to manipulation: When traditional anchors lose their hold, individuals become more vulnerable to misinformation and harmful narratives.

A bleak future? The meaning crisis isn't an inevitable fate but left unchecked; it could lead to a future characterized by:

- Further polarization and societal divisions leading to dystopia: Individuals clinging to disparate belief systems could exacerbate societal fractures.

- Rise of fringe ideologies and emerging cults: Desperate for meaning, some may seek solace in extremist groups, which all purport that they are well-meaning or, worse, embrace harmful belief systems.

- Technological dystopia: Unchecked technological advancements could further blur the lines between reality and simulation, amplifying feelings of detachment. We are already witnessing this phenomenon with AI's ability to generate deep fakes and influence elections and the risk of your job being replaced by an AI machine.

A broader, more pervasive public discourse emerges to dive deeper into these two phenomena since the erosion of our agency is replacing something far more sinister. It's like a virus, neither living nor dead, that has penetrated our society. It feeds on everything that is healthy and can no longer be expelled by taking a pill. It is no longer a question of taking a blue or red pill. That option has long ago expired. We need a new adventure but one that causes a part of you to die so a new you can emerge.

GLOBAL RISKS

To face our crises effectively, we must clean up. For that, we have the faculty, and resources. But we need two more calls to action. We need to wake up, and we need to grow up. I wrote this book in an Asian Capital and on an Island, spending half my time between each. The capital city, with 10 million people with skyscrapers bustling with business activity, luxury shopping malls, thousands of restaurants and entertainment venues on one side and grey-brown smog choking its residents, clogged arteries with bumper-to-bumper traffic, lack of clean tap water, and burning landfills and polluted rivers and coastline on the other. 80% of the nation's economy runs through the capital. It is a testament to humanity's progress and its unintended consequences.

The Island, with a population of 4 million, with its beautiful beaches, blue ocean, lush greenery, rice paddies, hundreds of surf breaks and diving spots, and crystal clear blue skies, made me aware of what we are losing. With its frantic tourism development to cater to 30 Million visitors by 2030, choked arteries, shoulder-to-shoulder day clubs, escapists, crypto cowboys, and ever-decreasing water supply, The Island is becoming a crisis zone. I realized that even the Island of the Gods is not spared from what will come.

Having lived and worked on all continents except Antarctica, I have found Indonesia the most incredible place on Earth. I found love here and discovered people who are so friendly and filled with unparalleled creativity. One word for me describes the Indonesian people best: flexibility. Indonesians have an incredible capacity to find alternatives for almost any challenge, and their problem-solving skills are the best I have ever seen. Sorry, Mckinsey and Company, but they even outclass you. People here are generally happy. The food here is amazing, and it's still the most biodiverse country in Asia despite its mining, oil, coal, palm oil plantations, and industry akin to our prosperity and doom. It's a country full of contrasts and represents a window into the world from where I can watch and read the views of all countries, rich or poor. I could not have written this book if it was not for Indonesia and its people.

The optimism for the future is palpable all around you, for many do not see the risks, and I realized that this must be the same for many people in their respective countries. Most people don't think further than their borders, and their worldview is based on what they experience within their arena. The arena within which they have agency. There is a gap in understanding an integrated worldview as most people are predominately ethnocentric even though we are a global civilization. Here, I also experienced a profound sense of grief because, armed with my knowledge of the wastesphere, I talked to people who lived on the frontlines of our waste—shark fishermen who worked like slaves on foreign fishing vessels. Men and women living next to open landfills or what I call trash mountains daily collect plastic in toxic conditions to send to recyclers who would pay cents for their efforts, barely enough money to feed themselves, let alone afford medical care. The recyclers would only take the PET components of the plastics found while the rest was left rotting with other waste like textiles and other industrial and household waste.

We are achievers.

Humans now control the planet and are masters of our nature. We can defend ourselves against any predator. We can cure many diseases. We can climb the highest mountains and dive into the deepest parts of our Ocean. We can fly around the planet. We can live anywhere we like.

We have the best food systems and the best technology. We have electricity almost everywhere. We have acquired enormous amounts of wealth. We are connected like never before. We have access to information at our fingertips. We have so much wealth that we freely give to people experiencing poverty and those who suffer from disasters. We donate to causes to protect what we almost made extinct. We even receive a tax return for it.

If needed, we can build entire cities in the harshest climates known to man and insulate ourselves from the elements, even if we live in a world where the average global temperature is +45 or – 50 degrees Celsius. We have the technology, we have the materials, we can reuse materials, and we have the architects, engineers, scientists, health professionals, economists, entrepreneurs and philosophers, actors, performers, and so much diversity and variety within our civilization to overcome any challenge. The world is beautiful, so be quiet with your doom and gloom and be rid of yourself. Most of our global population believes this to be true, even if they recognize and accept that climate change is real. I was one of them, a skeptic who had doubts about how bad things were. While Climate Change is widely recognized as a crisis, I still observe a severe lack of understanding of our combined cascading metacrisis.

What is more concerning is that we are not sufficiently addressing our global existential risks. I went from feeling 80% is acceptable, 20% is insufficient to, 80% is terrible, and 20% is hope. Welcome to living in between worlds.

I've experienced close contact with wildlife from an early age. Love for nature grew both on land and underwater. I started scuba-diving in 1994. After around 400+ dives, I stopped in 1998 while in Grand Cayman. I stopped because my favorite animal, the shark, was no longer present when I went diving.

After the last five years of research and diving, I realized something so complex and life-threatening that I could no longer keep it quiet. I'm a fool, as defined by the age-old tradition of the tarot. According to the Tarot, the fool likes to venture into the unknown, experiment with new things and ideas, and learn along the way. The fool is forever curious and never gives up; the fool keeps going, experiences new events, and makes discoveries that the fool would happily share with whoever is listening. The fool is a complex being with emergent properties, unconstrained by complicatedness. We need more fools.

I feel comfortable being the fool. As a fool, I spent a lot of time reading material from experts, having a look-see for myself, speaking with loads of people, and above all, having an open mind. This is difficult as one has to untether from the socio-economic systems and technologies that bind us.

Embracing the concept of the fool and perhaps even delving into esoteric lore, I discovered that to understand, one must first unlearn, break down, and confront our own shadows and blind spots. Our civilization is reaching an unprecedented stage in human history: we are on a path to self-terminate our existence for the following reasons;

1. Our planet and ourselves are so heavily polluted that it seems impossible to fix.

2. We have exceeded our planetary boundaries and continue to overshoot our planet's ability to regenerate.

3. We need economic growth to continue to finance debt, i.e., to pay interest on our debts and increase the wealth of a growing population.

4. Our global institutions are treating the symptoms, not the root causes.

5. Growing sense of meaninglessness in a society addicted to instant gratification and subject to Limbic hijacking.

Humans, not aliens or a meteor, have created these existential termination risks.

We face self-induced catastrophic risks because we cannot continue the exponential growth of 2%-3% when we have exceeded our planetary boundaries and continue to overshoot and pollute our planet.

We are on a path that will lead to:

1. Dystopia

2. Catastrophe

Both of which we are starting to witness today. We are close to living in a dystopic world. The breakdown has begun; it's not evenly distributed, and ethnocentricity still reigns supreme in our post-modern world.

We are on a path toward a cliff where we stand either to stare into the abyss or, if we get our act together, a ledge we can jump down to with minimal injury. Part 1 of this book has provided enough evidence to support the previous statement should you still have doubts. There is no doubt that we are seeing signs of collapse. It is not evenly distributed—another reason the metacrisis is hard to address. Those who contribute the least will suffer the most, as has always been the case in humanity's history.

One of the key underlying causes is our exponential growth in tech. While nukes were of primary concern during the Cold War and even today, we now also have to factor in our economic system, which was created to reduce the risk of nuclear war. But in doing so, we have created an even more dangerous beast that has allowed us to deplete our nature, leading to the 6th mass extinction event that includes us. See chapter Triumph. All this is thanks to growth in tech, energy use, and our economies.

Technology has shaped humanity's behavior and our relationship to our natural world since the dawn of man. We developed tools like the plow, which fundamentally changed how we viewed animals. We were once animistic, still visible on murals that endured the test of time. Bulls were revered, and their spirit was respected, but all that changed when we cut off its balls, put them in front of a plow, and whipped it all day.

Spears, bullets, and guns did the rest, so we did not have to hide in caves around a fire from animals that could kill us in seconds. Fast forward to today, we live in a completely different world, far removed from the healthy, livable dirt we used to dwell in. Thanks to our highly integrated and fragile global supply chains, production, and global technology, we are now a global civilization, the first in our collective history.

As an ex-cowboy selling data network speed for over two decades to provide faster access to your mobile devices, I can tell you that we live in a world where tech builds tech without us. A chip engineer has no idea how the latest chip is created because the tech does it now. Software is developing new software on top of those chips at speeds our brain can no longer comprehend.

We desperately need imagination, but what do we do? We ask the available large language models to imagine because it's faster, and we don't have to think. We call these machines artificial intelligence (AI), although I sometimes wonder what exactly is intelligent about what they do. At best, they are information processing machines that farm us from what we have issued into this world via online platforms. Information originated from our distributed intelligence and knowledge, but they have so far skipped rationality and wisdom, a key aspect it does not yet possess. We are using the machine to regurgitate information available within our civilization. It cannot think and feel independently and, therefore, cannot be Intelligent. At best, it may be able to pantomime caring and feeling. AI will always be a machine tied to finite resources until it can be biologically integrated into a being. Something the singularity enthusiasts are aiming for. Welcome to the cyborg, but I don't think that is humanity's destiny.

At best, we will likely have better sex dolls that can recite books when we need a bedtime story. The movie Surrogates and episodes of Startrek come to mind when I think about AI. As a Techie Consultant, I can see a world where the constraints on consumerism and the wastesphere force us into a virtual world where we can visit the Jungles of Asia, Africa, and South America without leaving our living room. We don't need to fly to Paris or Rome anymore because we can now have virtual visits to all the museums and wonderful architecture. Our Virtual World will stop climate change as we don't have to move anymore; we don't have to buy stuff except for food and water because we never have to leave our homes. We will need a treadmill to stay healthy, but other than that, we wouldn't need much. Our whole world will be reduced to bits and bytes controlled by the corporations that win the AI wars. Our reality will be fake, beautiful, untouched perfection. At the same time, the earth becomes one big farm to feed us on one side and a mining operation to support the solar-powered super data centers that host our artificial intelligence machines on the other. Where the few undomesticated animals left are stuck in zoos, our Surrogates can visit.

We need to correct a few misgivings and the confusion that exists in public discourse when it comes to Artificial Intelligence. Again, history is a great teacher. Humanity has always been fascinated with AI. It can be traced back to Greek Mythology with Talos, a bronze being that protected Europa while she was in Crete. In ancient Chinese history, it was said that engineers would create mechanical men to impress the Emporer. But it was Thomas Hobbes, an English Philosopher in the 17th century, who imagined an all-powerful sovereign who would subdue people to guarantee their security. This sovereign was Leviathan, the Old Testament monster the philosopher likened to a "mortal god." Those who deify artificial intelligence say it could become the new Leviathan.

I'm not against AI because it's a technological evolution from humanity's capacity to create technology, and like the plow, it will fundamentally change humanity's behavior in terms of social, cultural, and economic structures. Of that, I have no doubt. But AI is not all-powerful. At least not yet. Will it ever reach God-like power? We shall see, but one thing is clear: once again, we failed to analyze potential negative consequences and implement measures and fail-safes to prevent them from manifesting.

There are two types of AI. One is low AI, and the other is high AI. Things like calculators and computers represent low AI. Both were once actual jobs people performed. High AI is what Hobbes was talking about. An all-powerful being that could make decisions for itself and guide humanity. Our current AI, which most people will recognize as large language models or artificial general intelligence, sits in the middle. To become high AI, it must master and evolve to embrace Logos, which one can argue is well on the way to accomplishing. It must also master pathos and mythos. We can only achieve that if we overcome technical and energy challenges. It also has to become auto-poetic, I.e., The ability to embody emergent properties that are inherently within Nature's capacity. Call it biological. It should be able to reproduce independently from the hardware it's tethered to. Since we are not there yet, can we argue if we should leave it up to AI to solve the metacrisis, or perhaps the question should be, how can AI help us solve the metacrisis, and what are the risks? These risks of our current technology stack are not well understood. While we have barely managed to halt assured mutual destruction, we now face additional risks. Nukes are hard to build, but access to A.I., once deployed in the cloud linked to my treehouse with WIFI combined with some basic synthetic biotechnology from cheap-to-acquire CRISPR gene drives, I can genetically manipulate entire wildlife populations that can not be reversed other than by making them extinct. No Lab is 100% safe and can, if it so chooses, design weapons no one can control or prevent unless you live in a society where everything is monitored, including your visits to the bathroom. Beware the risk of dystopia if you wish to control these threats.

You might find this fantastical, reserved for science fiction, but let's take an example. Let's say someone or a small group collects Vibrio Bacteria, as described in chapter Water, and with today's available technology, could transfer the flesh-eating components of that bacteria and combine it with SARS-COVID-19's most effective mutant or a pathogen we haven't even heard of and release it during the opening of the Olympic Games. How would you prevent this from happening?

Technology is inherently neutral; it is not bad, and it is not good. A screwdriver is a tool used within a technological ecosystem (saw, wood, screw) and can also be a weapon. Technology, no matter how sophisticated, is merely a tool we humans use. We have hackers. Some are state actors, so let us add some AI. Technology changes our behavior and relationship to the world around us, and its major risk is mental health issues. The biggest risk we face with technology is that it has become so powerful, controlled by a few, that it is not balanced equally with Wisdom.

I propose the following to understand our global civilization and current global risks. Apologies for being reductionistic here but reductionism can be useful to a degree. Think of our civilization as a **three-legged stool** where the seat is a **doughnut** where in its center, we dump all our shit into the Biosphere, creating the waste sphere and, by extension, our meta crisis.

The first leg of our stool is our Technology stack. Without Technology, humanity would not be where we are today because it enables us to change our nature to fit our needs. Food Technology Systems, Information Technology, Construction, etc., and we do an amazing job at creating so that it starts making itself. Enter Robotics, Automation, and Artificial Intelligence.

The second leg is our culture, institutions, economy, governance, law, health, education nature, military, arts, etc., which should manage our technological, financial, and economic ecosystems, security, and the nature which we try to support with management systems under the law with justice.

The third leg is where wisdom resides. It's where we make sense of the world: discernment and coherence. We look at the big picture. Here, we collectively decide what is sacred to us, what it means to show constraint, and what sacrifice means.

We need to understand the risks of each leg of the stool, the supporting rungs, and how they are interlinked. Here are some.

Leg 1: Nukes, Exponential Growth of AI Technology, Synthetic Biology (e.g., DNA manipulation), Distributed Tech proliferation. Development of chemicals, etc.

Leg 2: Exponential economic growth, failing institutions to handle global crises, information wars, polarization, pollution, unintended consequences, mental and physical Health. Perverse incentives in game theory and multi-polar traps. Power asymmetry, Lack of Coordinated decision making.

Leg 3: loss of wisdom; Values, constraint, sacrifice, loss of the sacred, meaning in life, meaning of Life.

These risks converge inside our doughnut, where we run in multiple races to get ahead in a post-truth society where facts are distorted to suit a particular camp, where we continue to dump our shit over the side and refuse to face the dark side.

To design our way out, we must include all three legs of the stool and the doughnut, plus incorporate 2nd, 3rd, and 4th order causal analysis of potential unintended consequences.

We need to build design principles and criteria for collective and collaborative design because many minds and hands are needed to navigate out of our metacrisis. We are now well on our way to reaching a population of 9 Billion, not a tribe. Can the Dunbar principle be used in design and scaled globally?

To Awaken, we must beware the Beast; do not welcome it in.

What is the beast? A part of the famous poem "Howl" by Allen Ginsberg from 1956 explains it like no other. It is the source of our predicament. What lies beneath our metacrisis currently has no name in our global civilization. It is spoken of by maybe 300 to 500 thousand people worldwide who know it well. It's the core, the root cause of where we are today, and scholars can now link it directly from old texts who predicted our predicament. These texts were written more than 2000 years ago. The one story we know is the story of the Ark of Noah. Still, few know of the phases that preceded the flood and the role technology played in each phase, particularly the unintended consequences of technology. The Ark is viewed in our psyche as the good of technology. We have forgotten what preceded it, and now the question reigns: Will technology save us or lead us to our end?

Excerpt from Howl:

What sphinx of cement and aluminum bashed open their skulls and ate up their brains and imagination?

Moloch! Solitude! Filth! Ugliness! Ashcans and unobtainable dollars! Children screaming under the stairways! Boys sobbing in armies! Old men weeping in the parks!

Moloch! Moloch! Nightmare of Moloch! Moloch the loveless! Mental Moloch! Moloch the heavy judger of men!

Moloch the incomprehensible prison! Moloch the crossbone soulless jailhouse and Congress of sorrows! Moloch whose buildings are judgment! Moloch the vast stone of war! Moloch the stunned governments!

Moloch whose mind is pure machinery! Moloch whose blood is running money! Moloch whose fingers are ten armies! Moloch whose breast is a cannibal dynamo! Moloch whose ear is a smoking tomb!

Moloch whose eyes are a thousand blind windows! Moloch whose skyscrapers stand in the long streets like endless Jehovahs! Moloch whose factories dream and croak in the fog! Moloch whose smoke-stacks and antennae crown the cities!

Moloch whose love is endless oil and stone! Moloch whose soul is electricity and banks! Moloch whose poverty is the specter of genius! Moloch whose fate is a cloud of sexless hydrogen! Moloch whose name is the Mind!

Moloch in whom I sit lonely! Moloch in whom I dream Angels! Crazy in Moloch! Cocksucker in Moloch! Lacklove and manless in Moloch!

Moloch who entered my soul early! Moloch in whom I am a consciousness without a body! Moloch who frightened me out of my natural ecstasy! Moloch whom I abandon! Wake up in Moloch! Light streaming out of the sky!

Moloch! Moloch! Robot apartments! invisible suburbs! skeleton treasuries! blind capitals! demonic industries! spectral nations! invincible madhouses! granite cocks! monstrous bombs!

They broke their backs lifting Moloch to Heaven! Pavements, trees, radios, tons! lifting the city to Heaven which exists and is everywhere about us!

Visions! omens! hallucinations! miracles! ecstasies! gone down the American river!

Dreams! adorations! illuminations! religions! the whole boatload of sensitive bullshit!

Breakthroughs! over the river! flips and crucifixions! gone down the flood! Highs! Epiphanies! Despairs! Ten years' animal screams and suicides! Minds! New loves! Mad generation! down on the rocks of Time!

Real holy laughter in the river! They saw it all! the wild eyes! the holy yells! They bade farewell! They jumped off the roof! to solitude! waving! carrying flowers! Down to the river! into the street!

Allen was heavily criticized for Howl, published in 1956. I came to realize that collective consciousness exists. There is an awareness or collective intuition of the underlying beast causing all our risks. We see repeatedly how works like these have been suppressed and actively ignored by optimists, including myself.

Moloch: "Sacrifice **your** child so you may continue living and win in war."

Sustainability: "We borrow the use of the earth from **our** children in the hope they may prosper."

Sauron: "The one ring in my possession will bind **all** the others into perpetual darkness."

Moloch, to me, is the Sauron of our time. We must cast the One Ring that binds all others into darkness, into the fires of Mount Doom. Tolkien provided modern mythology with his fantasy novels, which have been read by over 100 million people and are more familiar in today's culture than the long-forgotten old testaments' God from Caan, Moloch. Perhaps our times require a mythological being that would resonate with our global civilization, including non-Western cultures.

I propose to reintroduce Moloch in public discourse, a malevolent mythological being that resides in our shadows persists in our culture and is still hidden from view but ready to be exposed because we have managed to unleash the genie in the bottle that Thomas Hobbes once proposed. From this evil, we may design a transformed mythology that restores the wisdom found in all cultures, past and present. We are currently deep in a global war. It may not be kinetic, but the one war that reigns supreme is our technology war, and Moloch is directing it. While he remains invisible, you can feel its presence everywhere. My experience working in the technology sphere for over two decades has shown me that we rejected the notion of the divine from holy scripture. Some factions within our industry have devoted themselves to a new god. Another faction embraces the genie principle as a more benevolent view, often ignoring that the so-called good they wish to distribute contains harmful unintended consequences. This technology god looks shiny and benevolent on the outside but is Moloch in disguise and manipulating us with its influence.

What is Moloch's influence over our Technology stack?

A large part of the reason we are in this predicament is because of our technology. We can catch more fish in one net than a whale can catch in a month. We can collect more grass in a day than a cow can. We produce more milk at dairy farms than a herd of wildebeests on the plains of Africa.

Our technology drives our economic systems and our societal systems. Thanks to automation, it is so powerful that it practically runs itself and has become a beast tied to perverse incentives. Without perverse incentives, there is immense value in technology. We need to learn how to pause, but it may be too late as our systems do not see an advantage in a pause, fail-safe analysis. Eating or being eaten dominates our tech entrepreneurial landscape.

The most incredible inventions of our time are social media, e-commerce platforms, and AI. It's also easiest to commence with to explain our metacrisis. When it was first designed and rolled out, nobody considered doing a physiological, psychological, or nature deep dive regarding its possible adverse effects on society and our planet. They could not have known as the development was intuitive, and the people or companies working on the code were locked in an arms race to get the platform out as fast as possible due to financial pressure (burn rate), game theory dynamics, and multi-polar traps: competitive threats and value sacrifice. Most importantly, the premise of these developments was rooted in doing good because we are inherently good people. Our focus was on efficiency and convenience. What could be easier than sitting naked in front of your laptop and ordering the latest gadget in three steps?

We played our part beautifully in the highly competitive data networking space by increasing speed and bandwidth. Moore and Metcalfe, we worshiped you as we deployed 3G, 4G, 5G and started to design 6G.

Where is Moloch in all of this? That sneaky invisible presence started to exert its influence in the user techno space with the economic system it had already infected. While users could use the platform for free, the company was left with a cost that needed to be recovered. Venture capitalists (VCs) were eager to pump money into these ventures. They did so, hoping they would reap enormous returns as quickly as possible. Enter Moloch"s most beloved agent: the perverse incentive to maximize short-term profit and its emissary, the fiduciary obligation of the board to meet shareholder demands, and to top it off - the jewel in the crown: Increase shareholder value. These shareholders, often institutional investors like pension funds, asset managers, and family offices, have a fiduciary responsibility to maximize returns to meet their financial objectives. These funds compete with each other. Enter game theory and multipolar traps—a perfect system created to destroy the commons as consumption of things exploded. We became addicted. We would have withdrawal symptoms if we left our mobile devices at home. The horror of feeling naked is unbearable.

Global enterprise is now a giant ship where a CEO can be replaced if it does not conform to shareholder demands. High AGI replaced OpenAI's CEO. It would be the joke of the century, I would imagine. But it is one of Moloch's many goals. How did he get a grip on our current tech? Enter the world of algorithms and AI that could synthesize massive amounts of data to keep the user hooked, increase eyeballs, and sell more products. In a competitive environment, it was essential to optimize your algorithms that would hook its users to maximize screen time, like and comment feedback loops to optimize even further, and target users to ads that could lead to them buying more stuff. What is even more concerning is how large sections of our civilization have been limbically hijacked. Limbic hijack—hacking the brain's emotional centers to elicit a desired reaction; in the social media business model, limbic hijack compels a behavioral reaction to generate monetary profit driven by engagement. The better you were as a company at harnessing the power of technology, the more profit you would make and beat your competitors. Again, Limbic hijacking is not new. It was certainly not invented by social media companies. Enterprises and even governments have been doing it for centuries with advertising and propaganda. Remember this one; "Drink more milk. It's good for your bones." Just FYI, almost half the global population is lactose intolerant. Milk is not a staple for humans.

We consume information based on our likes, which results in our current crisis: polarization, post-truth dynamics, narrative warfare, and the rise of demagogues, which has damaged friendships, torn communities and families apart, and added insult to injury, further damaging the planet. That's how Sauron broke the fellowship of the ring, with Boromir representing humanity, who pays the ultimate price, in case you need more clarification. One defector is all it takes for Moloch to emerge in full force. What many people don't understand is that Moloch is not AI. It is using AI to motivate us to build a body. Its influence is to enslave us further disguised as progress so we can solve many problems for the benefit of a handful of people. Our leisure time spent online has become unpaid work with our constant feeding of behavioral information. Let that sink in for a moment.

The sheer amount of energy required to facilitate this growth of technology is almost unimaginable, and the need for more energy is even more fantastical. When these companies were made aware that their business models were causing harm to society, particularly children and young adults who became addicted to social media, they were met with enormous internal challenges. They could change, but it would significantly reduce profits and even risk becoming unprofitable, violating their fiduciary responsibility to its shareholders. The competitive landscape would prevent them from doing so, and the free neoliberal markets would simply kill them, so they were locked up in industry-wide multipolar traps. They know that the only way to prevent mass rebellion is to speed up the adoption process and make the technology more invasive.

Dystopia is not far behind. Technology companies that are most advanced in Artificial Intelligence are tricky to regulate. They earn more revenue than many countries' GDPs and, as such, exert enormous power over politicians. Add to that the energy, agricultural, automotive, chemical, pharmaceutical, and financial giants, whose world vision is so tight that they threaten the core foundations of a participatory democratic society. Our ability to govern is threatened. All these companies are run autocratically. There is no democratic structure. Their influence over politics cannot be underestimated. These companies are locked in endless battles for market share and profits and will pressure the system to extremes and sometimes falter when the law catches up with them. They are trapped, and they know it. Only a dystopian regime can reign them in when it threatens the existence of their form of government. It is also, therefore, no surprise that those on the extreme left and right are advocating for dystopian measures. Do we want another dictator? Let's call Borat, shall we?

Multipolar traps exist in all industries. Take the automotive industry. Their whole business model is designed to sell more cars. To maintain relevance, they have to transition to electric vehicles as regulations worldwide will prevent them from producing more fossil fuel internal combustion engines. The race is on to stay competitive with little regard for the damage they cause to nature. The only item they change is the fuel source, but all else has to be extracted from the earth, even the batteries they need, which results in more pressure on our planetary boundaries and wastesphere. Only 20% of all cars are recycled. The energy needed to scrap them is also not well understood. Collaborating to reduce overall car use by supporting public transport infrastructure will hurt their profits and growth. We produce around 80 million cars per year with a CAGR of 5%, and without expanding automobile infrastructure, we increase congestion, lowering productivity. At the same time, our labor is at risk of being lost to AI. Awareness is growing, and calls for change are steadily becoming louder. Systems change is required, yet we struggle to design systems leading to a nature-positive world. Biomimicry is showing promise in architecture, and Dhonut economics and regenerative ecosystem design are equally promising. The challenge, however, is our financial system.

Understanding the difference between complicated such as the computer and complexity as evident in Nature is slowly growing in some corners of the globe. Still, its required growth trajectory is not emerging, and Moloch is responsible. Our institutions lack global coordination skills, and few understand the need for integral theory and practice as that worldview, popular in the nineties, has diminished, mainly because of its hierarchical design, where relinquishing dominance is its biggest challenge. Developing integral thinking is a major challenge in a post-modern world unfamiliar with the risks of global collapse.

These multipolar traps have contributed to our exceeding planetary boundaries, and we are now helpless to fix them. Why? Because we lack the skills, our computer-centric problem-solving thinking has left us devoid of rationality, wisdom, and imagination. Despite our best efforts, we are stuck and cling to a belief that we can fix everything by addressing the symptoms. We can, but not with the same thinking that got us here. We can't fix climate change by planting trees or sowing sulfate aerosols or reflective particles into the atmosphere. Lowering temperatures with geoengineering is changing the climate. We can't change climate change with electrification. We can't fix ocean dead zones by reducing our greenhouse gases; We fundamentally need to change how we move, work, and play and what we eat. To do so, we must defeat the Moloch. It is now exposed, and we should focus on it to find a way to rid ourselves of this evil. We urgently need to understand what unintended negative consequences mean.

We could develop a new Logos, Pathos, and Mythos. Like the three-legged stool supporting the donut, which is a reductionistic view of our complex civilization greatly eroded. Unfortunately, it appears that explanations in today's world of communication need reductionism to get the point across. We also see that cognitive distortions have increased since 2007 and risk exponential growth as our metacrisis manifests itself like the hideous head of Moloch with AI as the evil Eye over our civilization.

We should develop and expand integral development that could produce new enlightenment to solve our wicked problems. Moloch needs to be defeated. We need to develop a planet B civilization grounded in Wisdom, hopefully utilizing the best of planet A so we don't have to start from its ashes.

LOGOS

Words have meaning and shape our thinking.

We are saddled with debt, for example. This thought invokes the thought that our debt is carried by a horse or mule instead of *being burdened with debt*, which makes it more personal and automatically changes how we think about debt as something personal.

The weather is grey and wet - it invokes a thought of cold, rainy weather. It is regarded as something negative, but to a farmer who is suffering from drought, it would be a blessing.

Store sales are up 15%, which invokes positivity in those who like shopping or are active in retail. To someone who advocates for nature conservation, it means more resource depletion and pollution.

Deforestation invokes less horror than *killing trees*.

We caught a fish today vs. *We killed a fish today.*

Slaughterhouse vs *meat processing plant.*

We have sanitized and scrubbed our language so it is smooth and shiny and cannot offend. We like to smell the roses but are afraid of a bloody thumb, so we genetically engineer our language to remove the thorns so that only the rose remains.

In times of crisis, words become important when you want to send a message. Done effectively, it can change how we think, talk, and act. The dominant narratives are still focused on prosperity, material wealth, and human-centric thinking.

Some examples:

GDP Growth, consumer spending is up, the housing market is recovering, coral reefs and rainforests are asset classes, geoengineering, and recession.

Climate change vs Ecosystem collapse thanks to rising temperatures. We don't want climate change, but we are okay with seeding the stratosphere with material that will change the climate.

Stories bind us and provide insights that could change our sense of reality. We have become experts at language manipulation. Have you noticed by now that I only used the word environment when I had to, when the word was part of the name of an agency like the EPA? I used nature instead of the environment. The word environment is a word meant to describe what we can see, smell, hear, and touch. It's a clinical word to describe what our external senses can detect. Nature is infinite and resides within and outside us, which you can see, smell, hear, touch, and feel emotionally, spiritually, connectively, and collectively.

Climate Change, which initially started as Global Warming. We did not like that word, so we changed it to climate change, only to see it change again over the last twenty years to the climate emergency, global boiling, and climate crisis. Yet the term climate change persists as we do not want to create a panic. The lulling effect of language is powerful, and several techniques are used that we need to become familiar with so that we become more literate about the information we consume.

The field of Ecolinguistics provides us with some guidance. I recommend a deep dive into this topic if education or storytelling is a large part of your activity. These stories reside deep in our consciousness, and we typically don't pick up on word choice unless we are discerning critical readers. Today, we tend to review news, articles, and scientific papers at face value. We don't analyze them unless we are part of a scholarly group or specialization course. We live by the stories we are told. We unconsciously absorb words that shape our thinking, acting, and behaving.

The Stories We Live By is an ecolinguistic course developed by Professor Arran Stibbe from the University of Gloucestershire. Ecolinguistics provides a beautiful perspective of our cognition and societal cognition. Five dominant narratives are found in all media, including AI. This is unsurprising, as all media, including AI, depend on Human input and output. Large Language Models are, after all, trained on human narratives.

The five dominant narratives we live by:

The Prosperity Story promotes material acquisition and money.

Example: We have GDP growth again. Good news: consumer spending is up, the housing market is recovering, store sales are up, tourist travel is growing again, and influencers are promoting more products than ever before. The growth of BEVs and AI is exciting. All of these stories hurt our ecological spheres.

The Religious Story focused on the afterlife and human spirituality rather than the world around us.

The Security Story builds up the military to protect relationships of domination.

Examples: Energy and resource security in Nickel, Lithium, and Cobalt. Strengthen our borders because geopolitical tension is rising. We require supply chain protection.

The Secular Meaning Story reduces life to matter and mechanism.

Examples: We have reduced everything into units, numbers, assets, currency, and percentages that we can plug into spreadsheets and databases and run models. Data is king. We have become excellent administrators of our world. Data has become our conviction as the sole source of truth.

The most dangerous story we live by is The Human Centrality Story, where we continue to use our domination and colonizer view.

Example: Geo-engineering. The Amazon Bioeconomy is the last frontier for our global economy.

These stories are currently dominant. If we are to change as a civilization, we should change our stories to focus on valuing all life and our supporting spheres.

We need a different kind of imagination and creativity that breaks away from the five major narratives that dominate our world. We are an incredibly creative species; we've chosen to ignore this capability with our busy-busy behavior in pursuit of material wealth.

Logos has dominated our Civilization for thousands of years. Pathos has built our capacity to collaborate, empathize, and sympathize as individuals and as a group. It speaks to our emotions. Mythos gave us wisdom and everything true, good, and beautiful. Logos has provided us with the technologies that helped us survive until our technologies started threatening our survival thanks to the wastesphere. Language is Humanity's superpower. It is how we differentiate from our fellow species. The use of language has delivered many benefits and caused many wars.

The metacrisis is a mysterious, wicked problem. It's a planetary and human sickness for which we have yet to find a cure. To find the cure, we should endeavor to decipher it. The metacrisis we face – a web of interconnected challenges, from pollution to social-economic inequality, meaninglessness, and delusion is blanketed in misinformation, fake narratives, and competing agendas. Where the sole focus and belief in science and technology will promise to produce the golden egg. We need a new Rosetta Stone to decipher the code and unlock possibilities to navigate out of the metacrisis. The ancients understood the power of three. You can find this power all over the world and in many forms. Here, I will focus on the trinity of Logos, Pathos, and Mythos, which are essential for human beings. We are invited to accept this again to embody the True, Good, and the Beautiful.

Logos isn't only about cold, hard facts. It's about understanding the architecture of information, the interconnectedness of data, and the ability to discern truth from fiction. We live in an age of echo chambers and fake news. We need protection against the manipulation of facts, a sextant, and a compass to navigate us through conflicting narratives, questionable research methods, and the perverse incentives they are tied to. We live in a post-truth world swamped with information so vast that we cannot tell the forest from the trees. What is right and what is wrong? We are inundated by points of view and opinions that either resonate with one group or antagonize the other. We are constantly at war, most often online. Some have argued that WW3 has already started, and it's called the narrative wars of the 21ˢᵗ century—the choices are either to use our current narrative, like Sue for Peace, or perhaps a new narrative, such as a Dialogos of Peace and Unity.

So, why is a new Logos crucial to tackling our metacrisis?

Dismantling the power that feeds us instant gratification: Our current narratives are fractured, siloed, and often built on shaky foundations. We speak different languages of "truth," making collaboration and collective action nearly impossible. Logos, emphasizing integral thinking and evidence-based reasoning, can help us bridge these divides. By demanding proof, questioning assumptions, and seeking common ground, we can build a foundation of shared understanding – the first step towards lasting change.

The end of algorithms designed for profit: The algorithms that shape our online experiences often prioritize engagement over truth, trapping us in filter bubbles and amplifying extremism. Logos empowers us to challenge these algorithmic biases, seek out diverse perspectives, and evaluate information critically. We can become active consumers of knowledge, not passive recipients of curated narratives that further divide us.

Reclaiming the Power of Storytelling that increases our attention span: While facts are essential, they are not the whole story. Logos, in its purest form, encompasses the art of logical argument and persuasive storytelling. By weaving facts into compelling narratives, we can make complex issues relatable, inspirational, and invitational to build a shared purpose – crucial ingredients for tackling any crisis.

But wielding Logos effectively comes with challenges.

Confirmation Bias:

- Echo chambers: Algorithms and social media curate content based on past behavior, creating virtual spaces where we're primarily exposed to information confirming our beliefs. Stepping outside these echo chambers and actively seeking diverse perspectives requires conscious effort.

- Emotional attachment to narratives: We often build our identities and worldviews around specific narratives. Challenging those narratives can feel like an attack on our core beliefs, triggering emotional resistance and making it difficult to engage in objective reasoning.

- Confirmation bias in disguise: Disinformation often masquerades as objective information, using biased sources, cherry-picked data, and emotionally charged language to exploit existing biases. Deciphering this requires keen critical thinking skills and a healthy dose of skepticism.

The Weaponization of Logic:

- Logical fallacies: Manipulative individuals and groups can wield logic deceptively, using fallacies like strawman arguments or ad hominem attacks to sway opinions and win arguments. Recognizing these fallacies requires familiarity with various argument structures and an awareness of common manipulation tactics.

- Half-truths and cherry-picking data: Facts can be selectively presented or misinterpreted to support a particular agenda, creating a misleading picture of reality. Developing data literacy, understanding research methodologies, and seeking information from diverse sources are crucial safeguards.

- Emotional manipulation: Combining logical arguments with emotional appeals can be a powerful tool for manipulation. Identifying and separating emotionally charged language from factual reasoning is crucial in avoiding being swayed by biased arguments.

The Slow Burn of Change:

- Entrenched narratives: Powerful interests often invest heavily in promoting specific narratives, making them deeply entrenched in society and culture. Shifting these narratives takes time, sustained effort, and a multi-pronged approach.

- Complexity of issues: Many aspects of the metacrisis are complex and interconnected, making reaching a consensus on possibilities difficult.

Finding common ground and building coalitions amidst diverse perspectives requires patience, empathy, and skillful communication.

- Disinformation fatigue: The constant barrage of conflicting information can lead to disengagement and apathy. Maintaining motivation and commitment to truth-seeking in the face of this fatigue requires individual resilience and community support.

Remember, mastering Logos is an ongoing journey, not a destination. By acknowledging these challenges, equipping ourselves with critical thinking skills, and fostering a culture of open dialogue and evidence-based discourse, we can harness the power of reason to navigate our complex world and pave the way for a brighter future.

While the challenges of wielding Logos effectively in the digital age are significant, here are some potential possibilities to consider:

Combating Confirmation Bias:

- Media literacy education: Promote critical thinking skills and awareness of media manipulation tactics in educational curriculums and public programs.

- Support diverse news platforms: Actively seek out and consume news from various sources, including those with different perspectives.

- Fact-checking platforms: Utilize credible resources to verify information and identify misinformation.

- Open dialogue: Engage in respectful conversations with individuals holding different viewpoints, focusing on evidence and mutual participatory logical reasoning.

Countering Weaponized Logic:

- Logical reasoning training: Develop strong critical thinking skills by studying logic, argumentation, and rhetoric.

- Source evaluation: Assess the credibility of information sources by examining their expertise, affiliations, financiers, methods, influences, and potential biases.

- Data literacy: Learn to understand research methodologies, identify flawed data analysis, and interpret information critically.

- Emotional awareness: Recognize and manage your emotional responses to information, avoiding decisions based solely on feelings.

Overcoming the Slow Burn:

- Collaborative storytelling: Use compelling, accurate, and emotionally engaging narratives to build empathy and understanding across diverse groups.

- Coalition building: Identify common ground with individuals and groups holding different perspectives to collaborate on shared goals.

- Long-term engagement: Remain committed to truth-seeking and critical thinking, even when facing discouragement or fatigue.

- Celebrate progress: Acknowledge and celebrate successes, however small, to maintain motivation and inspire continued action.

Additional Posibilities:

- Support organizations: Back groups promoting media literacy, critical and integral thinking, and evidence-based decision-making.

- Advocate for regulations: Push for policies that hold social media platforms accountable for combating misinformation and incentivize them to promote diverse perspectives.

- Embrace personal responsibility: Commit to actively seeking truth, engaging in civil discourse, and holding yourself accountable for your own biases.

In conclusion, all of the above means we will likely develop memetic immunity. Unfortunately, no vaccine is available to inject that immunity into our system, but it would be amazing if we could.

By implementing these possibilities individually and collectively, we can overcome the challenges of wielding Logos in the digital age and create a more informed, critical, and truth-seeking society where meaning and purpose for the good of All is restored. Remember, it's a continuous process, but by empowering ourselves and others with the tools of Integral thinking and open dialogue, we can pave the way for a brighter future where reason, understanding, and collaboration guide our path.

So, how can we navigate these challenges and harness the power of Logos?

1. Practice Humility: Recognize that we all have biases and actively seek out information that challenges our assumptions.

2. Cultivate Curiosity: Ask questions, explore different viewpoints, and engage in respectful dialogue with those with different perspectives.

3. Become a Discerning Storyteller: Learn to craft compelling, factually accurate, and emotionally resonant narratives.

4. Amplify Trustworthy Voices: Support organizations and individuals committed to truth-telling and critical and integral thinking.

Pathos Holds the Key to Our Shared Narrative

Pathos is the essence of emotion and empathy, transcends mere information to connect us at a visceral level. The fire in the belly of a climate activist's plea, tears rolling down a child's cheek yearning for a safer world, and shared laughter ignite hope and foster collective action. In the multifaceted dilemma of our metacrisis, pathos serves as the missing link, the bridge that combines disparate voices into a shared purpose.

So, why is pathos crucial to changing our narratives and tackling our interconnected challenges?

The Language of Connection: Data and reason are vital, but they often leave us cold, unable to ignite the spark of collective action. Pathos transcends language and cultural divides, speaking directly to the human heart. A mother's grief over a polluted water source resonates across borders, and a shared cry for justice against inequality echoes in diverse communities. By tapping into the emotional core of issues, Pathos builds bridges where facts alone cannot.

Apathy and paralysis: Faced with the immensity of our metacrisis, apathy can easily creep in. Facts become statistics; challenges feel insurmountable. Pathos cuts through this despair and breeds hope and compassion. A child's innocent question about the future or a community leader's passionate speech awakens a sense of shared responsibility. Pathos motivates us to move beyond mere awareness and into action by stirring our emotions.

Orchestration: Our narratives are fractured, echoing in isolated chambers. Pathos allows us to transcend these divides by developing empathy and understanding. We discover shared values and common ground by sharing our fears, hopes, and experiences. The laughter of children playing in a newly planted community garden the tears shed at a vigil for victims of injustice can unite through careful narration.

But wielding Pathos effectively comes with its own challenges:

Manipulation: Emotion can be exploited. Fear can be weaponized, and anger can be misdirected. Navigating the ethical use of Pathos requires mindfulness and authenticity.

Comfort: We gravitate towards emotions that resonate with our existing beliefs, creating comfortable but ultimately unproductive echo chambers. Actively seeking diverse perspectives and uncomfortable truths is crucial.

Emotion: Emotional highs can fade into apathy. Sustaining momentum requires channeling fleeting feelings into concrete action and long-term engagement.

So, how can we navigate these challenges and unlock the transformative power of Pathos?

Practice Empathy: Step into the shoes of others, actively listen to their stories, and acknowledge their emotional realities.

Cultivate Authenticity: Share your experiences and emotions honestly, fostering genuine connection and trust.

Find Flow in Shared Narratives: Seek out and participate in conversations that evoke shared emotions, fostering a sense of connection and purpose. This is where entering the flow state during Pathos conversations with thought leaders becomes crucial. In this state, we truly connect with the emotional resonance of the message, allowing the speaker's passion to ignite our commitment to action.

Amplify Diverse Voices: Seek out and share narratives from various perspectives, ensuring your understanding is inclusive and multifaceted.

Remember, Pathos is not a solo act. It's integrately woven from countless individual narratives. By cultivating empathy, practicing authenticity, and engaging in meaningful conversations, we can integrate shared emotions that will rewrite our current narratives and propel us toward a future where compassion, collaboration, and collective action guide our way.

Mythos, Mythology, or simply Myth in today's dominating worldview of society almost borders on becoming a dirty word. Myths are regarded as mere fantasies now, and their deeper meaning is reserved for scholars. We also see this in the hollowing out of religions, gradually eroding towards nihilism. Yet Mythos is essential if we are to emerge as a post-tragic global civilization. Within Mythos resides a key element, the pursuit of wisdom, often measured in terms of what is good, true, and beautiful. But what do we mean by these three terms?

While the terms "good," "true," and "beautiful" have been extensively explored in philosophy and religion, where their psychological meaning is multifaceted and often debated is again relevant for humanity faced with existential risks as defined under the metacrisis.

The Good, the most potent of virtues, is not simply the absence of evil. It is the active pursuit of the betterment of all beings. It is compassion that extends beyond humans, borders, justice that uplifts the downtrodden, and a deep respect for the sacredness of all life. By embracing the good, we can heal the divides within our communities and restore the balance of nature and the world.

When embraced in its completeness, the True transcends mere facts. It encompasses the stories we tell ourselves and each other, the myths that bind us together and give meaning to our existence. True stories resonate with our deepest selves, revealing the interconnectedness of all life.

The Beautiful is not a superficial adornment. It reflects the "what cannot be described" order that governs the universe. It is in the intricate melody of music and dance of nature as life interacts with air, water, and soil, the selfless act of love, and the enduring strength of the human soul. When we cultivate our appreciation for beauty, we reconnect with the spring of well-being of life itself. It holds magical and infinite potential of imagination.

Interconnection and Individual variations:

It's important to remember that these concepts are often intertwined. Seeking "the true" might contribute to understanding "the good," while appreciating "the beautiful" can be intrinsically rewarding (perceived as "good"). Individual differences and cultural contexts significantly influence how these virtues are interpreted and pursued, but at the core, they are common to all Life. The virtues that I refer to are:

Compassion and Kindness: These involve recognizing and understanding the suffering of others and being motivated to help.

Justice: Striving for fairness and treating others with what they deserve.

Honesty and Integrity: Being truthful and acting in accordance with supporting for All Life of their support systems.

Courage: Bravery and determination.

Temperance: Moderation and self-control.

Forgiveness: Letting go of resentment and anger towards others.

Prudence: Good judgment and wisdom in making decisions.

Love: A deep affection and care for others.

Recently, we have seen more and more discussions within the regenerative space where the power of storytelling is discussed. We also see the emergence of indigenous wisdom coming forth into the limelight. In each, there is a discussion about the meaning of words and how they have changed over time and, from a more radical perspective, developed new words that fit our current times and could influence our thinking and behavior. A field that resides with linguistics and ecolinguistics sciences. I would add one more ingredient: Symbolism

One of the most potent mythical stories found in almost all cultures and even in religions worldwide involves a Cauldron. I was first introduced to the Cauldron by reading the cartoons of Asterix and Obelisk and the Smurfs, where the cauldron is used for good and evil, and I learned that a cauldron is coeval. The Cauldron is featured in many fairy tales, which signifies change or transformation to obtain a desired outcome. Mythology includes elements of sacrifice and constraint to provide resources, as in Nordic Mythology, or a Connection to the divine with the Ding in Chinese Mythology and the Druid's Cauldron for abundance, inspiration, and transformative knowledge. The Cauldron was used to symbolize birth from the womb (creation from darkness), Transformation for something new to emerge, knowledge, and power. Without Obelix and the potion's power, they would never have been able to hold off the Romans. During my time involved in business transformation, I found that the objective to transform never materialized. Once I understood the symbolic meaning of the Cauldron. I realized that transformation is only ever an emergent property from causes, ingredients, and actions that produce outcomes, often ignoring the emergent negative consequences or byproducts. When I mentioned this, my fellow consultants thought I was crazy, which indicates that many had forgotten the meaning of symbols used in stories meant to educate us and how they can be applied to today's complicated challenges.

Using words shapes your thoughts, how you speak, and how you act. What if you "put yourself into the shoes" of a fish, a tree, a piece of land, the atmosphere, or a biosphere? If you can grasp that expanse, what would those words invoke in such a mind?

During my research, I found an interesting side note related to the Greek word Evangelion, meaning good news, which was translated into English as God Spell "The Good Story," which we now know as Gospel and Spell. When I thought about this, I realized how powerful a story can be when written well. If done exceptionally well, its power could be considered magical, I.e., giving birth to a new form of thought, action, and belief that cannot yet be explained.

Words have meaning; take care of how you use them. This is difficult but a craft worth pursuing during these times.

INTEGRAL THEORY

As with our technology, humanity has evolved in the field of development. Individually and as a civilization. We've been shaped within our cultures and societies. So far, we have exposed our limitations and Moloch, preventing us from tackling the metacrisis effectively. Where did it all come from? It's easy to say that it's because of our behavior and how we have been educated, but what if it's a deeper aspect of our humanity that we ignored, have forgotten, or chose not to pursue?

I pose a simple question. Is the universe a complicated set of building blocks or a complex dynamic system of holons?

Of course, the correct answer is both, but how many people have heard of Holons? I was never taught it in school, and in public discourse, I've yet to hear the term being used in everyday communications. During my years as a consultant, I could have been more valuable if I had known what holons were. This is understandable as the difference between the building blocks and holons of the universe is primarily debated in Philosophy and not in a technology firm that thinks in bits and bytes. The current consensus is that Holons comprise the Universe's building blocks. A Holon is anything that is simultaneously a whole and a part of a greater whole.

To simplify, the belief is that we humans are individual holons. The Atom in our body is a whole that comes together to form another whole called molecules, which come together and form another whole called cells, which come together to form organs that come together and form an organism. We are organisms and highly evolved at that. Each part of us is a holon. At every level of scale, we observe that reality is not made up of things and processes. It's not made up of parts but holons. At every moment, wholes are creating new wholes and more new wholes with new qualities, characteristics, and behaviors that the constituent wholes cannot explain. In other words, each holon as a whole is greater than the sum of smaller wholes.

The science of holons includes physics, chemistry, biology, math, ecology, sociology, psychology, philosophy, theology, linguistics, and economics. All life and its relationships are a type of holon. Our civilization has segregated or reduced the study of holons to each respective field, so we now mainly look at holons as Lego blocks.

Arthur Koestler argued that humanity's capacity for greatness was often undermined by its tendency for self-destruction, and based on my research, this is the case today when confronted with our wastesphere, ecological overshoot, social injustice, and destructive economic practices. What I found fascinating from his work is that evolution continuously optimizes efficiency, where holons are the wholes that drive these efficiencies. This contradicts how we view efficiency today, focusing on single objects or processes. In the field of efficiency, a crucial revenue earner in consultancies, we have practices specializing in process efficiency, technology efficiency, customer service efficiency, cost optimization efficiency, and many more. The focus is often on parts or components but rarely analyzed from the perspectival realization of holons. As I've explained in the previous chapter, Global Risks, imagine if we addressed the mobility dilemma related to the automotive industry from this perspective. We would be increasing public transportation and producing smaller cars.

In the 1980s blockbuster science documentary Cosmos, American astrophysicist Carl Sagan said, "If you wish to make an apple pie from scratch, you must first invent the universe." I thought he was joking. I would have to be immortal, as the universe is over 13 billion years old. Now that I understand the basics of Holons, it is starting to make sense. Apologies to Charles Darwin, but evolution is the emergence of holons combining to make bigger holons that are all in relationship with each other and dependent on each other, which is infinite as new emergence manifests itself as part of evolution.

From atoms to organisms implies that there is a hierarchy which, from the holon perspective, can be defined as a growth hierarchy, which is a developmental type of hierarchy, unlike the more familiar hierarchy that we are used to, which is the domination hierarchy, from single cell organisms to apex predators or for example societal hierarchies from President to the person on the street. A holon growth hierarchy is based on the principle that each holon combines with similar holons to produce a bigger holon, ultimately leading to a stronger and more resilient holon. From puppy to dog, from tadpole to frog, and from sapling to a tree. Or from atoms to organisms. From organisms to community. Nations are not holons as they are imposed upon us with borders and governance structures. Holons, such as societies and cultures, are at risk of the infection of hierarchical structures that limit a holarchy's ability to transcend. We should be careful not to confuse the two hierarchies. Holon growth hierarchies show us that no matter what level of the hierarchy, you are also dependent on the lower levels of the hierarchy. If you remove all the cells from the hierarchy, the organism will cease to exist. If you remove all organisms, communities will not exist, but atoms and molecules will ultimately remain.

This makes sense because that is how we care for the holons within us with our food. We nurture holons and desire to grow as holons to become more resilient. Contradictory to a sense of being a holon, we have long shifted to a dominator hierarchy where the lower levels are oppressed. As Individuals, we suppress our deepest fears and bad behavior. We succumb to the temptation of fast food that harms our lower holons, like our liver. In a community, we risk falling for suppressive characteristics that manifest racism, colonialism, societal ranking, haves and have-nots, and the systems we developed to support domination. We pursue greatness while we have become self-destructive.

Should we not ask ourselves if we should become holarchies as a system aligned with the universe versus the dominator hierarchies in politics, religion, and economics we have become so accustomed to?

Integral theory, developed by Ken Wilber, offers a bold framework that attempts to do that. It's not a simple solution, but it's a powerful lens through which we can examine the complexities of our world and potentially navigate the "metacrisis" we find ourselves in. Integral theory is not new and has been debated for many centuries. Ken Wilbur draws on many developmental experts and the works of Jean Piaget, a Swiss psychologist known for his work on child development, particularly the Theory of cognitive development, which describes the nature and development of human intelligence.

A distinct set of qualities becomes universal based on the understanding of holons and their value and what each holon possesses.

- Reality as a whole is not composed of things and processes but of holons.
- Holons have four fundamental drivers
  - ☐ Self-preservation: An inward drive towards their agency
  - ☐ Self-adaptation: form a community
  - ☐ Self Transcendence: An upward drive called eros
  - ☐ Self Embrace: A downward drive which we call agape
- Holons emerge
- Holons emerge holarchically. A sequence of holons
- Each emergent holon transcends but includes its predecessor.

- The lower sets the possibilities of the higher; the higher sets the probabilities of the lower

- The number of levels determines if it is shallow or deep. The number of holons on any given level determines its span.

- Each successive level of evolution produces greater depth and less span.

- The greater the depth of the holon, the greater the depth of its consciousness.

- Destroy any type of holon, and you will destroy all of the holons above it and none of the holons below it.

- Holarchies coevolve

- The micro is in relational exchange with the macro at all levels of its depth.

- Evolution has directionality, such as increasing complexity, differentiation and integration, organization and structure, relative autonomy, and humans' capacity to shape their nature.

- Increasing telos. Emergence is itself emergent.

Based on the above qualities, I realized that rocks, weapons, AI, and current governments are not holons.

Integral theory contains three components: Quadrants, Stages, and Waves. These can be applied to individuals, businesses, politics, and our global civilization's many cultures and societies. Ken Wilber's central premise is that everyone is correct to some degree; hence, all views should be considered within this framework of which holons and their characteristics form an integral part of the growth development of self, culture, and society from an internal and external perspective.

Integral theory paints a grand picture, encompassing numerous aspects of reality divided into four quadrants, each representing a distinct way of knowing:

- Upper Left (interior-individual known as I):

- Upper Right (Exterior Individual as IT):

- Lower Left (Interior-Collective as WE):

- Lower Right (exterior-collective as ITS):

Integral theory emphasizes that a comprehensive understanding requires considering all four quadrants, not only focusing on one at the expense of others.

There are 10 stages of integral development.

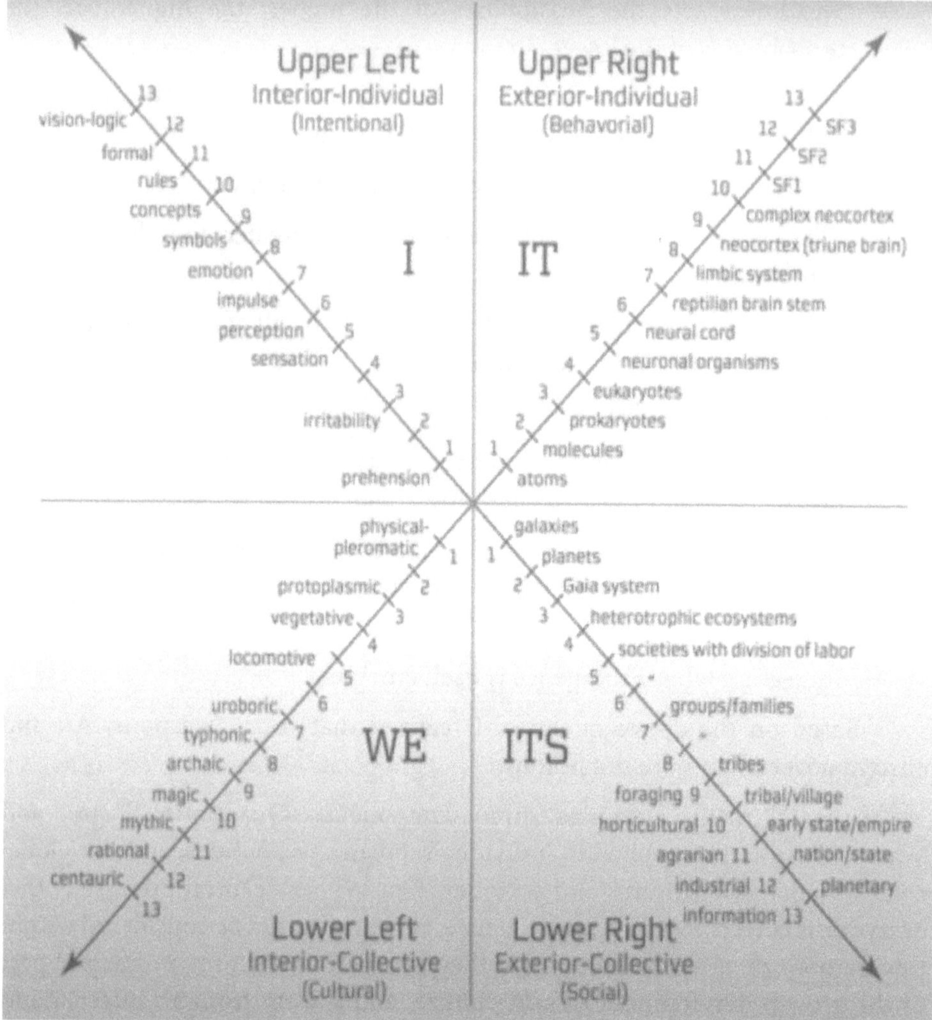

Pre-personal stages:

1. Archaic: This stage focuses on basic survival needs and experiences like hunger, pain, and pleasure. Each quadrant primarily operates in the present moment, with limited differentiation between self and other, and begins to learn through reflexes and simple interactions with their nature.

2. Magic: Egocentrism reigns supreme in this stage. Development a sense of self, but struggle to understand the perspectives of others. Magical thinking prevails, where they believe their thoughts and actions can directly influence the world around them. This stage also sees the blossoming of language and imagination.

3. Egocentric: solidifies the senses of self and becomes increasingly aware of their desires and needs. However, understanding social norms and the impact of their actions on others remains a challenge. Play becomes central, offering opportunities for social interaction and the development of empathy.

Personal stages:

4. Ethnocentric: This stage marks the emergence of group identification and adherence to societal norms and values. Understanding the rules and expectations of their nature, often conforming to authority figures, emerges. The world is viewed as right and wrong, with a limited understanding of different perspectives.

5. Worldcentric: Abstract thinking blossoms as questions arise to challenge established norms so they develop their values. They become more aware of global issues and injustices, often pursuing social change and individual expression. This stage can be marked by idealism and rebellion as they navigate a place in the world.

6. Reasonist: Logic and rationality take center stage. Individuals in this stage prioritize objectivity, critical thinking, and problem-solving. They focus on building careers, establishing families, and making sense of the complex world around them, often colonizing parts of the complex and making it complicated so it can be measured and controlled. Understanding systems and analyzing information become key strengths.

7. Postmodern: This stage critiques fixed ideas and embraces relativism. Individuals question power structures, challenge rigid ideologies, and acknowledge the limitations of reason. They value diverse perspectives and explore alternative ways of knowing and being. Deconstruction and openness to ambiguity are characteristic of this stage.

Transpersonal or Transcultural stages:

8. Integral: This stage integrates insights from previous stages, leading to a more holistic understanding of oneself and the world. Individuals recognize the interconnectedness of all things and embrace multiple perspectives. They strive for balance, inner peace, and contributing to the greater good.

9. Indigo (emerging): This proposed stage emphasizes systemic change and the well-being of all life forms. Individuals in this stage are deeply concerned with global issues and work towards transcendence that benefits the collective. They integrate reason and intuition, fostering collaboration and finding creative approaches to complex challenges.

10. Coral (hypothetical): While not fully defined, this stage is theorized to represent a transcendence of individual limitations and a deep connection to all life forms. It signifies. A state of unity consciousness, where compassion and wisdom guide actions with profound impact on the world. This stage is sometimes proposed by those who see our technology as the bridge to enable this for our human species and not for all life. The image of the Cyborg comes to mind that either creates hope for some or horror for others.

Remember, these stages are not rigid boxes, and individuals and groups may move through them at different paces or even revisit aspects of earlier stages throughout their lives. Integral theory's value lies in the diversity of human development, offering a framework for understanding ourselves and navigating the complexities of the world around us.

Last, the various waves flow through each quadrant and stage.

Premodern Wave:

- Dominant worldview: Archaic and magical modes of thinking. Emphasis on tradition, hierarchy, and belonging to a community.

- Key characteristics: Animism, myth-making, limited individual identity, focus on survival and basic needs.

- Examples: Early human societies, hunter-gatherer cultures, tribal communities.

Modern Wave:

- Dominant worldview: Rationality, individualism, and progress. Emphasis on science, technology, and individual rights.

- Key characteristics: Secularization, rise of nation-states, focus on logic and objectivity, separation of mind and body.

- Examples: The Enlightenment, the Industrial Revolution, and modern democracies.

Postmodern Wave:

- Dominant worldview: Deconstruction of fixed ideas, relativism, and social justice. Emphasis on diversity, questioning authority, and deconstructing power structures.

- Key characteristics: Rise of critical theory, multiculturalism, naturalism, focus on marginalized voices.

- Examples: Civil rights movements, feminist movements, globalization trends.

Emerging Integral Wave:

- Dominant worldview: Integration of reason and intuition, holistic understanding, and global responsibility. Emphasis on interconnectedness, systemic thinking, and collaboration.

- Key characteristics: Blending traditional and modern knowledge, focus on regeneration, spiritual awareness, and collective well-being.

- Examples: Post Capitalism movements, mindfulness practices, collaborative problem-solving initiatives (still emerging).

It's important to note that:

- Waves are not linear or deterministic: Societies don't always neatly transition from one wave to another, and elements of older waves often coexist with newer ones.

- There's an ongoing debate: Each wave's characteristics and specific timelines vary depending on the interpretation and focus of analysis.

- The integral wave is still emerging: It's not fully defined or universally accepted, but it represents a potential shift towards a more integrated and regenerative future.

Understanding the wave framework can help us recognize broader societal trends, anticipate potential challenges, and participate in shaping a more positive future. However, it's crucial to remain aware of its limitations and engage in critical dialogue about its implications.

I've only presented a forty-thousand-foot overview of integral theory, and for those who wish to dive deeper, I can recommend the work of Ken Wilber on this topic. I added it here to promote further thoughts on the matter and how it can be applied to the metacrisis. Integral Theory is a frame that provides no answers, only a method and sets of processes that can address the many wicked problems we face today.

However, there is still a missing piece, which is our capacity for sensemaking.

SENSE MAKING

> *"Sometimes we must be satisfied with the soup that is set before us, and not desire to see the bones of the ox out of which it has been boiled."*
>
> *George Webbe Dascent.*

In small pockets of humanity easily exceeding millions, spread around the world, a call is becoming louder and louder. Its call sounds like a desperate need for a new enlightenment. A new way of thinking that almost feels like it must be forced into existence because the crises are bringing us closer to the edge of a cliff. Add to that the feeling that we are running out of time. I can't help but notice distinct signs of desperation.

Discussions about new logos, pathos, and mythos are growing to address the meaning of crisis and combat nihilism. Integral Theory is questioning how we operate as individuals, businesses, and governments faced with wicked problems, a lack of sense-making, and the pursuit of something new. We need Planet B, which is an uncolonized complex system that is tied to evolution. There are works, of course, from well-educated experts that are well worth a read. Still, they often ignore or dismiss key components of our civilization and nature, such as the waste sphere, technology sphere, wisdom, and a globally integrated participatory governance sphere.

How often do you read books that discuss toolkits? With every problem or challenge we face, we as a civilization are quick to propose a tool or solution kit. It's almost as if we are carpenters who feel naked without our tool belt. While tools, otherwise known as technologies, can help to solve complicated things, they are hardly equipped to solve complex problems. One of the reasons for this is our lack of sense-making. Sensemaking has become enormously complicated.

The biggest challenge we face is our growing lack of trust in news. Most news we consume is propaganda, a narrative warfare for some agencies, and not an excellent sense-making source. This is the case when one compares the news narratives from the Murdoch media empire vs. Media outlets like the Atlantic, Mother Jones, MSNBC, and The Guardian. There are not many amongst us who watch both because we align ourselves with what matches closest to our beliefs, knowledge, or lack thereof, and our biases. Hence, we have a polarization crisis, and in the extreme, we become susceptible to brainwashing.

While writing this book, I've tried my best to provide facts from sources I trust and think are trusted by most people. I accept that it's not perfect and that some people would claim that I cherry-picked data. Perhaps our meta crisis is not as bad as it appears in this book, or the waste sphere is only a figment of my imagination. Everyone is entitled to their opinion, and I welcome a mutually respectful debate. I tried to leverage history and historical facts as much as possible and my own experiences as sources of truth. I also believe that most people are aware of all the positives in the world. We are, in essence, a positive and hopeful species. We are also a species that often ignores the opposing or dark sides of who we are. We do not want to be confronted with our dark side. We need to discuss both in the proper context. One of my struggles is how to make sense of it all. Both the positive and the negative that is not biased or based on pleasing one camp or another.

Sense-making has become difficult even when I researched specific elements of our wastesphere. At first, I read scientific papers at face value because I trusted the material without asking if it was trustworthy. It was only after I started comparing research methodologies, the scientists themselves, who they were influenced by, and how they were funded that I realized that even science papers had to be read with a grain of salt until I could gather scientific papers from many other sources that produced the same claims and even then I still had my doubts. Call this critical thinking at its best and worst because of increasing doubt.

To illustrate the above, I spend considerable time researching plastic pollution. One paper developed by Dutch researchers found that our plastic pollution was not as harmful as other researchers claimed. Reading their research methodology made it clear why they could make that claim. They collected data by counting the amount of plastic floating from rivers to the ocean. They completely ignored what was flowing downriver below the surface. They assumed that all plastic floats. They counted the floating plastic in a few rivers and then extrapolated them to encompass the globe. This research was immediately picked up by a section of the media that supports the belief that our pollution crisis is exaggerated. The producers of this material immediately used this research as proof that the plastic pollution crisis was overestimated. Were these researches wrong or right? From all the beaches I've visited all over the world these last five years, I could not find one river or beach that was not polluted with plastic. My eyes were not deceiving me. What I saw is my reality, and that is what I'm sharing.

Now, I'm faced with a dilemma: I can't trust the information I receive as 100% trustworthy. It is hard to find sources that get to the core of what is undisputable collaborated fact quickly without all the subjective noise often found in many science, business, religion, and political narratives. It is almost as if there is a war going on with sense-making. With over 8 Billion people today, the amount of information available to a single person is so immense that it is now impossible to process all of it and make sense of it. It is as if we now need to build tribes of up to 150 people to collectively process the information available and make sense of it to make better decisions. I tried using AI, but even that machine struggled to build the type of information networks I needed to ensure that wherever the information came from was true. All views and claims should be considered, especially concerning our wicked problems. The commonality between different claims or opinions should be synthesized to build unity and mutual consensus to improve our collective decision-making.

We have natural ecosystems and information ecosystems where we have access to various sources of information. First, from our families and friends verbally but more often from social media. We receive information from the news, other media, governments, political parties, businesses, religions, and books. Some are even more than happy to receive only information from AI as their source of truth. Add to that our knowledge, values, beliefs, and biases to leverage this ecosystem that provides us with agency together with those we have welcomed into our Arena to make what we believe well-informed decisions. Anyone who disagrees is expelled from the Arena, and then we start throwing shit at each other creating more conflict. Our information ecology is broken. To confirm this, one must ask where our information comes from. Why do people and groups share information, and for what purpose? Is it to convey a truth or to promote truthfulness, or is it meant to deceive, confuse, and promote lies that benefit a particular camp?

We no longer ask these questions. Our attention span is now less than 10 seconds. We stick to headlines and tweets and aimlessly scroll over information, often missing the meat of the content. We are now developing apps that reduce the contents of books to less than 15 minutes so we can grasp the essence. We merely smell the perfume without knowing its ingredients. How can smelling perfume improve our decision-making?

Dr Iain McGilchrist wrote a few beautiful books. One is called The Master and His Emissary, and the other is The Matter with Things. In these books, he convincingly argues that our society, mainly our dominant Western style-oriented society, is depressed thanks to the pursuit of wealth and power. We have become predominantly Emissaries because we are obsessed with manipulation.

The Emissary dwells in the left hemisphere of our brain, and The Master dwells in the right hemisphere of the brain. The left favors manipulation and has become dominant thanks to our survival instincts and the consistent urge to be reductionistic and reduce everything to things we can grasp.

Albert Einstein's famous quote: Everything should be made as simple as possible, but not simpler—is a brilliant example of how we misunderstand his meaning- it is precisely our ignorance of The Master because we have made things simpler. You cannot make things simple without wisdom. I would even go as far as saying that the Emissary has imprisoned His Master and is starving him to death.

I propose that sense-making starts with releasing The Master imprisoned in your mind and bringing forth the Good, True, and the Beautiful. This part of the brain understands the wholeness of the Universe and that not everything needs to be understood. It understands the relationships between objects and systems and the beauty of the natural world in all its colors. The Master sees the whole as more than the sum of its parts. The reality of the right side is opposite from the left's Google Maps-like depiction of reality.

Developing a Cathedral mindset can help tremendously. The presence becomes alive with wonder and awe because you accept your mortality, which The Master understands as humanity's most significant gift. At the same time, the Emissary hates it and seeks Immortality at all cost.

A balance must be found between The Master, who needs to reign His Emissary in and educate it to dispel Moloch like a cancer that has grown gradually to a stage where its host is almost terminal and could consume both sides of the mind. The Master loves the world of pathos and mythos, and we desperately need more of that.

EMERGENCE

The sheer gravity of our civilization's challenges – climate change, biodiversity loss, pollution, and other global risks described in the previous chapters– can feel overwhelming. Amidst the darkness, there is a spark of hope. I know that despair is not the answer. We are not people who give up. If we did, there would be a story in our history that confirms this, or worse, we would have met our end long ago. The story of David and Goliath would not exist. You may agree that Goliath is not some simple giant but a complicated, invisible, destructive influence. I call Moloch or Sauron the real enemy, if you prefer. We have to rise up to confront these challenges head-on. Our mission should be to defeat Moloch once and for all. The whole of humanity depends on it. We need a new fellowship and new alliances. We can write a story that will be told through the ages of how we managed to subdue Moloch and make it functionally extinct. We are excellent at making things extinct, so why not Moloch?

We should also realize that as we emerge, we need to accept that we cannot solve all our wicked problems overnight or even within a decade, as some might make you believe. We are in a predicament, which is a huge difference. It is unrealistic that we can forever remove chemicals and microplastics within a few decades, or the whole of the waste sphere, for that matter. What we can do is develop a cathedral mindset where we start to restore or, worse, need to build a new foundation on which our future civilization can be built that is solid and avoids all the mistakes we made in the past.

To avoid doubt, what I mean by a Cathedral mind has nothing to do with Christianity. It is pantheistic and universal. It is a mindset that encompasses all of humanity. I understand that visualization is important, so if you are from the faith of Islam, think of the Masjid al-Haram; if you are Buddhist, think of Borobudur; or if you are Hindu, think of the Srirangam Ranganathaswamy Temple; or if you are a Taoist, the Seitenkyu Temple, or if you are from an indigenous tribe, the land in which you live all of which were not built in a day.

Cultivating the Cathedral Mind

Imagine your mind like a colossal cathedral reaching towards the heavens. Its intricate arches represent interconnected disciplines, its stained-glass windows illuminate diverse perspectives, and its soaring spires pierce the veil of ignorance. This, my friends, is the "cathedral mind" – a collective intelligence where individual brilliance transcends its limitations and unites to elevate civilization, and it prevents Moloch from entering.

The challenges we face today demand more than individual solutions. The metacrisis cannot be solved with point solutions – We need more than science. We need a new philosophy, technology, art, engineering, care, wisdom, and every corner of human ingenuity that elevates us to a new emergent worldview shared by all cultures and societies. The siloed thinking of the past can no longer hold back the tide. We need minds that resonate, collaborate, and build upon each other like stones seamlessly forming a cathedral's magnificent arch. We should also realize that the work requires generations. Those who start at the foundation will not live long enough to see the final result. This should be accepted as part of the roles we all should be advised to perform. Those who reach the top rafters will realize that the cathedral will never finish, like Gaudi's Sagrada Familia. It will hold all the good, true, and the beautiful in complete harmony, infinitely complex and never-ending. The structure has no roof. This is important because closing the structures as fixed will lock in power, and when power is contained, it ultimately corrupts. Moloch creeps into the cracks of resistance. The structure signifies constraint, sacrifice and possibilities. An open roof invites one to be in harmony with the elements.

There is one symbol that represents the cathedral mind like no other. It can be found in all cultures and beliefs, even atheists, believe it or not. That symbol is the Tree of Life. It represents the complexity of life and so much more. To keep it universal, the Tree of Life holds all the virtues that were once displayed or described as statues in the likeness of ourselves or what I call the wise and enlightened.

People used to revere these wise individuals for the virtues they represented. These virtues were once celebrated. Nowadays, there are only a few places left where this is the case. You may find this strange and unnatural today, but deification is more active than ever. The only difference is that our desire for a deity has shifted to celebrities who do not embody those same virtues and hence cannot provide the wholeness and emotion of awe and wonder, even if you think they do. The so-called ecstatic experience from a live concert is artificial because it provides no value or meaning to life within Earth's spheres. It's just fun for fun's sake, so let's not make more of it, and don't think your life is a mess if you can't afford or obtain a ticket. Remember I talked about scarcity earlier?

The benefits of fostering a cathedral mind are manifold.

Imagine tackling a complex challenge with doctors, engineers, artists, scientists, the clergy of all faiths, and philosophers sharing perspectives. The doctor might diagnose the ailment, the engineer devises a treatment, the artist imagines and manifests inspiration, the clergy conveys wisdom, and the philosopher examines ethical implications and deeper understanding. The synergy from this collaboration unlocks innovative solutions we wouldn't have found alone, yet even imagined.

A cathedral mind embraces diverse voices; it develops a richer understanding of human needs and experiences. The economist with a cathedral mind considers poverty not in currency but through the lens of the artist's portrayal of its human cost. This fosters empathy, leading to technically sound, compassionate, and inclusive solutions.

A cathedral mind thinks of centuries to come with a firm footing in the present, equipped with the right and wrongs of the past, weathering storms and adapting to changing times. By cultivating a collective memory and learning from the past, the cathedral mind builds resilience for future generations. Imagine tackling climate change with the scientific prowess of our generation but also the accumulated wisdom of past civilizations that thrived in harmony with nature.

Developing a cathedral mind requires dedicated effort. Here are a few pillars to build upon:

- Embrace cross-disciplinary learning: Encourage dialogue and collaboration between seemingly disparate fields. Let artists inspire engineers, and philosophers challenge economists.

- Nurture integral thinking: Encourage questioning assumptions and exploring and integrating diverse perspectives. This fosters intellectual humility and openness to new ideas.

- Build collaborative platforms: Create spaces for open exchange, whether online forums, community workshops, or international summits. Let ideas flow freely and cross-pollinate.

- Repetition as a method to enhance the mind's profound understanding.

Remember, the cathedral mind isn't built overnight. It's a continuous process of collaboration, learning, and building upon your own and each other's strengths. But as we cultivate this collective intelligence, we pave the way for a future where humanity, like a magnificent cathedral, mosque, temple, or forest, stands tall and united and illuminates the path to a brighter tomorrow. All are connected via a naturally formed mycelium network.

To build this grand edifice of collective wisdom, let us begin, brick by intellectual brick. For in our shared understanding lies the key to not only surviving but thriving in the face of the challenges that lie ahead.

As I wrote at the start of this book, all birth starts in darkness, and in darkness, we find our threats that we must overcome. It all starts with ourselves to dig deep and recognize the shadows we carry with us as baggage. These shadows were formed as we grew up; some are severe and detrimental to our health, and some will have less severe shadows, but we all have them. Why do I know they exist? All we need to do is look around us and see the world we have created, which is magnificent, but we also know deep down that it has come at a cost—a cost we can no longer ignore, for we are likely to lose so much of what once was. The process of loss is a gradual one, persistent, and will manifest in grief, subtle but growing each decade. We have to endure and navigate through it. The task ahead will be fraught with peril, making you nauseous.

Transcending Fragmentation: Building the Cathedral Mind with Logos, Pathos, Mythos, Integral Theory for individuals, family and groups and sense-making.

The metacrisis demands minds that exceed the limitations of individual thinking. We need a collective intelligence as vast and enduring as the structures it evokes. This mind, constructed from diverse disciplines and perspectives, offers hope for navigating the complexities of our times.

But how do we cultivate this cathedral mind? How do we integrate the fragmented knowledge and experience into a cohesive whole? Here is where the powerful quartet of logos, pathos, mythos, and integral theory comes into play. It also fits nicely with my earlier reductionist view of civilization as an integrated doughnut supported by three legs.

Logos: The Pillar of Reason and Analysis

Logic and reason form the foundation of the cathedral mind. Scientific inquiry, data analysis, and integral thinking provide the scaffolding upon which all else rests. Logos allows us to understand the intricate workings of the world, from the subatomic level to the vastness of the cosmos.

However, logos holds only one of the legs of civilization. It risks becoming trapped in the minutiae, losing sight of the bigger picture. This is where the other elements come in.

Pathos: The Pillar of Emotion, Empathy and Community

The cathedral mind resonates with the human experience. Pathos, the power of emotions and shared stories, infuses it with empathy and compassion.

Art, literature, music, and personal narratives tap into our collective feelings, allowing us to connect with the human and nature costs of challenges and the potential for positive change.

Narratives for Meaning and Wisdom

Myths and stories are not mere flights of fancy; they are potent tools for meaning-making. Mythos allows the cathedral mind to create narratives that connect the disparate pieces of knowledge into a coherent whole. These narratives provide context, purpose, and inspiration, guiding us toward a shared future vision.

Integral Theory: Bridging the Gaps

Integral theory provides the framework for integrating these seemingly disparate elements. It proposes a multi-level, multi-perspectival understanding of reality, encompassing biological, psychological, social, and spiritual dimensions. By acknowledging the interconnectedness of these levels, integral theory helps us build a cathedral mind that is both comprehensive and nuanced. It would fit nicely into the Doughnut.

What Emerges from the Cathedral Mind?

When logos, pathos, mythos, and integral theory work in concert, something remarkable emerges:

- Holistic wicked problem-solving: By viewing issues from multiple diverse perspectives, the cathedral mind can identify root causes and develop possibilities that address the symptoms and the underlying systems at play.

- Enhanced creativity and innovation: The cross-pollination of ideas from diverse disciplines fosters new possibilities and approaches, leading to breakthroughs in fields ranging from science to art.

- Deeper compassion and understanding: Through shared narratives and empathy, the cathedral mind cultivates a sense of global responsibility and collective action for the betterment of humanity and the planet.

- Resilience and adaptability: By integrating lessons from history and diverse perspectives, the cathedral mind builds adaptability and resilience in the face of ever-changing challenges.

Building the Cathedral Mind: A Continuous Journey

Cultivating the cathedral mind is not a one-time event; it's an ongoing journey of collaboration, learning, and growth. Here are some critical steps we can take:

- Encourage cross-disciplinary learning: Break down silos between disciplines and promote dialogue between scientists, artists, philosophers, engineers, and all walks of life.

- Foster critical thinking and open-mindedness: Question assumptions, explore diverse perspectives, and challenge echo chambers.

- Create platforms for collaboration: Utilize online forums, community workshops, and international summits to exchange ideas and build understanding.

- Embrace diverse narratives: Share stories from different cultures and backgrounds to foster empathy and a more inclusive vision of the future.

- Integrate integral theory frameworks: Utilize integral frameworks in education, leadership training, and organizational development to cultivate holistic thinking.

The cathedral mind is not a utopia but a powerful metaphor for the collective intelligence we need to navigate the complexities of our world. By harnessing the power of logos, pathos, mythos, and integral theory, we can build a future where humanity thrives, not only survives, in harmony with each other and our planet. It's time to start laying the bricks, one thought, one conversation, one collaboration at a time.

ARISE

The world I have painted for you with my words is one that is severely sick. To most, it is not visible, which for some may invoke horror, and for many, something we can ignore like a headache we can dispel with an Asperin or three. Now that I have added the need for us to develop a cathedral mind, it may make you feel dizzy and disorientated. It may even make you nauseous. This is good because you can grasp the enormous change required to develop it. This is a positive development. You may get so nauseous that you may have the feeling of throwing up. Like when you have food poisoning.

Think of it this way: we and the planet are the same Being. The waste sphere is the poison on our planet and is now within the being. The being is starting to feel sick but has no idea from what. Maybe it is a virus or something the being ate or drank. The feeling worsens; the being drinks water from a plastic bottle filled with microplastics, and the nausea won't disappear. The being lies down on a bed and starts to sweat. The Being starts scraping the collective brain, determining what could have caused it. Then comes the realization that the being is going to throw up. It's still distant, a slight rumbling in the beings stomach but strong enough to lift itself from the bed and walk to the bathroom, where the being decides to hang over the toilet bowl. There, the being waits, hoping it will disappear, but the feeling persists. The being does not want to throw up. It hopes it will go away, but no, it gets worse; the final moments are the worst; the being sweats even more to try and cool down, and then there it comes. All the toxins the body wishes to expel explode into the toilet bowl. The being repeats it a few times and slowly starts feeling better. The sour smell swarms its nostrils, and it flushes so the smell goes away. The water, now stagnant, absorbs the toxins. The sweating stops. The being feels strong enough to stand but too weak to leave the bedroom, so the being lies down again. The process repeats for several days, and the being finally discovers that it could have been a virus of 8 Billion souls and you are no longer a part of this Being.

This extreme example can apply to relationships as well—relationships we have with each other and with our nature. I'm not talking about toxicity. I'm referring to the feeling before an event where we feel most vulnerable, no longer have control, and are forced to let events happen as they come. This experience is found in couples as they get to know each other and sometimes between close friends as they reach a stage in their relationship where their vulnerabilities, their weaknesses, perceived or actual, get exposed that will either lead to an eventual breakup or an integration of the relationship into a functional whole. This profound experience lies at the beginning of an awareness that elevates us beyond ourselves. We become one, and we face the challenges united. We see this when small groups meet severe challenges that threaten their survival. Now imagine if that can be scaled beyond the Dunbar number.

For those unfamiliar with the Dunbar number, I offer a brief explanation: The Dunbar number, proposed by anthropologist Robin Dunbar, suggests a cognitive limit of around 150 people with whom we can maintain stable intimate social relationships. Our brains can only handle keeping track of that many people and their connections to each other.

Imagine if we could exceed the Dunbar number so that our civilization becomes whole and agrees that we are all in this together. Assume that was possible. What would that look like? Would we have a Global Commons that could be managed in an integrated participatory democratic governance structure where place, peace, and belonging are planetary health-centric? Do we all agree that our religions are not that different and can unite us in the principles of the Good, The True, and The Beautiful? We agree that an economic system that prioritizes planetary health over profit is better than the current one.

I've often thought about planetary unification ever since watching the first Star Wars movies. My conclusion so far is that we would need multiple inhabited planets of similar collective intelligence competing with each other. One planet united against another, similar to two football teams competing for the World Cup. Planet A vs Planet B. Or our civilization slowly collapses over several decades or even centuries where few people are left. Let's say 2 billion people have survived and built a new civilization from the ruins of the old. A phoenix reborn from the ashes, if you will.

As Albert Einstein once said, A smart person can fix a problem. A wise person prevents it.

Preventing or minimizing collapse remains our only option so far. Transformation of our civilization is inevitable, like it or not, for we have lots still to unlearn. Fortunately, there are many roads to travel to transform a civilization. With a collective cathedral mindset, this may even be possible to accomplish, but be prepared for the long haul, and please keep Moloch at bay until defeated.

We can arise as activists. We don't need to start a revolution, even a peaceful one. People tend to get hurt or, worse, get killed. Let us stick to peaceful activism.

What I have found to be the most effective methods when researching activism are peaceful protests that focus on humanity and our rights and topics that resonate with people at home. Suppose we were to demonstrate the right to live waste-free and without pollution so that it no longer harms us and nature. By focusing on our shared beliefs and what we value most, we can achieve the required change faster. By doing so, the net beneficiary is not us but our planet. Nothing stands out more than the freedom to live a healthy life, free from toxins.

Protesting to make politicians change has hardly ever been effective, even less so with business leaders. Remember that they have their seats to protect. I would advise that protests focus on recruiting the wider public and convincing them that what they are calling attention to affects the public directly but in a way that resonates and is something they can relate to personally. A poster with a bird that has thrown up plastic or a bird cut open to show plastic in her stomach does not make the effects of plastic pollution personal. I know this is sad but true. On average, a person will feel outraged about the state of affairs related to pollution for around an hour. They may even discuss it with friends, and then it quickly simmers away and is forgotten.

Politicians fear one thing the most, no matter which color they represent, and that is when their constituents turn against them. They know they have to change when they start losing large chunks of their support. Politicians do not fear protests; for them, it is a test to see if it will spill over to broader society, and if that happens, when it reaches the tipping point, they will be forced to take action. Gandhi did it, Martin Luther King did it, and the students in Thiamin Square did it. Their protests gained broad support from the public because what they were protesting resonated with the public. Protesting for something is better than demonstrating against something. Americans started pulling out of Vietnam because they were losing the war. The Vietcong under Ho Chi Minh would not give up, and no number of bombs and soldiers would wipe them out. Yes, the anti-Vietnam War protest helped turn public sentiment, but I think newsreels of body counts and the number of injured coming home were more effective. What tipped the scale, in my opinion, were the local communities witnessing firsthand how soldiers struggled when they came home. The main reason the war ended was that The United States could not win this war. It did, however, teach us something important.

Since the vast majority are not experiencing climate change, biodiversity loss, and pollution personally, it is challenging to convince the polarized public of how critical the situation is. One way is to make them feel it. Physically and emotionally. Facts matter, and science can provide the cold facts, but pathos and mythos have the most impact. The closer to home, the better. A starving child around the corner from your house has more of an impact than one on another continent. One thing that unites all humanity is health. We all want to be healthy, and if our nature, food, and water are making us unhealthy because of our waste sphere, then that should be where we start. Health and the right of children to live without waste are universal. Pollution is something everyone understands. We need to change the narrative of greenhouse gas emissions to pollution.

Here are a few suggestions that I could come up with

People have a right to clean water

We have a right to clean air

We have a right to healthy land

No more plastics in my body

No more pesticides in my body

No more forever chemicals in my body

No more heat waves

No more extreme weather

No more floods

No more dirty air

No more polluted rivers

No more plastic beaches

No more landfills

No more burning of waste

Protect our children's health.

Keep our children healthy.

No micro-plastics = healthy children

No Forever chemicals = Healthy children

Don't waste our food

We have a right to healthy food

No more plastics in our food

No more chemicals in our food (meat, vegetables, fish, fruit)

Our waste is affecting our health.

Our waste is polluting our food.

Our waste is polluting our water.

We want more durable products.

We want better quality clothes.

Whatever you choose, ensure the messaging informs the public. Some of these slogans will make people curious and raise their interest. Few people know that we all carry forever chemicals, pesticide residues, and micro and nano plastics in our bodies, causing all sorts of harm. Some will read up on it online. Others will start to talk about it with others. Bad news travels faster than good news. Public opinion will change and will have a direct effect over time. When that happens, politicians will change, and more people will be inclined to support the movement.

We know where the cause is coming from and who is responsible. Focus on the reason, and those responsible will change and be held accountable.

Symbols have always been a powerful communication tool throughout human history. It is a language that is globally understood and simple. Using symbols to address a crisis may be worth investigating to mobilize a global population to act in unison.

Since we discussed Tolkien, who provided us with fantasy mythology, I once again returned to his writing as he deeply understood the power of symbolism.

Legolas was given the Bow of the Galadhrim, a mighty bow that improves aim and increases the speed its arrows leave towards its target. It is meant to symbolize increased singular focus and momentum to neutralize one's enemy. The hobbits were issued silver belts in the book and daggers in the movie—both symbolically mean willpower, courage, and strength. Samwise was given a rope. The symbolic meaning of the rope is to be able to carry on and carry a burden that is thought to be beyond your weight or ability to carry, and yet the rope proves you can, and you can use it time and time again. Gimli was given three strands of Galadriel's hair. A symbol for improving things, to make things better than before. Frodo was given the light of Erendhil, the elves' most beloved star. Symbolically, this means to provide light when you find yourself in total darkness and despair and gives you the courage to confront your worst fears, both external and internal. Aragorn was given a sheath of his sword Anduril and a green gem in a silver brooch. This symbolizes that one should claim one's rightful place on this earth to benefit all who dwell on it and serve and guide one's community to live in harmony and peace with each other and nature.

All were given elven cloaks that changed color based on their surroundings. They kept you warm and cold in any climate, and you could pass hostile territory undetected and even confuse an enemy's aim. Its symbolism is obvious. Be like nature, and nature will protect you from those who seek to harm you. On the flip side, they could also symbolize a way to avoid Sauron's evil eye. So, choose your symbols carefully.

Creating symbols can have enormous power. When everyone understands them, they can be powerful and lasting. The modern peace sign was first used in 1958. Gerald Holtom designed it for the campaign for Nuclear Disarmament. The raised fist, or clenched fist, symbol was first used in Budapest in 1912. It is regarded as the oldest protest symbol and is still seen globally.

Would creating a symbol that would personify humanity's struggle to combat waste and associated health crises be effective? Would the universal symbol of the Tree of Life be effective?

Change does not happen because a leader, in any field, proclaims a solution or desire. That is not what I have found. It's the individuals and small groups of people you have never heard of that initiate change often because of a leader's mistake. Take the example of Ronald Reagan's speech before the Berlin Wall on July 12th 1987. He uttered the now-famous sentence during his speech: "Mr. Gorbachov, Tear Down This Wall." But nothing happened. East Germany was dealing with an exodus of its youth traveling south and trying to cross the Iron Curtain border into Austria. East Germany's political leadership was crumbling, and an inexperienced officer held a press conference to appease the press by saying the Government was working on a solution. A Western journalist asked, but what about The Wall? The officer responded that the Wall would be opened. What he meant was that it would be considered. He messed up. Brave East Berliners tested it out that night and managed to cross the border, thanks to the border guards' confusion as they had not received any orders due to a lack of communication. Mr Gorbachov was sleeping then, and when he awoke and was informed, he decided that it was East Germaqny's problem, not his. The officer became famous for just a moment. I don't think people today know his name: Gunther Schabowski, and the first East Berliners that crossed the border that night remain nameless.

HEALING

How do we heal our relationship with Nature?

All these examples of the destruction of nature have one thing in common: we have distanced ourselves from nature so much that we have lost our intimate connection with it. As explained in the chapter on governance, it all started with a little plant. Our colonizer mind is a mind of manipulation; we remove the complexity from Nature and make it complicated so we can measure, manage, and control it. We build boundaries around what we have manipulated so we keep complexity out. In the case of Wolves and monkeys, it's guns; with sharks, it's overfishing for scalene that you put on your face and lips; with Birds, it's called pollution; and with flies, we use insecticide. It's universal.

We should restore nature and increase biodiversity. In that case, we will eventually also see the return of species that belong in that ecosystem, which means that interactions between humans and animals will become commonplace. I, for one, can't wait to see it happen. For these interactions to be safe for both us and the species, we have to be able to control our instincts. No matter where we live, humans can kill any animal. There is no need to prove that anymore.

Elephants are intelligent animals with strong bonds to their family members. They have emotions proven long ago as they mourn for the loss of their kin. They have fun when you see them having a mud bath. They are social beings. When they first encountered humans, they were not scared. They knew that no animal could kill them. However, when we started killing them like fish in a barrel, they quickly learned to fear us, and they still do. This is learned behavior. All wild animals will try to avoid us unless a particular need or lack of a critical resource like food or water requires them to venture into territory that was once theirs. Farmers in Kenya and Tanzania often complain of Elephants ransacking their fields full of crops. Considering that this region has suffered from drought for a long time, it is natural that farmers are protecting their water sources.

When wolves were reintroduced in Yellowstone Park, we witnessed a remarkable restoration within the ecosystem as they restored the balance so all species could thrive. All these examples amplify the fact that rewilding is essential to restoring ecosystems. Planting trees is okay, but one should always factor in the impact on the ecosystem.

So, for biodiversity to have a chance, we should learn to become emotionally attached to our fellow species. With emotional attachment comes compassion and love. That's why people who work with animals love them so much and find it hard to part from them. It is as if a relationship was imprinted in them through their interactions.

We are far from reaching emotional attachment with our species. One example is when people petition an animal species to obtain "personhood," meaning these animals have the same rights as humans. We approach this from our perspectives. We are still a species that seeks to control as opposed to serving. We have yet to master the skill of being in service to our fellow species. We like whales, so we should protect them and give them rights. Why not for all species? The answer, of course, is that this will be impossible to enforce, and it is unrealistic because we could be arrested for the murder of a fly. The mindset is based on protection and enforcement, yet one should ask oneself: Why is enforcement needed in the first place? Achieving emotional connectedness to our fellow species is the only answer, and enforcement is no longer required when that is achieved. One would show respect when an animal has to be put down, or a tree has to lose some branches so people may continue to pass by without getting hurt from falling branches.

The last item I wish to address is viruses. We know that viruses can skip from one species to another. COVID-19 and Ebola are good examples. Becoming one with nature increases the risks of other viruses not known to us that could affect us and cause detrimental health issues. We need to be prepared for this if we are to restore our biodiversity with continued human population growth. That's why I recommend we spend more on prevention research than research that focuses on understanding. Evidence and reason can often estimate risk well, but only a value judgment can determine acceptable risk.

"Easy for you to say." I work in a skyscraper on the 28th floor and live in a high-rise apartment in the city. I don't have an elephant in the room, so how can I connect?" Good question; asking this question is a good start. It's easy; all you have to do is become aware of nature. I'm sure there are botanical gardens, nature areas, and parks where you live. Go there and observe nature, look for insects and birds. Do this often enough, and you start to get a feel for the place; you will find familiarity with what your fellow species are doing while you are there. And if you are fortunate, you may even experience a curious squirrel or a bird paying you a visit and check you out.

Another option is to have a plant in your home or place of work; for professionals, I recommend a plant at work, in your office, or on your desk. If you are a mobile worker, i.e., you don't have a fixed desk, which is common, your place of residence is an excellent start to keep a plant. If you feel confident, buy a lovely leafy plant; if you are not confident or a mobile worker who travels a lot, buy a cactus, but one that flowers. Take care of it like it's your most-priced possession. Don't let anyone else care for it. It is your plant. If it dies, you apologize, dispose of it respectfully, and start over until you get it right. Let's see if you can make it flower for those with cacti. Cacti need special conditions to flower. If something is off, they won't. Take it as a challenge and reward yourself if, after a year, your plant has grown. It is funny when you take care of something, you automatically get attached to it.

People can do this all over the world. It's not difficult, but reading about it and doing it is a big step. Connecting with nature is part of the healing process that humanity has to pass through to become regenerative. He who eliminates waste shall find much reward in himself and nature. It only takes one action to make a difference and progress from there.

How do we heal our relationship with society?

To be able to heal is first to identify the root cause. I would argue that the root cause is manipulation, humanity's modus operandi since its dawn when it still lived in Hunter-Gatherer tribes. I would argue that manipulation lies at the core of the metacrisis. What I mean by manipulation is our ability to make the complex complicated. This has been a key necessity for our survival. It cannot be denied, but once we understand that this manipulation caused unintended consequences, we can reframe the problem at its core. It requires a new form of governance and, in this case, a new governance structure for the medical health industry. Suppose we don't transform healthcare fundamentally from maintaining mental health issues via medication to healing mental health permanently. In that case, this will be the number one illness of the 21st century, like cancer was the illness of the 20th century.

We know the causes, as I've described, and we also know the possibilities. Still, because of Moloch, we are stuck in races that undermine our ability to implement these possibilities. The medical sector has yet to unite, using a cathedral mindset to overcome this health crisis. As with our relationship with nature, we like to shoot first and ask questions later. Instead of taking the time with patients who are suffering from mental health issues, we are quick to prescribe medication. That's how pharmaceutical companies make profits and recover research and development costs. The more they sell, the more profits they earn, making their shareholders rich. The doctors and therapists who prescribe these medicines are stuck in the same trap because they have to provide a living for themselves and their families. Who suffers? The patient because the root causes are not being treated. The objective of the medical profession, once well understood during the shamanic healing traditions of old, was to cure permanently, like setting a broken bone and alleviating pain during the process of giving birth. Medicines were temporary as a support mechanism to heal a patient permanently through additional health support.

Today, medications are prescribed to keep the patient addicted. This is a consequence of our manipulation mindset. Keeping a patient on medication is more profitable than curing their illness. The task before us requires us to change how the medical industry is governed fundamentally. It needs to transform into a structure that prioritizes curing before profit. To do this, Moloch has to be defeated. Once defeated, a new healthcare structure may emerge where there are no more defectors.

An example would be starting with a transformed patient intake process. Instead of filling out a form that takes at most 20 minutes, we should expand the intake process to 3 to 5 hours, followed by 2 to 3 sessions more. The expanded time will allow health professionals to conduct a deep dive into the domain of manipulation and diagnose if their mental issues stem from other people, like family, school, work, or society, or are from the use of many daily technologies that they use such as processed food and drinks, vicinity to harmful substances like plastics, forever chemicals, pesticides or other forms of pollution within our wastesphere. Could the issues stem from technology use, such as online social platforms, games, and AI, or excessive use of the hardware these games, applications, and platforms run on? I could go on as there could be many causes, many of which I have already captured in previous chapters, where humanity's manipulation of our world has resulted in negative consequences that may be affecting our mental health. Treating the root causes with the primary objective of curing people is the solution. This may take a generational approach; hence, the dominant harmful pursuit of quick fixes should be subdued.

Healing the Relationship with Your Mind and Body.

Once you realize that society, technology, the use of medication or drugs, doctors, and therapists are only there to support you as part of your healing process and obtaining the ultimate cure, it is you who must do the most work. All healing starts with the realization that something is wrong and worse. The feeling that you are sick. The second part is acceptance, and the third is the motivation to seek help. Is this easy? Not. If it were, there wouldn't be an intervention often initiated by your closest friends and family.

The hardest part of dealing with mental health is confronting it. Part of the integral theory regarding the I in the upper left quadrant is to conduct a clean-up or what others call shadow work, where you draw out the manifestations of Moloch. You draw it out, give it a seat opposite you, and start a conversation with it. You ask it questions like what, why, when, and where to get to know it, like you would with an enemy. You decided to get to know it better to detect its weaknesses and learn how to control it. It's a skill you have because it has been passed to you through generations. The art of manipulation for good resides within you. Once you have confronted the shadow, you can absorb it once more, learn to live with it, and recognize how it tries to manipulate you.

At first, this could be a horrifying experience, and by horrifying, I mean a complete disorientation of who you are and an inability to make sense of things. So, do not start by yourself. Have someone with you who can reassure you. A professional would be best. No One takes Ayahuasca by themselves unless you are an idiot. A one-to-one session with someone you trust entirely can help draw out your shadows one by one if you can engage in a flow-state dialogue.

The flow state is a powerful and elusive experience characterized by complete absorption in the present moment. The flow state is gaining traction within the medical community, and 30 to 50 years from now, people will laugh at the following paragraphs as the flow state will likely be a condition that can be invoked with little effort.

Imagine yourself fully immersed in an activity where time melts away, and your mind becomes one with the task. You perform effortlessly, almost instinctively, driven by intrinsic motivation rather than external rewards. Challenges feel stimulating rather than daunting, and your focus narrows, filtering out distractions and worries. Thoughts cease to be internal chatter and instead blend seamlessly with your actions. A sense of joy and peace washes over you, fueled by the sheer pleasure of being fully engaged. In this state, your self-awareness fades, replaced by a deep connection to the activity and a sense of mastery over it. When you finally emerge from the flow, you feel energized, fulfilled, and delighted by the experience, with a lasting sense of accomplishment and clarity.

All healing processes that you can do starts with one small step after another. Think of it as a journey where, once you have started, you can, at some point, look back and see how far you have traveled and what you have accomplished. However, as we've seen with the COVID pandemic, people have started to wake up and realize that they were living hollow lives under the rule of a massive political and economic machine that no longer serves their best interests. Many have tried to break this hold, as we saw with the great resignation period during the pandemic, where hundreds of thousands of people left their jobs and careers either to find another meaningful job or change their pursuits to a new life of meaning. This change also came with a feeling of guilt, perhaps not conscious in most but certainly deep down, where many experienced the feeling that something has to change and we can no longer continue as we are Because if we do, we are all fucked. This realization, in some cases, led to anxiety and despair, so the road towards healing is not an easy one. Part of the journey is acknowledging those feelings and forgiving yourself. Similar to the process of shadow work described earlier.

Think also from the perspective of the cathedral mind to generational thinking where what you embody in health inherited from your ancestors can be improved so that the generations after you can improve on it further. That is how wisdom accelerates generationally. It is time we attune to this mode of being. It will make you feel better. It certainly worked for me.

Your body is a great teacher. Each cell has a neighbor and combined form a function; some become organs, all tasked with specific specializations controlled by the mind and vice versa. Each cell and organ has a sense of place, a deep connection to its function and purpose. This sounds philosophical, but it also makes biological sense. Research has shown that the microbiota in your gut directly influences your brain. Your hormonal balance regulates your feelings and emotions, and from it springs the mind. You would want to avoid any disruption in this balance so when you think of the wastesphere; you understand the risks we face. The mind cannot function properly if the body is unhealthy, and vice versa. And we have a lot of work to do on our minds. The most powerful aspect of who we are is our mind. It's from our mind where all is created and understood. However, we have been misusing it for quite some time, or perhaps a better way of saying it is we have started to suppress half of our brain with our mind, and it's time we reversed it.

For humanity to survive, we not only need a whole new manner of thinking, but we also need to heal and embrace the wonders of our world.

OPPORTUNITIES

"Waste is not waste until you waste it."

Will.I.Am from the Black Eyed Peas musical group is credited with this statement:

Brilliant from a guy whose music I sometimes listen to on SoundCloud and Spotify. For me, at least, it opened my mind. What if we could turn the waste we emit into our air, water, and land into value? Ideas are formed, possibilities are found, and because there are so many of us, I'm convinced there will be people who will come up with new ideas to eliminate our wastefulness.

When we acquire a skill, it eventually becomes part of our subconscious. Take, for example, learning how to ride a bicycle. At first, you consciously struggle with balance and try to keep your bike straight on the road so you don't crash into a tree. You learn how to turn left and right, when to speed up, and when to brake. All this learning happens consciously until you have mastered the skill. After that, it becomes part of your subconscious, and riding a bike becomes as easy as walking. We don't think about it. Ryding a bike becomes part of our subconscious, instinctive behavior.

To eliminate waste, we should first learn not to waste anymore and develop products and services that cause no harm. Once that has been accomplished, will we become genuinely regenerative?

Humanity can do almost anything with the power of imagination and wisdom. We are opportunistic by nature. We should stop manipulating ourselves, our civilization, and our nature. Manipulation is a crucial tenet of our being, and we should learn to control it and transform it into a benevolent tenet. As we have argued, technology drives our behavior, not vice versa. Technology is controlled and operated by technology companies ranging from agricultural tech, food tech, consumer goods tech, pharmaceutical tech, automotive, information, and digital tech, stuck in competitive races for dominance that is increasingly poorly regulated. This has to change.

We can see more and more innovations from creative people being developed and implemented. These technologies are for the benefit of our well-being. A shift is happening, nascent, and seeds have been planted, ready to spring to life and see a new light. On the other hand, the Old World continues to destroy itself, blindly following the path that will ultimately lead to its inevitable self-termination as the systems we depend on collapse. The global AI race is well on its way, and since we have proven countless times that our civilization ignores the risks in pursuit of wealth, it will lead to another catastrophe. Another stock market collapse is inevitable. We keep pumping more money into the system to maintain growth. With the latest drive to define value to an evolutionary way of life, which represents Nature, and convert it into an asset class, we can continue our obligation to pay off the debts of the previous crisis, which only accelerates our demise. It is sad in a way that we still need the old world; the technology and the processes. To change will take time, hence the need for a cathedral mindset. The pain and suffering that come with this change will depend on how long it will take for us to cross the chasm of adopting a new way of life.

We are witnessing more and more innovation in material science, where our agricultural waste is transformed into alternative products to replace the more harmful ones. There are so many examples now, which is encouraging, and it is only a matter of time before these new materials come to scale. Some examples are Avocado seeds, Bagasse, Banana skin, and Pinanple tops, which used to be discarded and turned into biodegradable plastic. We see increased use of seaweed and fungi as a source for replacing single-use plastics, and the list goes on.

CO2 emissions are used as a source to make other products like diamonds. They are considered some of the most precious materials used for many applications. You and I know diamonds from being used in jewelry, but they are used for so many other things. How about outfitting your house with diamond windows? Too much? Or as a screen protector for your mobile phone? Better?

Diamonds are made from carbon, heat and pressure deep inside our Earth's crust. They are the hardest material known to man. On Mohs scale that measures the relative hardness of material from 1 to 10, a diamond is rated as 10. There are now a few companies that make diamonds from our CO2 emissions. A company claims that for each 1-carat diamond they produce, 20 tons of CO2 is removed from the atmosphere. They are working to become a fully carbon-negative operation in the next few years, aiming to pull 100 million tons of CO2 from the atmosphere within ten years. Source: earth.com

That would mean that this company would produce 5 million carats in 10 years.

Creating a diamond begins with atmospheric collectors pulling air in and capturing the CO_2 in a special filter. That CO_2 is synthesized into hydrocarbon raw material. The material is then placed into reactors, which create the perfect environment for diamond growing, which takes about three to four weeks. The raw diamond is then sent to diamond cutters to be cut and polished and then to goldsmiths to set into gold and platinum jewelry. They source their energy from renewable sources.

The diamond industry would have a fit with this. They fought for years against synthetic diamonds. Imagine the outcry when they finally become aware of diamonds being made from our CO_2 emissions. The value or the appreciation of diamonds would plummet. Diamonds would become worthless. Who would want to wear a diamond from the emissions that caused our climate to change? Or one could argue that the diamond bought as a gift contributed to climate action.

Don't worry about the Beers and the Diamond Jewelry Industry. Most diamonds are useful elsewhere. They are used in industries for drilling and cutting purposes. They are used in the automotive industry, medicine, audio equipment, and heat sinks. If these diamonds become more readily available, I'm sure there will be scientists or engineers who come up with other applications that are beneficial to us and nature. Finally, they can be reused, and if they are processed in a Zero-Waste system, and micro-nano particles don't end up in us and our fellow species, we may have found an elegant solution to rid ourselves of 1.15 trillion metric tons of excess CO_2. That would be around 57.5 billion carats that could be produced. Or if you all line them up, it would be 368000 Kilometers long. The circumference of the Earth is 40075 Kilometers. You could wrap this diamond necklace 9.18 times around the planet.

We have vast quantities of excess CO_2 ready to be harvested from our atmosphere.

It currently takes 1200 kWh to remove one metric ton of CO_2 from the atmosphere and about 650 – 1100 kWh to grow a 1-carat diamond. Total energy use would be 23100 kWh for every 1 carat. This does not include the energy used for synthesizing, for which I could not find any data. As I said, it takes a lot of energy, mostly from direct air capture. An average house uses between 9000 and 12000 kWh of energy per year. As long as the CO_2 is captured from the atmosphere and not directly supplied by fossil fuel companies and as long as the energy sources used are renewable, such as solar, hydro, wind, and other replenishable nonharmful fuels, then we may be able to use that material for value, if we stop our greenhouse gas emissions. Energy use needs to become more efficient if Harvesting CO2 from the atmosphere is to be a viable solution to lower Atmospheric CO2 concentrations.

Let's be clear: I do not favor carbon capture technology as an excuse for the fossil fuel and dependent industries to keep emitting greenhouse gases, especially how it is discussed today, where captured CO2 from our air is forever dumped underground. I agree with Al Gore and many experts that carbon capture technology will not stabilize the atmospheric system.

Another point worth stressing is that our Energy demand is also not sustainable. While wind, water, and sun are renewable energy sources, the technology to harness these renewable sources is not. Today, we are replacing one energy mineral with another, and again, we are not factoring in the externalities and causal effects that this will cause from Coal to Oil to Gas to Nickel, Cobalt, and Silica. You may be familiar with the Jevon's papadox. If you are not here, here is a short explanation. The Jevons paradox, also known as the rebound effect, is a counterintuitive economic phenomenon. It states that increases in resource use efficiency can lead to an overall increase in resource consumption. This happens because when a resource becomes cheaper due to increased efficiency, people tend to use more of it, often negating or even exceeding the initial gains in efficiency.

An urgent topic that needs to be discussed is reducing energy demand per capita over time. We can do this by extracting less because we produce longer-lasting products that do not harm nature because they are processed and exposed responsibly globally. The key is global, for if we had one defector, Moloch would have won again.

Biodiversity expansion opportunities.

My grandfather belonged to a group of Dutch entrepreneurs. They were called the Leather Barons and dominated the market from the 1930s till the early 1970s. My grandfather was forced to produce army boots for the Germans during the war. This made my grandfather an excellent recruit for the Dutch resistance movement. For one, he reduced the quality of the boots so they wouldn't last. He argued that high-quality material was hard to come by and that half his highly skilled employees had been shipped to Germany to work there. Second, he was allowed to travel from border to border to distribute the boots. His truck had a secret bottom where he could hide downed pilots and transport them to the coast, where U-boats would pick them up and take them back to England.

These barons prided themselves in producing the highest quality footwear. What they produced was meant to last forever. My father and his brothers inherited the business, and soon, the health of their business began to decline in the 60s. Not because they were bad managers but because they resisted the urge to change their supply from high-quality leather and soles to cheaper materials sourced abroad. They also resisted the urge to offshore production to less expensive, lower-skill production centers. Technological innovation made this possible as machines could now replace the labor-intensive aspects of production. Cheap, lower-quality, mass-produced shoes soon flooded the market. My father and his brothers lost market share and profits, ultimately leading to the business's demise.

Some of the brothers survived by partnering with the Italians, known for high-quality shoes in the 60s and 70s. Thanks to the Mafia and large Italian population centers in the USA, the high-quality, more expensive shoe market survived, but it was much smaller than it once was. My father went to Africa to set up leather-centric production facilities and later returned and started a successful industrial footwear and personal safety equipment manufacturing company. His primary clients came from Germany. Adaptation runs deep inside my family.

Since the 1950s, the world has focused on efficiency and cost. At the end of the 20th century and the beginning of this century, it was cool to be Six Sigma black belt certified, and transformation focussed on efficiency, and customer service was a booming business. Let's reverse this and start focussing on quality to last. With all our knowledge now related to efficiency, we could utilize this to produce higher quality, long-lasting products that would significantly reduce demand for raw materials and energy. These products may be more expensive initially, but my grandfather, smoking his favorite 18cm long Montecristo during a rainy Sunday afternoon, told me something I never forgot.

"Would you rather buy a pair of shoes that cost $100 that would last for three years, or would you prefer to buy a pair of shoes that cost $30 that only last six months?"

My Uncles adopted my grandfather's advice and effectively used it in their marketing campaigns—quality over quantity. In nature, it should now be evident that we should focus more on quality based on the principle of built-to-last versus fast, cheap consumption quantity. It will take guts, ingenuity, and innovation, but we don't have to reinvent the wheel. My forefathers understood this way before consumption became a planetary predicament as a key driver of economic growth.

As of 2024, we are stuck in a biodiversity race to the bottom where $800Bn is allocated each year to restore our Biodiversity while a total of $7 Trillion worth of activity is involved in extracting Biodiversity to meet our needs. We have yet to reach a stage where our Biodiversity is expanding on a global scale, and yet the awareness that Biodiversity expansion is a must is emerging. The challenge is how our Biodiversity will adapt to a changing climate. Adaption is not well understood. We know that Biodiversity does not adapt as fast as the current rate of climate change. We also know climate change will risk food supplies as weather patterns change. I emphasize here that humanity is part of our Biodiversity.

To illustrate the amount of action required to restore our Biodiversity and reach a sustainable level, I refer to a paper published on January 10th, 2024, called Mapping the Planet's Critical Areas for Biodiversity and Nature's Contribution to People. This paper concludes that we must restore 49% of our land area to support 90% of the Global Population. This report details how much effort is needed to restore our planet's Biodiversity and, by extension, Earth's health to sustain us.

The only way to reach 49% is to reduce our resource demand for raw materials. The 2024 Resource forecast report by the United Nations Environmental Program forecasted raw material extraction to grow by 60% by 2060. In the last 50 years, we have tripled our consumption of raw materials, devastating ecosystems. To increase Biodiversity, we should increase the lifetime of all technologies available to us. By technologies, I mean everything artificial. This will require significant design, manufacturing, distribution, use, and disposal innovation. This requires the following processes. End-to-end lifecycle assessments include 2nd, 3rd, and 4th level causal analysis and end-to-end extended lifecycle management. A product's durability is doubled or tripled; ideally, it lasts a lifetime.

Technology for good.

I hope by now that you understand that our use of technology has reached a stage where it is causing our civilization's collapse. The power of our technology can be put to positive use. Despite the social stress it has produced, it can also warn us of impending threats. News can inform us within seconds of emergencies. One of the critical capabilities we can adopt from our current digital technology is to use it for better decision-making.

Better decision-making means we have to take a neutral stance in using information. To improve decision-making, we should be open to aggregating all the available knowledge on one topic and the associated claims. We have to include the extreme claims and investigate if there are any truths to these claims.

We can use AI technology to provide a concise output that has eliminated all the biases, even those of the people operating the system.

We are seeing an emergence in the use of this type of technology. News and information feeds are optimized to provide both sides of the story. Algorithms and additional AI capabilities are used to balance the information you consume and are no longer based on likes, screen time, and other limbic hijacking techniques. The objective is to break the echo chambers many people are trapped in. Watching videos on YouTube of Policemen beating up people only provides a one-sided view of reality. Watching people beating up police officers on YouTube provides another reality. While any violence should be reduced or eliminated, my point is if you are fed both types of videos, you can form a more objective view and quickly realize that the central premise of violence in society is the issue, not the people and not the Police as separate groups.

Another use gaining traction is the advisory capacity this approach enables. Decision-makers can analyze different perspectives and even break persistent biases and beliefs when presented with a complete 360 overview that leads to a well-founded conclusion. This has enormous benefits to policymakers and legislators as it provides a method of digesting information objectively and reduces the influence of Public Relations firms and lobbyists. The Society Library, a not-for-profit organization in the United States, is an excellent example of this initiative.

There are many more, and I'm giving these examples to stimulate your imagination of how our technology can be used for our well-being in all sectors. The last one I will provide is networking technology, where you can better understand people's perspectives and influences. Take a politician. We are used to journalists informing us about politicians' behavior, both positive and negative, although, in our current society, negative news tends to claim the front page. Imagine if you could access a political representative's network. While this could pose privacy issues, we could still use their public profile to map out who they are connected to and who influences them. This could extend to as far as the organizations that are funding them. All this can help you understand their familiarity, views, and opinions on any particular topic without listening to them. This technology has been used for several years inside companies to map out relationships between employees and who influences them to various degrees. This can be done for good but sadly also for nefarious purposes, so I would tread this development carefully until a proper governance structure is implemented.

Our most challenging predicament is becoming waste managers.

Believe it or not, waste has value once you remove its harmful effects. Many are discovering how our waste can be converted into value that would regeneratively benefit the planet and humanity.

When you work as a management consultant, an age-old technique is sometimes used to change a client's perspective. It's pretty simple. Here is an example.

Imaginary discussion between client and consultant:

Client: "Human-caused CO2 emissions are a dangerous waste product from burning oil and coal, causing climate change, and must be reduced to zero."

Consultant: "What if I told you that CO2 emissions caused by humans from burning oil and coal are of value and can be used to make products that do not cause harm to humans, our ecosystems, and the climate?

Human-caused CO2 emissions are evil and must be reduced to save us. This is the consensus of the majority on Earth. The client would most likely be amongst them, thinking or saying that the consultant was mad and insane and should be fired. On the face of it, the client is correct.

CO2 emissions can be converted into products, and here are some examples of where these human-caused CO2 emissions are being used as feedstock: Fertilizer, Alcohol, Straws and Cutlery, Soap, Watches, and Fuel. This market is still tiny but will likely grow once we solve a few challenges.

1. *Making these products requires energy, and as long as we keep using fossil fuels that emit CO2, these products are not likely to grow fast unless renewable energy sources replace fossil fuels.*

2. *Any product produced must not cause unintended harmful consequences for everything on our planet. The following principles need to be applied.*

   a. *The rule of thermodynamics must be evaluated with any production process that uses waste, energy, supporting materials, the economic system, energy waste, produced waste, and recycling.*

   b. *Any non-biological nutrients introduced to nature do not cause harm.*

   c. *An end-to-end lifecycle assessment is mandatory.*

   d. *A complete lifecycle management process must be implemented and reported upon to be amended and improved upon when needed.*

   e. *Any waste produced is suitable for planetary crisis mitigation and adaptation, such as rising sea levels.*

f. Social justice factors such as inequality, abuse, and discrimination, to name a few, need to be avoided.

3. *Cost of the product: Market leaders will do everything they can to keep their market leadership and beat these products on price.*

4. *Availability of resources. Materials needed in support of production may not be as readily available. We see this to a certain degree in our current energy transition and electrification process.*

The best example is how waste can be converted into a product of high value that can never again cause harm to our planet.

A lot of effort is currently being made at start-ups sourcing waste to make products. Agricultural waste is another opportunity and requires more development as many of the products produced from It contain chemicals and plasticizers. It is unacceptable if we don't know the chemicals they contain and if they are safe.

Industrial and municipal waste to make new products is another opportunity, and I'm not talking about capturing Methane from Landfills. Not all are produced within a zero-waste system during its entire lifecycle. There will be waste, but we have an opportunity to minimize this. As Mark Twain said, "Continuous improvement is better than delayed perfection."

What would be awesome is to create a Zero-Waste or a regenerative label tag when a product meets the regenerative criteria, which is simple: The product will never cause harm to humans and nature from sourcing to end-of-life and final disposal.

Coming back to the client. Is it possible to turn a substance we regard as waste into a valuable product with the condition that it does no further harm?

What I found interesting is that products made from what we emit can be measured using a global productivity standard that is not used today. This is the waste elimination standard, which would be something like this: This product removed X tons of waste and what has already been emitted. For example, 1 liter of alcohol removed X tons of waste, or 1 ton of packaging material removed X tons of bagasse (sugarcane waste). Industrial waste that remains after recycling and is used for land reclamation or sea level rise adaptation removes X ton of waste for every square kilometer of sea wall. If we were to use waste as a metric in metric tons that is removed from our wastesphere, we can measure progress and reap the benefits, which is to restore the health of our planetary spheres. We should all become waste managers.

I'm aware that I'm discussing the extract part as part of a product development cycle. But rest assured, we are talking about extracting our current waste pile.

Opportunity: removing plastics, pesticides, and forever chemicals from our Biosphere.

This topic is challenging, especially when it comes to our ocean. We need to focus on this topic urgently. For rivers, I see no other way than to have water treatment facilities installed to filter out all these harmful substances globally. The technology is available, and biotechnology is a promising field to provide low-cost solutions. The water filtration market will be worth USD 33.65 billion in 2023 and 54.48 billion by 2030. The challenge is to make it accessible to countries that need them the most. As for the ocean, we have no other option but to continue to clean it up as best we can, even the microplastics, for if we don't, there will be no fish left to eat safely and no birds left for nature documentaries. The reason I say this while I'm writing this is that I see no global progress to eliminate plastic from our lives. We should focus on cleaning the ocean rather than conducting more research. We already know how bad it is. Should we continue to explore the ocean depths?

I often see the words, just transition, regarding energy and emissions transition. While there is merit in such a method, I strongly advise this transition to factor in how much of that adds to our waste pile during the entire lifecycle. Don't forget to responsibly dispose of end-of-life solar panels and wind energy blades. I still see these items ending up in trash heaps or buried underground.

How do we become waste managers?

How do you become a waste manager yourself? Educators, speakers, advisors, and specialists can teach you until they're blue in the face, but real change doesn't take hold until people change what they do. Plenty has already been written about reducing waste in books ranging from Zero Waste Society to all sustainability books. But in today's predicament, we need to go deeper, and that is in the way we use language. As described in the chapter Logos, Pathos, and Mythos, we need new stories to change our thinking and behavior.

Consider some practical examples below if you are a solutioneer and a nexus problem finder. Combined with storytelling, you could immensely improve the results from outcome-driven solution targets.

There are ten things that you can do to become a waste manager and help others become one, too.

1. Focus on the one and start from there. Choose one item that ends up as waste that you have complete control over, and apply the Zero-Waste principle.

Examples:

Pick one item

- Shower: Use the shower to make yourself wet. Close the tap, soap yourself in, and rinse your body. You will save water that ends up in a wastewater treatment plant.

- Finish your plate, and if you can't save it for later

- Give your shoes a 2ⁿᵈ life by having it made new in a shoe repair shop

- Wear your old T-shirts as pajamas; it's not as sexy lingerie, but I'm sure your partner will find a way to undress you.

- Pick three pieces of clothing and have a tailor make a new piece for you. It's incredible how a pair of jeans looks when made from three older ones. You may even start a new fashion trend.

- Buy less products with plastic wrapped around them.

- Put different kinds of fruit in one plastic bag instead of three.

    Anyway I hope you will find your own

For example, where I live, people buy instant noodles in plastic packs. Some people buy 20 packs at a time. My girlfriend used to do that every time we went grocery shopping until I showed her that you could buy a whole kilo in a single bag in another aisle. This single instant noodle packet adds spices and chili to yet more plastic sachets. We have these at home but in bigger bottles. She also learned that buying one kilo made no difference in preparing our food in terms of time. So, instead of throwing 60 pieces of plastic in the bin that ended up in a landfill in a month, she threw only one empty bag and two bottles of glass.

- Ask your favorite burger restaurant not to add lettuce and tomatoes if you will not eat them.

- If you don't eat the salad garnish with your meal, ask them not to add it to your order.

- If your kids can't finish their plate, eat it yourself. Or save it and have them eat it later. I know this might be tough, but I don't need to remind you that Food waste is a major issue. I see mothers still eating their kid's unfinished food in some countries.

- Buy less fruit and vegetables if you find them thrown in the trash.

- Avoid buying single-use drink bottles if you can buy a bigger one. It's cheaper.

- Buy clothes made from plant material that doesn't contain polyester, or buy a leather jacket made from grapes and husk waste.

- Watch TV in the dark and experience the cinema experience.

You can pick one item to start with. Once it becomes a habit, start with another, and so forth. Ultimately, you can implement a Zero-Waste policy in your household over time.

1. Set a goal and make it measurable.

2. Buy no new clothes or shoes this spring unless you have nothing to wear.

3. Delay the purchase of your next mobile phone by one year.

4. Drive your Tesla for another two years.

5. Extend the lifetime of your purchase as long as you can.

6. Measure energy consumption monthly and try to reduce it.

7. Visualize. Picture yourself covered in waste you have thrown in the trash for one week. Better yet, throw the garbage on your bed and sleep in it with eggshells. You see waste where it does not belong, which taps into your emotions and drives change. Repeat it for nine weeks and see how much trash you have reduced.

8. Your community. When you see someone throw a candy, burger wrapper, vape, or any item on the ground, pick it up, preferably with a tissue, carry it, and when you find a bin, throw it in there. When the waster sees you smile, show them the item that was discarded recklessly and wish them a good day. Social comparison theory shows that we look to others for guidance as to acceptable behavior.

9. Mobilize. Embracing a new behavior typically follows an adoption curve: early adopters, early followers, safe followers, and latecomers. However, there is a gap between early adopters and followers, called the chasm. You will need influencers to bridge the gap between early adopters and early followers. These people have the most informal connections and those to whom others look for directions. You find these influencers in schools, businesses, and any organization, even online. When you have enough early followers, the safe followers and latecomers gradually come on board without much effort.

10. Change the flow. When you make a shopping list, buy healthy food first. Don't follow the supermarket aisles and then choose the item on your list based on the aisle you are in. Leave the snacks and unhealthy food for last and ask yourself. Do I really need those snacks? Changing how you buy from healthy to not-so-healthy things makes you aware of what you also waste.

11. Subtract, not add. Stop buying or using one thing that you can do without. I want candy before dinner, for example. Remember to focus on what you waste. Delete those selfies that are the same from your phone.

12. Incentives: Treat yourself if you save money by delaying a purchase or extending the lifetime of a product. Tell yourself, if I don't buy clothes this spring, I can spend a weekend in the woods with my boyfriend where there is no WIFI access. You'll have unforgettable sex if he is any good.

13. Teach and coach well. Many behaviors have a skill dimension. Doing by example is an excellent teaching method. Explaining why you are doing it also helps.

14. Hire and Fire. Unfortunately, you will find friends and family that will not cooperate. When it comes to family, hire help to find someone they can listen to. With your friends, you could opt to fire them as your friend if the hiring process does not work. I know this sounds cruel, but remember, we have a crisis to solve, and sometimes drastic measures are required.

What is critical is that your actions need to be incentivized. When you pick an action, make sure you incentivize yourself. The easiest is if you can save costs. Reward yourself and go to the beach for a weekend. Start small and see where it leads. It may surprise you how easy it is. Ultimately, the more waste you eliminate, the more you save.

From a personal perspective to businesses and organizations.

How many of you working in companies or institutions like schools or government departments have a zero-waste policy? Some companies have, I'm sure. When we understand that what we as humans emit in waste; GHG, food waste, building waste, agricultural waste, water waste, plastic, pesticides, and chemicals is all connected, it should make sense that we can have a zero-waste policy everywhere. I think sustainability officers would be able to develop one. If you are an SME, start and don't wait for the law to come to you. What would happen to corporate social responsibility (CSR) and environmnetal social and governance (ESG) guidelines and reporting when not GHG but waste was the key metric we were dealing with in addition to reducing the need for valuable resources like water and nature? I do not see why we would not be able to do this. Businesses should consider the implementation of zero-waste as an opportunity that could be stimulated through incentives, like what we can do on an individual level. Businesses grow when the opportunity presents itself and the right incentives are developed. The net beneficiary is your health and that of the planet.

One other vital facet to consider is product development in a zero-waste world. The most straightforward example I can find is the tobacco industry. Sorry, yes, you guys again. 1.3 billion people still smoke in the world today. Eighty-two million vape smokers are included. That's a lot of cigarettes and vapes, which, by all accounts, end up as waste. I'm not here to ask you to stop smoking. Remember, the dose makes the poison. What I do have an issue with is twofold.

1. Cigarettes contain 7000 chemicals, and vapes contain 2000 chemicals. Not all of these have been tested for human and nature's safety, so we don't know what we are pumping into our bodies and in nature, but we now know what health effects smoking can cause. They are not dissimilar from what we find in the plastics, chemicals, and pesticides we ingest from other products. In essence, smokers are Lab rats. Poisoning ourselves is our choice, but creating waste from smoking is unacceptable, especially if it ends up in our nature. So I recommend analyzing all these chemicals for safety, especially concerning our nature.

2. Start producing a product that minimizes waste. Rolling cigarettes would be a solution with a pipe. Add a healthy filter so it can be consumed end to end—no more cigarette butts. The pipe could be made from air-captured CO2 or seaweed instead of plastic, so it lasts for years.

Vapes are more challenging since they require heating the liquid to create the vapor. If we can't find a solution based on zero waste, we should not have them. I apologize on behalf of the 82 million people who vape today. Guys, please don't kill the messenger.

In all aspects of our lives, we have become slaves to convenience. Convenience, as a result, creates more waste, so to transition to a Zero Waste culture, we can,

1. Change our products to become more durable

2. Change our products from singular usage to multiple, refillable, enduring products

In the Middle Ages, we used to have guilds. They are defined as associations of craftsmen and merchants formed to promote their members' economic interests and provide protection and mutual aid. Guilds were prolific throughout Europe between the 11th and 16th centuries as both business and social organizations. They had strict rules associated with product quality and setting fair prices.

Imagine if the millions of supermarkets, convenience, and pharmacies formed a global guild and decided that as part of their transition towards zero-waste decided that all products sold in their stores would no longer be available in single-use packaging. How much waste would be avoided when you had to scoop, weigh, and pay in weight for all products that could be sold that way? It would force their suppliers to change how they supplied their goods, and society would have to bring their containers. This transition alone would be massive, but it would reduce our total waste.

All of this work in a zero-waste culture requires opportunity and incentives. Opportunity resides in competition. Beat the competition, and your first incentive emerges. Incentives can also be stimulated. For that, governments can help by providing tax incentives. For example, reduce your plastic use instead of single-packet instant noodles, and make a single monthly package of 30 portions without individual packaging. By reducing a company's plastic use, you get a tax break. Let's change the name of the environmnetal minister to the minister of nature and zero-waste.

This can be applied to all sorts of products that create waste. The average lifetime of a mobile phone is three years. Move it to six years. Would this have an impact on revenue, profits, and employment? Yes, of course. However, we will need many waste managers, and a shift in where people will be employed will occur. Furthermore, extending your phone's lifetime to six years might be better for your business in the long run if the opportunity and incentives are right.

After all, extended producer responsibility (EPR) will likely eventually apply to all products globally, not only plastics.

EPR laws are being enacted into law more and more. For the moment, they cover packaging. It is not hard to imagine this will eventually be extended to other products that create waste and cause harm to us and our nature.

Does your government, or if you are a civil servant, have a Zero-Waste Policy?

We know that laws against littering and polluting have been implemented. Laws that cover EPR are being implemented, and even an Ecocide Law has been enacted. What would be great if these laws and more concerning our wastesphere became global?

Failing this, it will be up to the small hands in this world to turn the wheel in the right direction.

That leaves enforcement, and that remains a challenge. As long as governments have an education department and a public awareness department, they can leverage these organizations to implement programs that educate. Will it work? Hard to tell. I'm not yet convinced that EPR laws will work, for I know of a government that has said that EPR is already covered in their waste management law, which states that producers are responsible for the disposal of packaging that cannot be composted or is difficult to compost. Yet I find their packaging in nature everywhere today. This law was enacted 15 years ago.

Labeling is another incentive that has proven to be quite effective. What if we introduced a regeneration label on all products, from food to what we wear and use? It may not be perfect, but it could be a good start. This regeneration label would have to meet the following criteria.

1. No substance was used in growing and production that harms nature and thus us.

2. The product will not cause harm to nature during use.

3. The product will not harm nature when recycled.

4. The product will never be harmful to nature when it is finally disposed of

5. Global democratic coordination, oversight, enforcement, and standards.

Consumers could then choose products that are good for the planet and us. This, of course, would be adapted as new embodied thoughts and behaviors emerge.

AI as a waste manager

As I've argued, technology changes our behavior and relationship to our planet. We have seen how consumerism caused planetary overshoot. What incentives exist and could be expanded upon in countries with the highest overshoot? The countries with the highest overshoot are also the wealthiest. The Incentive would have to address all the negative consequences of our consumerism and how these consequences can be minimized. I would argue that this will become a reality over the next 10 to 15 years as we use AI more and more. We will increasingly become homebound, where going out is no longer essential. We can have meetings that are so real that they are almost the same as meeting people in the flesh.

We would have AI monitor our health, mentally and biologically. So we can balance what we consume mentally and physically. We would be home-schooled for life, where children would have an AI tutor and a remote Human Teacher as an intermediary who would also work from home. Adults can access courses that teach how to acquire a cathedral mindset and learn about ecology, health, and new forms of governance. Many would be employed as data governance officials monitoring Data sovereignty and Data Ownership in a participatory democratic governance structure. Our AI will become our health and physical trainer. All this will result in less waste. We would eat healthier; we would need fewer clothes because our avatars would be dressed; we could go diving in the Galapagos without getting wet; we could walk through the Amazon without sweat, and, as a result, reduce air travel. We would have our food delivered so we don't need cars anymore, and the list goes on. We would truly be linked to the machine. This is possible, enabling us to become nature-positive and reduce pollution substantially.

It would pose enough incentives to turn our predicament around correctly and incorporate everything we have discussed. The Metacrisis may enter a new age if we can keep Moloch away. The analysis of such a future would have to be carefully investigated because it all depends on our energy use. Suppose the AI incentives can reduce the energy demand of our manufacturing, food, and clean water production and reduce it so much that the AI energy requirement is less than the energy used for the production of physical goods and the associated logistics. If that proves to be the case, we may have a solution if we can also. Minimize the waste that AI will produce. Another key question is whether we will have enough material resources to build and maintain these machines.

The Incentives would have huge implications because we would no longer need so much infrastructure. We would need less mobility infrastructure as it will be reduced to pure logistics. Our labor requirements would change dramatically. This is already happening but not at scale, and the socio-economic implications have yet to be assessed. What is missing is a voluntary system governed by consensus, not enforcement.

FLOWSCAPE

In 2021, curiosity led me to take a course called Large Marine Ecosystems (LME) Assessments and Management. I wanted to learn more about our ocean. I wanted to know what attributes affect the health of a marine ecosystem. The world has 66 large marine ecosystems, mainly within our country's economic exclusion zone (EEZ). This course helped me to think of a single challenge and its relationship within the system, how it affects the other components, and, more importantly, how addressing that challenge would impact the entire system.

This course does not cover the whole ocean, for there is no legal jurisdiction related to its entire management. The ocean outside EEZs belongs to our planetary common good, which the United Nations oversees. Ocean regions such as the Indian, Pacific, Atlantic, Arctic, and Antarctica are managed by commissions focusing mainly on fisheries. There is currently no permanent ocean commission. Between 2013 and 2016, a temporary ocean commission issued two reports: one about the health of our ocean and the second about priorities to improve its health. In June 2023, the UN's 193 Member states adopted a legally binding Treaty to protect the high seas. This treaty covers the ocean beyond the boundaries of the EEZs. The feedback so far indicated that within this treaty, there is enormous potential for opportunity to restore the ocean's health, but as some critics say, it lacks teeth. The treaty was ratified in September 2023.

Large Marine Ecosystems' health is decreasing. Scientists have known this for years. Dr. Kenneth Sherman of NOAA National Oceanic & Atmospheric Administration's National Marine Fisheries Service and Dr.Lewis Alexander of the University of Rhode Island pioneered the concept of large marine ecosystems in the mid-1980s. They designed a modular approach, now adopted, to prompt large-scale action to overcome the downward trend of LME goods and services, primarily to mitigate the degradation of LMEs in the face of the accelerating effects of climate change, biodiversity loss, pollution and to achieve integrated adaptive ecosystem-based management (EBM) of LMEs

EBM involves a paradigm shift from single species or single sector management to entire ecosystem management and integrates a science-to-policy process. Operationalizing the EBM concept is the aim of the LME Approach. The LME Approach provides a five-module strategy for assessing and monitoring LMEs and taking remedial actions toward recovering and regenerating degraded goods and services in LMEs. The modules are focused on the application of suites of indicators for measuring LME socioeconomics, productivity, governance, pollution & ecosystem health, and fish & fisheries, which are incorporated into a multi-country LME strategic planning process through the development of a Transboundary Diagnostic Analysis (TDA) and a Strategic Action Programme (SAP).

The five modules are all connected, so it's essential to understand what these modules focus on.

1. Productivity module. This module focuses on an LME's carrying capacity for supporting fishery resources. Its measuring parameters are mainly photosynthetic activity, zooplankton biodiversity, and oceanographic variability. In this module, systematic measurements are made to monitor and assess the status and changes of these elements. The information obtained not only reflects the natural conditions of an LME but also indicates its ecological impacts.

2. Fish and fisheries module. The focus of this module is on the changes in biodiversity of fish communities, which not only impact fisheries in an LME but also affect other ecosystem components. In this module, systemic surveys are conducted to obtain information on "changes in biodiversity and abundance levels of the fish community as well as their causes.

3. Pollution and ecosystem health module. This module deals with marine pollution, a significant cause of the degradation and deterioration of nature and resources in LMEs. The monitoring and assessment of "the changing status of pollution and health of the entire LME are conducted in this module. Systemic monitoring of data on water quality and biological indicator species is used to measure pollution effects on the ecosystem and detect emerging diseases. The health of LMEs is examined based on ecosystem indices such as "biodiversity, stability, yields, productivity, and resilience."

4. Socioeconomic module. This module addresses the human dimensions of LMEs. It mainly investigates the socioeconomic development of the human communities connected to LMEs, especially the industries and human activities closely related to, or depend on, the LMEs. The output of this module is the social science-based, socioeconomic information of LMEs.

5. Governance module. The governance regimes for LMEs are formulated mainly based on the information obtained from the above four modules and international rules and systems embraced in relevant global and regional agreements applicable to the areas concerned. Policy, legal, and institutional reform is made, and other measures are taken at the regional and national levels to improve the governance of the LMEs. The guiding principle of an LME governance regime is adopting a holistic, ecosystem-based approach to managing and protecting the marine environment and resources. Attaining this requires the integration of scientific findings with socioeconomic considerations in the management of LMEs. Accordingly, an LME's management plans are developed and evaluated not only based on scientific findings but also on the socioeconomic elements of the human communities concerned, including their socioeconomic conditions and the socioeconomic impacts of management measures. Mechanisms for integrated management are established to harmonize the interest of nature resource protection and the long-term socioeconomic benefits of the coastal communities concerned. The governance module, a work-in-progress, is based on international experiences gained from LME projects and integrated coastal and ocean management. The trend of the LME governance module is to move away from traditional sectoral, single-species approaches to a more holistic, integrated approach to marine management. The general goal is to promote the long-term sustainability of marine ecosystem resources.

The primary technical role of a TDA is to identify, quantify, and set priorities for transboundary environmnetal problems. The key steps in the TDA development process are:

" Definition of system boundaries

" Collection and analysis of data/information

" Identification & prioritization of the transboundary problems

" Determination of nature and socioeconomic impacts

" Analysis of the immediate, underlying, and root causes

" Development of thematic reports

" Identification of leverage points

" Drafting the TDA

The TDA provides the factual basis for the strategic component of the TDA/SAP Process strategic thinking, planning, and implementation of the SAP. In addition, the TDA should be part of a larger facilitative process of engagement and consultation with all the key stakeholders from the initial TDA steps to the subsequent development of alternative ideas during the formulation of the Strategic Action Programme.

The TDA is a mechanism to help the participating countries 'agree on the facts' - perceptions drive many conflicts, and removing these can be an enormous step. Furthermore, the TDA should be seen as more than an analysis of data and information. It is a robust process that can help create confidence among the partners involved.

The Global Environmnetal Facility (GEF) has financially supported 23 out of the 66 LMEs. Their support covers both the TDA and SAP of these 23 LMEs. The results have been remarkable, but the waste threats are still present despite the actions taken by the intergovernmental groups managing the strategic action plans. We are not measuring eliminating substances that do not belong there, such as GHGs, Industrial, Agricultural, and Municipal waste, and the associated Plastics, Pesticides, and Forever chemicals.

That does not mean that this approach is wrong. It's because we have yet to come to grips with wastesphere elimination. When a problem we have caused by creating so much waste through our throughput process is so huge, it helps to break up the challenge into smaller parts when you take an interconnected systematic approach, such as, for example, with the five modules discussed above.

As far as I know, we have yet to cross the bridge to implement Transboundary Diagnostic Assessments on our bioregions, of which there are 185. These 185 Bioregions include some LMEs, as they overlap in some parts of the world. Transboundary means not only country borders but includes borders between states, such as in the USA and India.

185 of Earth's Bioregions Source: oneearth dot org credit: Karl Burkhart.

Suppose we were to assess the health of each bioregion using the LME approach of assessing productivity and look at carrying capacity, which is water, air, and soil health, fungi, mycelium, and photosynthesis that is required for food resources for all species within that region including our own. Such an approach would be called Large Terrestrial Ecosystem (LTE) assessment and management.

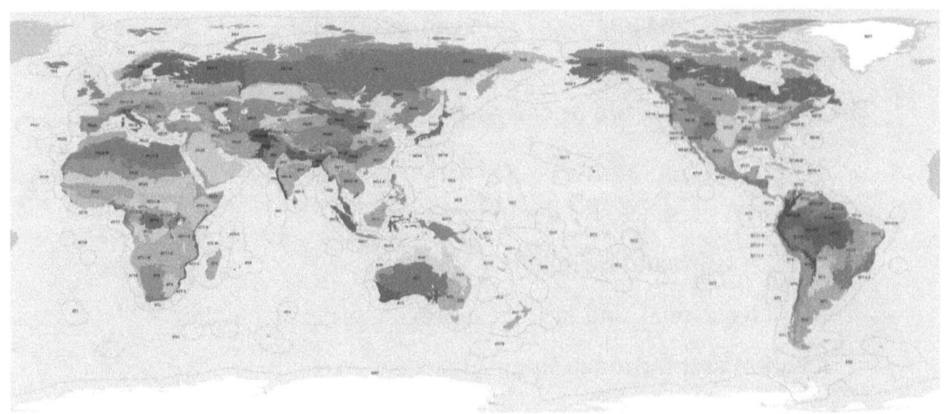

When we can monitor this, we can manage which would directly impact the food supply for all that reside in that region, which is covered in the module Plants and Animals. What would be the potential to grow endemic plant species again that would provide us with food and reduce our reliance on monoculture crops?

The same would apply to all the other modules. They have to be amended to suit the characteristics of each bioregion.

Imagine what that would mean for module 3: when a bioregion includes cities, agriculture, and industry. How would we tackle pollution differently when the focus is to restore the health of that region?

Module 4 would assess human's impact on the bioregion, including those that come to visit and are there temporarily. Finally, Module five, through collaboration, where bioregions include multiple countries, would foster close collaboration.

One of the essential exercises that forms part of the assessment is to find the root cause of why the state of a region is what it is.

Root causes are linked to the underlying social and economic causes and sectoral pressures. Still, they are often related to fundamental aspects of macro-economy, demography, consumption patterns, nature values, and access to information and democratic processes. Many of these may be beyond the scope of direct regional intervention, but it is important to document them for two reasons:

1. Some proposed ideas might be unworkable if the root causes of the problem are overwhelming or caused outside its borders.

2. Actions taken nearer to the root causes are more likely to have a lasting impact on the problem.

These root causes could be categorized into the following:

- Wastesphere

- Population pressure and demographic change

- Poverty, wealth and inequality

- National, regional, and or international governance issues

- Education and formulation of values

- Social change and development biases

- Development models and national macroeconomic policies

- Technology sphere used within the Bioregion

Assessments are all good and well, but without a strategic action plan, there is not much point in assessing. The bridge is there, for it would not take much to adopt the Strategic Action Plan approach and process adopted by the LME program TDA/SAP program.

The SAP is a negotiated policy document that should be endorsed at the highest level of all relevant sectors. It establishes clear priorities for action (for example, policy, legal, institutional reforms, or investments) to resolve the priority transboundary problems identified in the TDA.

Preparing a SAP should be a highly cooperative and collaborative process among the region's countries. The strategic component of the SAP process has two key phases:

1. Strategic Thinking:

    ☐ Defining the vision

    ☐ Setting goals or status statements

    ☐ Brainstorming new ideas/opportunities for innovation

    ☐ Identifying options or alternatives

2. Strategic Planning:

    ☐ National and regional consultation processes

    ☐ Setting strategies for implementation

    ☐ Action planning - Setting actions, timescales, priorities, and indicators

☐ Drafting the SAP

☐ Steps towards SAP implementation

Finally, ongoing monitoring and results assessment and adjustment plans as required.

A vital element of the SAP is a well-defined baseline. This enables a clear distinction between actions with purely regional benefits and those addressing transboundary concerns with global benefits. Another key element involves the development of institutional mechanisms at the regional and national levels for implementing the SAP and monitoring and evaluation procedures to measure the effectiveness of the process outcomes.

Addressing our challenge to rid ourselves of our connected wastesphere could be managed better from a bioregion level, even when the resource capabilities of that region are limited. It would also allow us to transition to regenerative practices within those regions and adapt to living within a region's natural boundaries. By doing so, the world would adapt to live within the planetary boundaries if everyone focused on eliminating the wastesphere created within their region. This would prevent corporations from exporting their wasteful activities to other bioregions when they do not meet the requirements set in each region. They would suffer the consequences in a particular region and at home.

It might create regional political, technology, and economic systems if the opportunities and incentives these transitions present are advantageous enough for us but also for our nature, for we must keep in mind that we are as much a part of an ecosystem as the fly, monkey or bird that is trying to eat your sandwich.

That leaves the transition from a globalized economy to a bioregional one that would likely pose the most significant challenge as not all regions have the same economic resources as defined today.

I would suspect, however, that by conducting a TDA and implementing an SAP, one could discover natural resources that contribute to eliminating our waste sphere. For example, one region could eliminate more GHGs naturally than another, such as those bioregions that contain expanding mangrove forests, wetlands, rainforests, kelp, seaweed, and other ecosystems that sequester carbon permanently. These nature-based possibilities could have significant value that creates a paradigm shift of what wealth means. Having vast resources of zeolite may help reduce methane from the atmosphere. These resources would be of immense value for regions that do not have those resources, or at least not in equal measure, especially those that emit the most waste.

Take Indonesia for an example. It has six bioregions within its borders, one shared with Malaysia and Singapore. They are:

IM18: Malaysian & Sumatran tropical rainforest, which includes Singapore.

IM17: Java and Bali Tropical rainforest.

AU15: Southeast Indonesian dry forest islands. (Includes East Timor)

AU14: Malukku and Sulawesi Islands

IM16: Borneo tropical forest and Sundaland heath forests, which include Malaysia

AU13: New Guinea & Surrounding Islands (Indonesia, Solomon Islands and Papua New Guinea

Within these bioregions, you also have the following LMEs: 35, 36, 37, and 38.

Conducting a TDA and SAP would have a significant impact on waste management.

Example:

IM18 Includes three countries; Sumatra has the largest rainforest. That rainforest can absorb X gigatons of CO2 while emitting far fewer GHGs from its activities. Sumatra would have a surplus capacity. Singapore, however, does not have a surplus, but it has the capacity and capability to dispose of solid waste that Sumatra does not have. Both Sumatra and Singapore are incentivized to minimize the wastesphere and share the objective of minimal waste. So, to compensate, Singapore could import Sumatra's solid waste to dispose of it properly. The abundance of Sumatra's rainforest benefits Singapore's actions to become net negative in GHG emissions, and Sumatra would benefit from Singapore's capability and capacity to eliminate solid waste. Both would work collaboratively to eliminate waste, leveraging the abundance of rainforests in Sumatra. Sumatra would be considered a wealthy region. Add to that renewable energy like solar, which Singapore imports from Sumatra, and you would have created a wealth ecosystem that can then benefit other regions that do not have that capacity. As a result, you would be well on your way to solving the nature crisis and restoring the earth's impacted spheres. Biodiversity benefits as it's in a bioregion's best interest to preserve and expand the value the abundance of biodiversity holds.

This could become a great equalizer, especially when you consider invasive waste entering a particular bioregion, such as GHGs or even imports of waste; for that, you can eliminate it permanently, and the unharmful leftovers are used for bioregion mitigation purposes. This could be a great collaboration exercise for economists, bioregional waste managers, and scientists. Products and services would be measured on waste and health impact, which can be priced in when products are transregional and extended producer responsibility measures and laws would ensure that a global producer of goods and services provides that any harmful impact is their responsibility to eliminate even including unintended consequences that could emerge over time.

There is now ample literature that discusses regeneration and regenerative design that would be helpful to use as implementation ideas and tools that will benefit regionality and how humans can prosper within it. I realize that TDAs and SAPs take time to develop. Each will take several years to complete. The time that, for some say, is running out, and for others, there is plentiful. We shall see, but at least for me, we should change our beliefs about wealth.

Creating ideas and providing suggestions is easy. Getting people to adopt these ideas is another matter altogether, which brings me to another emerging human capability that is hardly, if ever, discussed. I call it Flowscaping, which is related to the concept of Flowstate. Flow state, also known as "in the zone," is a mental state of complete absorption in an activity. In this state, people experience total immersion in the task at hand: They lose track of time and surroundings, and their attention is wholly focused on the activity. A feeling of energized focus: They feel fully engaged and motivated, and their skills and abilities are fully utilized. A sense of enjoyment: They experience a feeling of satisfaction and accomplishment from the activity. The results achieved can be described as phenomenal as success is amplified. It is as if nothing can go wrong, and you quickly achieve your objectives. Gamers who have experienced this state often seek it as they know how beneficial it can be.

The Flowstate has also been discovered within small groups of people. It has been detected between couples and small business teams who have worked intensively on solving problems, particularly in the consulting domain. From my experience working for a large tech company engaged in a major multi-million dollar deal, A key characteristic in addition to the individual experience of flow state is that communication flows smoothly and insights emerge almost on the fly, which enables the group to proceed further and even solve sticky problems.

You may wonder what all this has to do with bioregionalism. The above can also be experienced when you immerse yourself in the Biosphere. I have yet to achieve the Flowscape, as I call it, in places like the Jungle, in the mountains, or on a lake, but I have experienced it in the Ocean. First, while surfing and feeling one in the ocean, similar to the experience described above, and second, when I went diving. This experience cannot be confused with nitrogen narcosis, so you know. Flowscaping is precisely like above while you dive on a coral reef. You feel like you become one with the reef; you are, for the moment, part of their ecosystem. You almost feel everything is interconnected, and it's an emotional experience. Most striking is that when you are in the Flowscape state, your air consumption decreases significantly, and you swim effortlessly and are perfectly buoyant. The most incredible experience Flowscaping produces is interacting with the fish around you. They come closer and are more curious. They swim close to your mask or your camera to check you out. I've had this with turtles and even sharks. I know this experience is fundamentally different than regular diving for two reasons. When I'm not in a Flowscape state, the fish don't approach, and when it comes to sharks, they do not come close to you ever. But in a Flowscaping mode of being, they come closer, but not in a malevolent way. It feels like they treat you as one with their nature as if they understand your respect for the beauty that this world embodies.

I much desire the term Flowscaping to become recognized as a state in which people connect with nature intimately, not for its beauty but also to have the experience of interacting with its wildlife. I'm convinced these experiences will create an entirely different mindset of being one with Nature or, as some First Nation people determine, Nature as "A Way of Life."

How powerful would it be if people could evolve, embody, and integrate the Cathedral Mind with the Natural and Spherical Mind immersed in a flow state? What would we call such a mind?

MAGISTERIUM

Can our Global Civilization prevent the collapse of our current planetary governance structures? It is a question that requires attention, and the time for this debate should start as soon as possible. Confronted with the wicked problems that we need to solve, I can't help but observe that from a governance perspective, we are in a predicament. We are currently stuck in an impasse where the decisions we must make to address the metacrisis are insufficient. The only option, at least for now, is to place our faith in the courts to make the decisions our governments cannot. In 2024, there were around 2000 climate change cases globally, and 1500 were in the United States. There are currently 55 countries, mainly in Europe, Australia, and parts of Asia, with pending cases. Thousands of legal cases also involve the harmful effects of pesticides and forever chemicals. The number of cases of ownership rights for water, land, and healthy air around the world is staggering. This indicates a shift in the faith of our current governance structures, and, for those familiar with history, a return to a Judge-based rules system of governance that embodies virtues could occur to replace the current king-based system based on force. We would no longer have presidents, prime ministers, or supreme rulers in a hierarchy based on dominance and control but a Judiciary system that is governed from the local to the global within electable councils or courts. The challenge, of course, is how to ensure incorruptibility.

To change dominance into a subsidiary, we need an open debate about how we govern in the future, which should include the following spheres: The Technology Sphere, All Earth Spheres, the Waste Sphere, Economical, Cultural, Religio, and Societal spheres. That's a lot to take in, especially with Billions of people all having agency in all of these spheres. It can not be a single-sphere perspectival view, for example, a networked state governed by technology, a bioregional state governed by nature's principles, or a human-centric perspective. Its design will come from us and we have the imagination and ingenuity to put ourselves *in the shoes of* each sphere, from a plant to the soil to animals, to air, water, soil, and ultimately, to time. We should accept that we cannot control everything, no matter how much we desire this objective. It can not be done by one man alone, so all I can do is perhaps provide some inspiration that others can build upon to design governance perspectives that are a positive medium that is accepted in a 5.0 form of governance that encompasses All life and its supporting spheres. A term that I quite like for a name for a 5.0 form of governance is Magisterium of the Commons.

One must not forget Moloch, who has infected our globe with geopolitical tension, polarization, kinetic, moral, data, and economic wars. Psychologically, with rat races to the bottom, multipolar traps, nature destruction, addictive media consumption and gamification, and the deification of celebrities. Let's not forget the tension and degradation of the state-market regulatory and governance relationship.

While the Cathedral Mind embodies infinite Time, as the required changes are not a sprint but a multidecade adventure of discovery and experimentation into the unknown, we must supplement that mind with something infinitely more powerful. That something is to reestablish a relationship between the complex and the complicated. Perhaps one could argue and debate the relationship between the administrator and the master. Our current governance structures are based on the complicated, i.e.. The administrator has reduced everything to units, numbers, currency, percentages, graphs, and text plugged into machines to run models that help us make decisions on which we apply risk management. We need this; otherwise, we will have chaos, but we need more than the administrator.

I propose that we re-establish a relationship with the complex and seek a balance where both the complicated and the complex are equal to the Whole, which is infinite, never-ending, and always in an evolutionary state. The complex embodies uncertainty, which we should accept and embrace; wonders may emerge from uncertainty that no complicated system can produce. The complex embodies the bigger picture. It sees beyond things and bits and bytes. It can grasp relationships better than an administrator can.

To understand the concept of the Whole, we need to ask some fundamental questions.

What is the proper use of technology and its relationship with humans?

What is the proper role of Humans within a complex - complicated, balanced whole?

What is the proper role of Technology and Humans within Earth's Spheres?

How do we humans evolve towards wise, enlightened beings from an educational perspective that will define an evolved society and culture?

How do we govern the great economic transition where machines radically replace human labor functions since AI will most likely make some human tasks obsolete?

How can we transition those impacted to a life of freedom where they can prosper without the reliance on labor for money?

What would liberation from labor develop into as a positive outcome for people that embodies a new way of being one with the world?

These questions show that for a new governance structure for the planet and all its aspects to emerge, a highly evolved contextual modus operandi needs to be developed where the wholes within this structure are further contextualized, and specialization in any given subdomain is by default recognized as insufficient and not an objective. Simply put, those who can connect the dots and understand the relationships and tension between them would function better in such a governance model than one that relies on charts, figures, text, and models alone. A map is not a territory. The wholes should not be confused with domains as a domain alludes to a form of specialization that would reduce the capacity for complex understanding. These wholes would comprise all the main functions directly connected to the abovementioned spheres and include representation for each. All should be represented equally from a planetary perspective in the decision-making process.

That is not to say that domain specialization is not required. The domain expertise is a subset of the dynamics that flow from the Whole. These domains can be administratively governed in some bureaucratic institutions, which, depending on the benevolent potential of AI, would be run mainly by machines with human oversight. This human oversight could be run from the whole or the bureaucratic institution and act as an interface to the Whole.

For example, I will ask you to go back in time and think of a river. The entire River is a single whole where each of the earth's spheres are wholes that govern the River—our technology, economics, culture, spirituality, and society have relationships with the river, which is either a positive, we extract fresh water from it or a negative relationship, we pollute it. From so many wholes, you would have supporting domains of expertise that would provide the data and knowledge that can add to the contextual Whole where the River's health reigns paramount, for example, and where each contextual relationship enables the Whole, I.e., The River, to be governed positively. A healthy river is good for All life and can benefit our technology, economics, culture, spirituality, and society as a whole.

The emergent property of such a whole governance structure is wisdom. Wisdom is much more potent than expertise. Wisdom is always an evolutionary phenomenon that cannot be owned like expertise. If wisdom were something you could possess, it wouldn't be wisdom; it would fall back into expertise. In some respects, we have lost this understanding. As the Toaists say.

The Dao that can be spoken is not the eternal Dao.

Inevitably, we will have to debate the meaning of sovereignty. Sovereignty refers to the notion of freedom, liberty, equality, and the virtues embodied in wisdom. Sovereigns, which we once understood to be Kings, Queens, and Emperors, used to be ordained by the divine and were supposed to embody its virtues. That didn't work for long because power is such a powerful emissary of Moloch. So, we replaced feudalism with statehood. Today, a sovereign state manages its citizens as sovereign beings. The notion of sovereignty today means the capacity to make effective choices in a given context. These capacities are enshrined in Law and Order, which the sovereign state can change under certain conditions. The issue here is that these rules don't necessarily promote freedom, liberty, and the virtues inclusive of all spheres. Not even to an individual or a group. Sovereignty was predominantly a human-centric perspective and did not always include All. We lack a coherent planetary sovereignty that contains all the virtues.

This is understandable because we do not have a common global use of language that would allow for the emergence of a planetary sovereignty embodied with wisdom virtues that unify us and retain our individuality and that of our many cultures. A term used in one region may mean something else in another. So, for a new global governance to emerge, we need to develop a new common language with a whole dictionary of terms that mean the same for everyone. We need a global dictionary, like the global internet protocol called IP, that allows communication between all computer systems. Oddly, while we were excellent at connecting the world with our technology protocols, we never connected our human communication as a single protocol except through interpreters. Interpreters have a tough job because how do you translate a double meaning or a subtlety from the tone of one's voice? Imagine how many problems we could have prevented and solved if we had a common global language that we could agree to create. A completely new language. Our metacrisis is global, and we are a global civilization lacking a unified global language that helps us think, act, and behave for the betterment of All.

This leads me to the next evolutionary phase of Governance: the shift from paper-based to digital-based. We live in the digital age, but our contracts and constitutions are still based on written documents. The way we govern is still paper-based, which started with the Gutenberg printing press. We now live in the digital age. Don't get me wrong. I love traditions and history as long as they hold value for today's planetary values and what we should hold sacred. Without the shift to digital Governance, we won't be able to complete the whole structure. Today, we can send money securely around the planet, sitting behind our computers in our underwear. Why can't we all vote electronically from our homes in our underwear?

This transition will have profound effects that will fundamentally restructure our whole form of Governance, no matter what political system you prefer. The digitization of Governance would negate the need for representation as it is today, with members such as seen in authoritarian regimes or what we call lower and higher conferences of representation such as the House of Representatives and the Senate in the States or as in the case of many European democracies the Lower and Higher Assemblies that represent the people. Digitization, when appropriately implemented, would provide an efficient mechanism for people to participate in Governance and, in some way, restore their sovereignty. In addition, the Judiciary would be elevated to a higher level of Governance provided they are electable and have fixed terms. They would govern under the Global Commons with applicable customs to adopt. These Judges should not be compared to today's judiciary, which is predominantly human-centric. These Judges would have to embody the qualities and attributes that are able to govern all our global spheres and would guide rather than enforce the adoption of the Good, True, and Beautiful as a first principle.

The digitization capability would hold them accountable, with oversight from the people if they so choose to participate. The ultimate leadership would shift from a single person, chairman, president, or prime minister to a council where each member represents a part of the Whole. Think of the UN Security Council without veto power; it is electable globally using the Internet, and decisions are made collectively and via a circular voting system with no private and public funding for candidates.

Circular voting is not new; it is an emerging voting system where votes are not placed on people directly but on issues that electable delegates can debate and reach a consensus on democratically. Voters can check the box related to the level of priority for each of the positions, and from a tally, those issues that score highest would become part of the governance platform to manage. The style of governance will be issues-based, not delegate-based. Those elected for debate and consensus would require sovereign qualifications, which the education system must develop.

We also need to cover conflict. I mean a conflict that can not be solved with the global communications dictionary. This would mean that a fractural representation, perhaps even down to the Dunbar level or more, is required where these individuals are both wise and incorruptible. I use the Dunbar number because, in societies with less than 150 people, we can govern ourselves quite effectively and avoid corruption as the judiciary representative can be managed both top-down and bottom-up. Policing is another part of governance that should ideally be part of the judiciary, and it is here that block or holo-chain technology or its successors may become a valuable tool in enforcement. The wicked predicament remains when it comes to those countries that own nuclear weapons. Unless we completely remove them from existence, we will not see a new governance model emerge, or perhaps we will eventually evolve and become mature enough to dismantle all of them. Our record with respect to nuclear arsenal management has been one of playing with Moloch's favorite babies, and luck so far has prevented assured mutual destruction.

We should acknowledge that the 21st century will see a significant shift in global demographics where the populations of high-income states will continue to decrease. In contrast, those in Africa and parts of Asia will continue to grow. By 2100, Africa is expected to form 40% of the Global Population, and Nigeria will be the third most populous country after China and India. In addition, due to overshoot pressures, the High-Income countries will be faced with a choice to lower overall consumption of goods and energy, which, if not implemented, will hasten Earth's collapse. So, a shift in the power base of global custodianship will emerge, and this needs to be factored into long-term design.

This type of frontier proposal for Governance has not been publicly discussed in the halls of power. It reminds me of the Star Trek intro: To Boldly Go Where No Man Has Gone Before. We are entering a new frontier that requires a scale not seen before. While we can sense a transition evident in current public discourse within the metacrisis movement, we still face enormous resistance to change. The term surveillance capitalism comes to mind when discussing resistance factors, and as we have seen, the capitalist system is slowly eroding and taking civilization with it. Surveillance Capitalism is a view where data is gold. Personal data is a key resource that advanced technology like AI can collect, analyze, and ultimately use for profit-making activities by corporations. Our leisure has become unpaid work.

My first-hand experience working with telecommunications companies has shown how powerful this can be. These companies have your billing data and can analyze daily, weekly, monthly, and yearly call patterns. This data provides insights about who you call or text, which apps you use, and for how long so that they can use this data to provide customized services to you for profit maximization. The same applies to the App developers. Users can receive a weekly usage report on their phones. The power of Technology companies can not be underestimated, and the only faith, at this Time, lies not with governments but with the courts to do the right thing and constrain them. It is our last bastion, which one could argue is also under attack as Judges become susceptible to corruption. It's the age-old question: Who oversees the overseers?

The transition from the maximized and optimized administrative written literacy of Governance to the new digital literacy of Governance also requires a debate on private and public ownership in the context of our planetary health. With information being relegated to the query domain thanks to AI, humanity inevitably will have to evolve towards the wisdom sphere. At least, this should be the result, as what you know and, to a lesser extent, who you know is no longer all that relevant. With wisdom, I mean the ability to become exquisite choice-makers for the benefit of All life and its support spheres. Cognitive scientists call this the ability to become good relevance realizers. However, this can only become a reality if we can improve our capacity for sense-making and meaning-making.

When it comes to sense-making and meaning-making, we should ask ourselves what spheres of thinking individuals should acquire to show enhanced capabilities of understanding discernment and shaping their agency for the training of wisdom to occur. This training includes mindfulness, imagination, dialogical and movement spheres of being, and how this enables digital information management without falling into delusions, conspiracies, and manipulation, which the current biased large language models are prone to do. To counter limbic and imagination hijacking becomes an essential ability.

Wisdom would facilitate the emergence of steering oneself and the collective toward the Good in such a way that we become tempted by the Good. Imagine if we could change our temptation from instant gratification to temptation for what is Good, True, and Beautiful. What would such a world look like? The task before us is challenging. For centuries, we have been educating people so that they can fit into society and function within its scope, like learning how to read, write, and calculate. This has served us well until we find ourselves in the Age of Consequences. To enable a new governance model based on wisdom or the ability to govern within the sphere of the Whole, we would require our education system to transition as well.

What would a new education system look like in the context of Spherical Thinking and Wisdom? A trifecta would emerge that includes the qualifications or, to use the more accurate root, Quality of the Judge, Pedagog, and Prophet, all bundled together. This new form of education centered on the concept of sovereignty for individuals, communities, society, and the Whole of Civilization would emerge. The Person who embodies wisdom within their sovereignty used to be called a Sage. A term that is viewed by many with some level of distaste. The sage that will eventually emerge will differ from the Sage of the global axial or even the post-axial revolution simply because we live in a different technological sphere.

There are plenty of great thinkers around. Still, they are dispersed and focused on problems that fall into specific domains where their wisdom makes significant inroads from which we can understand the transitions to make. We are still at the foundational stage in addressing the restoration of our Earth Spheres, which will take generations.

Our digital technology, when deployed in educational processes, may enable us to develop the architects of the future. A sovereign of ages past enjoyed what is called an aristocratic education. He had the best literacy, writing, calculus, biology, physics, chemistry, classical, art, and theology teachers. This aristocratic curriculum can now, or soon will be able to be provided by AI. AI technology would make this education style possible worldwide, improving educational equality. As an example, If I were such a student, the technology would enable me to simultaneously interface with Plato, Laozi, Confucius, and Buddha in a dialogue facilitated by a human educator like, for example, Dr McGilchrist, to discuss a particular topic, such as the Influence of Moloch. I can't do that today; believe me, I tried.

From a governance perspective, we could use blockchain to address manipulation, which is a product of administration with a nasty byproduct called corruption. It is an application that has not gone unnoticed; quite a few people have written about the potential of blockchain. The value of this technology is that it is transparent and, once registered on the public ledger, can no longer be tampered with. However, it is still a tool deployed within our current inadequate structures. When deployed within the concept of the Magisterium of the Commons, we could encode technology to provide the ability to oversee the overseers. This is useful because this technology does not care; it only provides visibility and has no agency to manipulate. This requires full transparency and access at the local, regional, and global levels during the transition phases, where Sages hold the corruptibility of those representing the Whole at bay with the assistance of these public ledgers. Moloch may not be defeated yet, so we need to maintain our vigilance during this process, but at least we have a mechanism to support the enforcement of the transition.

Ultimately, this transition to a new form of Governance comes down to design, and because Moloch resides within humans, we need to consider this weakness of being human no matter how wise we become. This requires a structure where we can produce tools to neutralize man's ability to manipulate at micro and marco levels. The domain of expertise applies so that the information and factual recommendations are presented to the Governance of the Whole, where it can be debated, and its decisions are ultimately stored in public ledgers. When designed correctly, you would have a continuous interface between the working expert groups that focus on particulars of a sphere and connect with the Whole, where it can be synchronized. This would allow recursive feedback loops to be incorporated at the local, regional, and planetary levels. By design, you would have levels of competence emerge routed in aristocratically educated sovereigns.

Global citizen participatory governance is not a far-fetched dream when our civilization is already hooked on endless scrolling on social media platforms. Social governance platforms pose an alternative: we, the people, are informed on matters that mean something to us personally and are relevant to the community and society. It would be a better use of our time than following celebrities around online.

WHOLONMIND

*"He who loses wealth loses much; he who loses a friend loses more;
but he that loses his courage loses all."*

Miguel de Cervantes

It won't be long before everyone demands change. It will no longer be those who protest on the streets or are engaged in a war of minds on social media and the halls of government. It's inevitable. As our crises worsen, the louder the voices of protests will be. The old narratives about prosperity for all based on economic and technological growth are no longer effective.

Our Administrative bureaucratic mindset is no longer sufficient, for if it were, we would have solved these crises long ago. Many claim to have technical solutions, and while many show promise, especially with converting our waste into durable, unharmful products or those actively involved in ecosystem restoration and waste management, we lack a globally coordinated effort to collectively address global risks effectively. We've known about these global risks for decades, yet they persist, largely thanks to Moloch and a lack of spherical thinking.

We discussed many spheres as a thread throughout this narrative. The Wastesphere, The Technology Sphere, the bio, hydro, litho, cryo, atmosphere, and the right and left hemispheres of the brain. We are a global civilization, and our earth is a globe. All of these spheres are connected through evolutionary holons. That's why I propose spherical thinking.

To give spherical thinking a home, we need to develop a Wholonmind that includes the spherical, cathedral, and administrative. We need to reduce the Administrative Mind. The Wholonmind is greater than the sum of what it contains, and who knows what could emerge. The awareness of the Metacrisis may emerge as a start. The trifecta within the Wholonmind is where each serves the other in unison. Here is where Integral Theory plays a critical role as the directionality from the I, It, We, Its quadrant both in vertical stages and horizontal waves flow up, down, left to right, and vice versa. It is a dizzying concept, but our mind is well suited to organize these into a coherent rationality and improved relevance realization that would enable us to obtain Wisdom within our sovereignty.

The challenge, however, lies with learning, adopting, and applying spherical thinking at scale. This could take generations. To scale, we should pursue wisdom. Wisdom is the only aspect of our sovereignty that we can possess that can defeat Moloch or at least keep it bound from causing harm. The world is changing, and many people in academia, economics, business, and society are working on tackling the subcomponents of the metacrisis. However, there are few that embrace the term metacrisis. Public discourse is still focused on Climate Change. As with any challenge and crisis, we have an uphill struggle, and I've found a way to display it in simple terms of how we can evolve during the digital age. Bioregionality may be a solution if it can integrate with Individuals, Communities, Society, and the Economy and scale up towards a governance structure based on Wholeness and a growth hierarchy aligned with evolution instead of our current domination hierarchy.

Local potential can positively impact nature and human health versus having everything controlled globally or top-down, as we've been used to for so many centuries. Aspiring to be as wealthy as your neighbor is not as good as living within local communities that can provide for themselves and within their means. Does this mean that poor people have to stay poor? No, it means that poverty should be defined differently, and wealth is not about what you own but instead defined as the total quantity of goods and services you can share for the benefit of all. This is not an economic question but a social question as well. The field of philosophy may provide additional insight. Changing human behavior and beliefs takes a long time. Much debate is still required.

One way to show how far we have yet to travel is to use the technology adoption curve developed by Geoffrey Moore. This adoption curve is familiar to professionals in the ICT sector. It shows that all new technologies eventually must cross the chasm to become successful. Our civilization is currently approaching a similar chasm, for we can no longer continue as we are. We need to adopt new ways of doing things. Our "ability to do" will be tested more and more. The abyss awaits us if we don't adopt a way of thinking, speaking, and acting within Earth's boundaries. We are merely forecasting our risks. If enough of us cross the chasm successfully and adopt spherical thinking, we may minimize destruction. An essential requirement is to understand that actions are interconnected and impact multiple spheres. When we have reached the majority, we have a chance to evolve as a species that is content to prosper within the boundaries that Earth has provided for us.

We are still in the visionary and first adopter stage to save our civilization. We must be realistic and accept that not everyone will immediately jump on the bandwagon. This will take time. The most critical part is to cross the chasm.

I hope the information provided here makes it easier to understand. To solve a problem, we should find the nexus of the problems, for there are many. While some already know this, many do not. I certainly didn't before I started on this journey. Since waste is part of each of us, we should make it known to all, young and old. Will this effort be successful? I cannot tell, but at least I tried to start from there since it's the closest sphere that connects with the core ingredients that we need for our survival: Air, Water, and Soil.

I cannot predict the future. No one can—at least not a hundred percent. From all the research, there is no doubt that we have arrived at the Age of Consequences. Those consequences will manifest themselves in ever greater intensity in the coming decades. There is no quick fix, so we should maximize our time to develop new skills, develop wisdom, and adopt Spherical Thinking.

Sadly, we are still on a path that does not bode well for us as I return to where I started. I cannot tell which catastrophe we will witness first. When I look at Water, we have two major converging dilemmas: the melting of the Greenland ice sheet and the melting of the Thwaites Glacier in Antarctica. Sea level rise will continue, but we don't know how fast it will rise. Melting Ice at scale is impossible to reverse in the short term, let alone stop. Our landmass will decrease; I am certain of this.

We will have to face these challenges, and we need to build resilience. We need resilience within ourselves in addressing the increasing levels of mental health issues and the resilience of our communities and societies, and above all, we must be prepared to provide our assistance to All life by whatever means available to us. Resilience is not building walls around cities to keep away the flood. Resilience is the wisdom to prevent the floods. Civilizations don't collapse overnight. Some events could accelerate its collapse, but most take decades, if not hundreds of years. We can sense a transition taking place. The pace is slow while our metacrisis is accelerating. Let us hope we can get ahead of the metacrisis collectively. We have much work to do.

Wisdom cannot be taught or imposed. It can only be shared. For wisdom to emerge, we need to grow our physical, mental, and spiritual health. I needed to learn a new language where my worldview was not centered and influenced by the dominant worldview, leading us toward catastrophe. Our worldviews are not cyclical. They are predominantly overlapping arcs by which we tend to create everything. We think, talk, and believe in birth, maturity, death, and the afterlife of All life and our systems. Graphs, maps, things, and pictures represent this thinking, behavior, and belief all too well. We have developed technology that is now so powerful that we don't know how to manage it. We lack the wisdom, neglected for so long, that is most needed right now. We cannot continue if we do not have a balance between power, technology and wisdom.

We do not know how much we should consume, but we do know how to make consumption full of things that are not good for us. This can be applied to our physical, mental, and spiritual well-being. This not knowing how much we should consume is our lack of wisdom. We have neglected and abandoned the pursuit of wisdom. To emerge, we should pursue physical, mental, and spiritual wisdom, a trifecta of being centered around the Wholonmind that contains an evolutionary cathedral mindset.

My proposal boils down to a requirement to change how we move, work, and play. Adaptation will be infinite. We will need to watch out for the healthy nutrition we need. All of this embodies the concept of the Tree of Life, which emerges from within us and manifests itself into a beautiful biodiverse arena from which we wisely may use its fruits. Our arena is symbiotic with life-supporting technology within the evolutionary House of Wisdom. A civilization that is in service to the giving and not the taking. That's the vision that comes to mind in the Wholonmind. It's universal.

EPILOGUE

I've now returned to my cave where I must rest my curious brain, which has compelled me to take this journey. My bones are sore, for I have traveled far, farther than I ever thought possible. Call me, if you like, a Foolish Spider, now grey and still vibrant, who has lost his will to spin webs for others; I, the fool, have severed my life from the shadow of the dead man's addictive pursuit of mechanization, scientific manipulation, endless bureaucracy, and narrative warfare. To understand and expose the many nefarious manifestations that now dominate our worldview and need to be broken. Let the world become a dance filled with music instead of a silent, meaningless equation or a graph predicting our doom.

As a Fool, I am nobody's servant and have chosen to live in a cave surrounded by the lush green, densely forested hills that reign south of the Capital. I will remain a hermit for a millisecond in cosmic time to weather the storm.

Without my web, namely, my contact with civilization must read perverse and irrelevant to you, still geared to the machine, while directly as workers, employees and managers tethered to corporations or indirectly as civil servants tethered to politicians. You chose your jobs because they promised to provide you with a steady income and leisure to render the moment that you now so adore as valuable as a part-time service.

Who am I, you may ask to warn you that artifice will be your undoing and machines are not real but a perverse set of tools to build your false Idols? And do I suggest that you should resign from your jobs for want of sufficient capital to set up a small farm or become romantic shepherds – after your failure to come to terms with the post-modern world? No, my webspinningness strips me from offering any practical advice.

I only dare attempt a statement of the problem: how you will come to terms with what is true, good, beautiful, and sacred in your arena.

My Wholonmind, still young and emerging, ponders what sacrifice and teachings are absorbed from your ancestors and what gifts are bestowed on your children, their children, and great-grandchildren when you are gone.

Surrendered to love, I can reflect on the many arenas where I've lost and won many battles. I utilize all that I have learned, from transforming gold into art, dealing in speed, diving with sharks, and saving whales from our mechanization's pollution, to emerge reborn as a Renaissance man and build a new arena in service to the sacredness of life for all.

Here I shall dwell in peace while the world rages against the dying of the light. Applying the insights of process metaphysics and action protocols, the practice of aligning with unfolding, and learning boundary craft, may well be the right challenge, which in the learning process will shape consciousness towards increasing the wellbeing of life. Only that aim will keep consciousness relevant and aligned with the telos of our time.

I invite you to write a global story that speaks to all of us. Can we do this?

We shall see, and I bid you well.

www.ingramcontent.com/pod-product-compliance
Lightning Source LLC
Chambersburg PA
CBHW051228130726
47988CB00001B/271